D1058869

The Manchurian Frontier in Ch'ing History

Harvard East Asian Series 43

The East Asian Research Center at Harvard University administers research projects designed to further scholarly understanding of China, Korea, Japan, and adjacent areas.

The Manchurian Frontier in Ch'ing History

Robert H. G. Lee

Harvard University Press
Cambridge, Massachusetts
1970

Distributed in Great Britain by Oxford University Press, London

Preparation of this volume has been aided by a grant
from the Ford Foundation

Library of Congress Catalog Card Number 70–95926
SBN 674-54775-6
Printed in the United States of America

TO MY MOTHER AND MY WIFE

The Manchurian Frontier after 1905

Pre-1858 boundaries are in shaded lines.
Area ceded to Russia after 1860 is shaded.
Locations of ethnic groups in the eighteenth century are shown by shaded lettering.

RUSSIA
OUTER MONGOLIA
INNER MONGOLIA
RUSSIA (Post 1860)
Sea of Okhotsk
Sea of Japan
Po Hai Bay
HOKKAIDO
SAKHALIN
KOREA
CHIHLI
CHAHAR
HEILUNGKIANG
KIRIN
FENGT'IEN
GREAT KHINGAN
LESSER KHINGAN
CH'ANG PAI-SHAN
SHIHOTE ALIN
REINDEER TUNGUS
MANEGIR
BIRAR
OROCHON
BARGA
ÖLÖT
SOLON
DAGUR
BUTEHA BANNERS
DORBET BANNER
JALAIT
KORCHIN BANNERS
GORLOS
SIBE
GUWALCA
MANCHU
HURKA
HEJE
SHAVEN HEJE
UNSHAVEN HEJE
KILE
KIAKAR
FIATKA
Nerchinsk
Mo-ho
Albazin
Aigun
Mergen
Tsitsihar
T'ung-ken
Sui-hua
Hulan
Bayensusu
Harbin
Alchuka
Pin-chou
Lalin
San-hsing
Petuna
Nung-an
Shuang-ch'eng pao
Ch'ang-ch'un
Kirin
Yung-chi
Ninguta
Kai-yuan
Hua-tien
T'ang-ho-kou
Chia-p'i-kou
Hun-ch'un
Shen-yang
Liao-yang
Hai-ch'eng
Ying-kou
Port Arthur
Dairen
Lin-chiang
Hoi Ryong
Shanhaikuan
Peking
Manchouli
Hailar
I-min
Pulo
Adi
Mu-ch'eng
Rusun
Fudzin
Olga Bay
Lake Kizi
Lake Hanka
Hulun Nor
Buir Nor
Hulun Buir
Argun
Amur
Zeya
Ud
Niuman
Kumar
Nonni
Sungari
Ussuri
Iman
Muren
Hurka
Sufen
Iodzyhe
Tumen
Hun
Yalu
Liao
GREAT WALL
WILLOW PALISADES
50°
45°
40°
55°
125°
135°
140°

Acknowledgments

The present study originated as a doctoral dissertation prepared for the History Department of Columbia University. I am most grateful to Professor C. Martin Wilbur, under whose patient guidance the dissertation was completed. While being revised for publication, it benefited greatly from the expert criticisms of Professors John K. Fairbank, David M. Farquhar, and Jonathan D. Spence. Like many students of Chinese frontier history, I am intellectually indebted to Professor Owen Lattimore, whose pioneering studies in this field opened many fruitful avenues of inquiry to the newcomers.

To the Research Foundation of the State University of New York and the East Asian Research Center at Harvard University, I owe many thanks for their financial support. To Miss May Wu, my gratitude for her editorial assistance.

E. P. Dutton & Co. has kindly permitted me to quote extensive passes from the Malcolm Burr translation of *Dersu, the Trapper* by Vladimir K. Arseniev (New York, 1941).

Contents

The Manchurian Frontier
in Ch'ing History

Introduction

The geographical extent of the Manchurian frontier zone in this study is limited to the areas which during the greater part of the Ch'ing dynasty (1644–1911) were under the jurisdiction of the military governors of Kirin and Heilungkiang. It specifically excludes southern Manchuria, which although geographically a part of Manchuria, has been an area of Chinese settlement as early as the era of the Warring States (403–221 B.C.) It also excludes the Mongol territories to the west, which were governed directly by the Mongol aristocracy under the supervision of the Li-fan yüan (Bureau of Dependencies).

So defined, the Manchurian frontier zone formed a distinct political and cultural entity. For a greater part of the Ch'ing dynasty, its ethnic composition and administrative structure differed from all other areas of the Ch'ing empire. By the latter part of the nineteenth century, however, it had become so sinicized that when the imperial government decided to integrate all the frontier regions more firmly within the national structure, the Manchurian frontier not only accomplished the transition without any difficulty but was chosen, along with southern Manchuria, as a region in which basic reforms in the administrative organization of Chinese provinces were to have their first trial.

It is the purpose of this study to show that, although political changes in the Manchurian frontier zone in the late nineteenth century came as a result of the convergence of such changes as economic growth, internal political development in China proper, and the contemporary trend in international politics, one basic factor of political change was the cultural changes in Manchuria itself, in which Chinese immigration of various types played a pivotal role. A major aim will be to trace the process of sinicization of the Manchurian frontier area from the early years of the dynasty to the time when it became the provinces of Kirin and Heilungkiang, essentially Chinese in population and in cultural outlook. I will also try to correlate, as far as possible, the administrative changes with the cultural changes, so that the political dynamics in the frontier region may be better understood.

Because sinicization involved not only the transplantation of Chinese institutions and customs into the Manchurian context but also the reaction of the indigenous population to the intrusion of Chinese culture into their midst, the social and political organization of the tribal peoples and the consequences of their contacts with the Chinese immigrants will also come under discussion.

Finally, the Manchu rulers considered the Manchurian frontier a special preserve and the Ch'ing court was slow in recognizing the necessity for the reorganization of the older political structure of the frontier after the changing social environment had, for a long time, rendered it obsolete. The decision for reorganization, when it finally came, was prompted by contemporary domestic and international developments. I will try to show how such developments affected the reorganization program and how the program in turn affected the distribution of political power in the frontier region.

The Geographic and Cultural Foundation of the Ch'ing Manchurian Frontier Policy

The political geography of the Manchurian frontier area underwent a series of changes during the Ch'ing dynasty. In the course of their struggle with the Ming empire, the Manchus, under the leadership of Nurhachi (1559–1626) and Abahai (1592–1643), attained sovereignty over the various Tungusic tribes that lived in the Sungari-Amur-Ussuri region. The northern boundary of this newly conquered domain, however, remained vague and undefined. Meanwhile, the Russians were pushing their way eastward to the Pacific. In about seventy years (1582–1648) they had advanced as far as some of their present Far Eastern boundaries.[1]

The convergence of the Manchu and Russian advances produced a series of armed clashes in the Amur Valley, which led to the conclusion of the Treaty of Nerchinsk in 1689 and the demarcation of the Russo-Chinese boundary.[2] As defined by the treaty the northern boundary of Manchuria, starting from the western end, was drawn along the Argun, a tributary of the Amur, then along the Amur to the mouth of the Kerbechi, thence up the Kerbechi to its source, and eastward along the watershed between the basins of the Lena and the Amur up to the source of the Ud. In the valley of the Ud, between the northern and southern branches of the Outer Khingan ranges, the boundary remained undefined, because none of the negotiators knew the exact topography of that region.[3]

Thus, the Manchurian frontier region during the early period of the Ch'ing dynasty may be roughly defined as the areas north of the Willow Palisades in southern Manchuria, east of the Mongol territories paralleling the escarpment of the Great Khingan ranges, south of the line as specified in the Nerchinsk Treaty, and reaching Sakhalin Island and the Sea of Japan to the east.

Actually, very little was known of this huge region by the imperial government, for its garrisons were established only along the Amur, Nonni, Sungari, and Hurka (Mutan) rivers. There were a number of *karun* (frontier outposts) located along the Argun and Amur rivers to guard against Russian incursions, but none below the confluence of the Amur and Sungari rivers or along the great stretch of seacoast fronting the Sea of Okhostk and the Sea of Japan.[4] Aside from a geographical survey of Manchuria conducted by Jesuit missionaries as a part of an ambitious project covering the major areas of the empire during the years 1708–1718, the Ch'ing court seemed to have evinced little interest in exploring the outer reaches of its northeastern domain.[5] By contrast, Russian exploration of the entire Siberian region persisted from the seventeenth to the nineteenth century. The decline of Ch'ing power in the latter part of the nineteenth century gave the Russians opportunities to acquire the territories north of the Amur River, as codified in the Aigun Treaty of 1858, and the territories east of the Ussuri and Songatcha rivers and down to the Korean frontier, as specified in the Peking Treaty of 1860.

The Manchurian frontier territory remaining after 1860 is a rolling plain surrounded by mountain ranges on three sides: the Great Khingan in the west, the Lesser Khingan in the north, and the Ch'ang-pai-shan in the east. Its southern limit borders on the low-lying hills that separate the Sungari Valley from the Liao Valley of southern Manchuria.

The region has a cold, dry winter and a hot summer. The growing season is comparatively short, averaging five or six months a year. The rivers are frozen over for up to six months of the year in the north and five months in the south. The monsoon rains fall in the summer months, averaging about twenty-five inches on the plain. The rainiest areas are in the eastern mountains where precipitation averages up to forty inches. The semi-arid western part of the plain may receive less than twelve inches a year. The soil of the Manchurian plain is rich in humus, thick and fertile.[6]

The rich natural resources of Manchuria had important bearing upon its historical development. Its mountains were covered by extensive forests, which provided shelter for many valuable fur-bearing animals and shade for the much sought-after ginseng plant. The rivers teemed with fish. In the early period of the Ch'ing empire they also yielded pearls for the imperial treasury. The settlers found the soil so rich that they could grow bumper crops without the application of fertilizer. Beneath the earth were coal and iron deposits for the making of tools and implements. Gold was found in the riverbeds and along the banks of swift flowing streams. Throughout the Ch'ing period the Manchurian frontier was a land of opportunities for those willing to brave the hardships of a pioneer life.

Until railroads were built, distance and the difficulties of transportation were important natural obstacles hindering the settlement of the Manchurian frontier by Chinese immigrants. The total area of Kirin and Heilungkiang (including Hulun Buir) after 1860 was about 326,000 square miles. Adding the approximately 361,000 square miles ceded to Russia,[7] the entire Manchurian frontier zone would cover the immense area of 687,000 square miles, not much smaller than the 766,000 square miles of the twelve midwestern states of the United States. Few roads traversed this huge domain of plains, mountains, forests, and marshes. Aside from the post stations maintained by the frontier authorities between garrison points there were no commercial accommodations for travelers down to the nineteenth century. During the spring thaw and the summer monsoon, the entire area was an impassable quagmire. The virgin forests and marshes bred countless mosquitoes, midges, and gadflies that taxed the endurance of men and beasts alike. Even after Chinese immigration began to fill up the empty land, travel in Manchuria was still a burdensome task. M. de la Brunière, a French priest, wrote in 1846 of his experience while going from Kai-chen via San-hsing (modern I-lan) to the confluence of the Amur and Ussuri:

> Those who know the country best never go out without a mosquito cloth—that is to say, without a thick, double wrapper, covering the head and neck, and having two holes cut for the eyes. As to beasts of burden, to make them travel in the deserts five or six days in succession, under the noon-day's sun, is to expose them to almost certain death. These insects swarm particularly in moist, marshy places, and on the banks of the rivers by which Manchuria is intersected. Beyond San-sim [San-hsing] they grow to a monstrous size, particularly the gnats and wasps. As to others, as far as regards the punishment they inflict, it matters not whether they be small or large. The houses are somewhat preserved from them by the cultivated districts which surround them, and by their being fumigated with horse or cow dung: but they are not completely rid of them till the end of September, the time of the severe frosts.[8]

Twenty years later, H. E. M. James, a British civil officer in India, noted that if there were a time when life was not worth living, it was summer in the forests of Manchuria. To fend off the insect pests, men at plow wore circlets of iron on their heads on which were stuck bits of burning touchwood, and they carried pieces of it in their hands as well.[9]

He also called the roads mere tracks, more or less defined, from town to town, including the imperial postroads between garrison towns. During the greater part of the year they were usually impassable for carts; traffic was confined to the winter months when the ground was frozen. On the main line of communication, the worst sections of quagmire and the streams were bridged by local guilds, and in the north and east by the military authority. But the difficulties were so great that commerce was severely handicapped.[10]

Despite these difficulties, the Manchurian frontier region was the most accessible of all the frontier lands to Chinese immigrants. It was located next to the population centers of north China and could be reached either by land or across the Pohai Bay from Chihli and Shantung. Its interior was well drained by navigable rivers. The traveler was not required to scale formidable mountain ranges as in the Tibetan plateau land of southwest China or to cross burning deserts as in Mongolia or Sinkiang. In sum, during the Ch'ing dynasty, the Manchurian frontier possessed all the natural resources plus the advantage of accessibility that made it attractive to the poverty-stricken and land-hungry peasants of an overpopulated China proper.

Ethnic Distribution

The spatial distribution of ethnic groups in the Manchurian frontier zone conformed roughly to the lines denoted by the Willow Palisades. The Willow Palisades were nothing more than lines of willow trees broken at intervals by garrisoned checkpoints and protected by a deep trench.[11] The first line was planted in the last years of Shun-chih reign (1644–1661). During the K'ang-hsi reign (1662–1722) new sections were added from time to time until two palisades had been formed. One line extended northeastward from Shan-hai-kuan on the Great Wall to Kai-yuan and thence to the vicinity of the city of Kirin. Another line ran from Kai-yuan southeastward to the Yalu River. The whole scheme was completed in 1681.[12] After its completion, the Liao-tung plain, the traditional area of Chinese settlements, was circumscribed on three sides by the palisades. West of the palisades were the Mongol territories. Above the Liao-tung plain and east of the Mongol territories was the homeland of the Manchus. North of the Manchus were the Tungusic tribes, dwelling chiefly along the banks of such major rivers as the Ussuri, the Nonni, the Sungari, and the Amur, and their tributaries. The non-Tungusic Dagur tribes were found along the banks of the upper course of the Amur River and in the Nonni River valley. Hulun Buir, geographically a part of the Mongolian plateau, was also the home of various Mongol tribes.

After the overthrow of the Ming empire, many Manchus were sent to garrison various parts of China proper, and others were stationed in the tribal areas in the north. Meanwhile, Chinese immigrants penetrated the frontier region and settled among the Manchus and the tribal peoples. Thus began an intermingling of ethnic groups which had important consequences in the frontier political development.

The Manchus

During the latter part of the fourteenth century, a Juchen tribe of Tungus stock migrated upstream along the Hurka River from the San-hsing region to the valleys of Ch'ang-pai-shan, where they settled at first in the borderlands of northeastern Korea and southeastern Manchuria. When they finally made their homes, during the fifteenth century, at the banks of Heta Ala (upper course of Hun River in modern Liaoning province), they were known to the Ming Chinese as the Chien-chou Juchen, a small vassal tribe near the Ming frontier in south Manchuria. Originally a nomadic people who lived by hunting and fishing and used wooden bows and arrows, they learned to farm after coming into contact with the Koreans. At first they depended upon trade with the Koreans and Chinese for farm tools and draft oxen. By the latter part of the sixteenth century, relying on Korean and Chinese captives for technical knowledge, they had begun to mine their own iron ores and make their own iron weapons and implements. These technological advances resulted in better grain yields and made agriculture a major element of their economy.[13]

Beginning in 1583, Nurhachi, the Chien-chou chief, led his people in a series of campaigns which ultimately brought all the Juchen tribes under his control. In 1616 he was proclaimed *han* (emperor) by his supporters. Thereupon, he named his dynasty Chin suggesting, by so doing, an historical connection with the Chin dynasty, also of Juchen origin, of the twelfth and thirteenth centuries. In 1621 he took the Ming cities of Shen-yang (Mukden) and Liao-yang, thus coming into control of a sizable Chinese population and a rich agricultural district. Following Nurhachi's death in 1626, his son Abahai carried on the process of territorial expansion. In 1635 Abahai forbade the use of the term Juchen and invented the name Manchu for his people.

At the time of Nurhachi, the Juchen society was composed essentially of clan and tribal units. As tribal differences were being obliterated by Nurhachi's conquests, the Juchen society acquired more and more the characteristics of a feudal kingdom. At the top of the social pyramid were the *beile* and *beise*, the great chiefs or nobles who monopolized military and political power. Below them were the *irgen* or freemen, who had the right to bear arms. At the bottom were serfs and slaves composed mainly of war captives, a large number of whom were Chinese and Koreans. Chinese, Koreans, and Mongols who submitted voluntarily to Juchen rule were also drawn into the ranks of nobility and freemen.[14] With the organization of the banner system, which began in 1601, the Juchen nation was eventually divided into eight banners in 1615, with each of the banners controlled by one of Nurhachi's sons and a nephew. This change centralized the control of the Juchen army and state into the hands of Nurhachi and his family. It was the first step in transforming what was then an evolving feudal society into a bureaucratic state.[15]

After the death of Nurhachi, the inherent centrifugal tendency of the original banner system became apparent. Abahai, who ascended the throne with the control of two banners, but without the prestige of Nurhachi, felt insecure among other banner masters, who theoretically were all his equal. It was by installing a separate civil government, organized along Chinese principles and staffed by many Chinese officials and which was under his exclusive control, that Abahai succeeded gradually in undermining the feudal prerogatives of the banners by stripping away their governmental functions.[16] By the time the Manchus completed the conquest of China the separation of civil and military government was firmly established and the state had become a bureaucratic empire in the Chinese mold.

Thus, sinicization of Manchu society had begun well before the Manchu conquest of China. But Abahai and his immediate successors retained an ambivalent attitude toward Chinese culture. Although they adopted the Confucian ideology, worshiped Chinese gods, and patterned their political structure after the Ming model, they also insisted on preserving the identity of the Manchus as a separate people. Abahai once rebuked a Manchu adviser for urging him to adopt Chinese clothes for the Manchus.[17] After establishing themselves in China, the Manchu emperors discouraged the Manchus from intermarrying with Chinese and naming themselves in the Chinese style. Above all, they wanted the Manchus to preserve their ancestral language and martial spirit.

But the mass migration of Manchus into China proper inevitably accelerated the sinicization process. It was only on the Manchurian frontier that the possibility of keeping alive the "original" Manchu ways of life existed. A picture of this frontier Manchu culture during the early years of the dynasty has been handed down to us by Chinese exiles. It is an incomplete picture but adequate to serve as a point of reference for our later discussion of the Manchu frontier policy.

The Frontier Manchus

There are several eyewitness accounts of the frontier Manchu society in the latter half of the seventeenth century, not long after the Manchu conquest of Ming China. The earliest, written in 1660, was by Fang Kung-ch'ien, a Chinese official exiled to Ninguta in 1658 because his son was implicated in the state examination scandal of 1657. Another was written in 1721 by Wu Chen-ch'en, who was born in Ninguta in 1664 and lived there until 1681. Still another account was written by Yang Pin, the son of Yang An-ch'eng, who was exiled in 1662 on charges of sedition. Yang visited his father and recorded the scene at Ninguta as he saw it around 1690.[18] Because Ninguta was the administrative capital of the frontier region from 1653 to 1676, life there probably represented the best that the frontier could offer at that period.

A garrison town, Ninguta was built on the bank of the Hurka, which flows into the Sungari, an important tributary of the Amur. In 1660 it was surrounded by a low wooden palisade measuring three li (one li is approximately one-third mile) in circumference and guarded by four gates. At the center of the town were several thatched buildings which served as the headquarters of the military government. The compound was protected by walls constructed of broken stones, which would collapse whenever it rained. The banner soldiers lived within the palisade. As an imperial favor, obtained through the kindness of the garrison commander, the exiled officials were permitted to reside within the walled town. The rest of the population lived in several nearby villages.[19] In 1666 a new town was built. It was surrounded by two walls: an inner wooden wall measuring two and a half li in circumference and an outer mud wall ten li in circumference. The mud wall soon collapsed and was not rebuilt. The offices and private residences of high military officials were located inside the wooden wall, and the soldiers and civilian population lived within the mud wall. In 1690 the town boasted only about four hundred households.[20]

The villagers farmed lands provided by the government. Farms that had been cultivated for six or seven years were abandoned in favor of virgin soil, which was plentiful. Rice could not be grown. Millet, barley, bran, buckwheat, and kaoliang were the common crops. Wine was made from glutinous millet. Wheat was introduced but seldom ripened in time to be harvested. Tea was a luxury. Fishing was ordinarily done by harpooning from a canoe lighted by torch during moonlit nights. Firewood was obtained from the forest. Sesame oil or the oil from the seeds of *Perilla ocymoides (su-tzu)* was used for cooking. For lighting, the stem of the flax plant was smeared with a mixture of millet chaff and the residue of the seeds of *Perilla ocymoides,* which had been pressed for oil. The natives did not know the art of beekeeping. It was the Chinese exiles who taught them how to extract wax from honeybee combs for the making of candles. Horses, canoes, oxcarts, and sleds were the common means of transportation.[21]

The region was surrounded by primeval forests. In building a house, the framework was constructed of rough-hewn logs bound together with ropes. The roof was thatched with a species of long slender grass called locally roofing grass. The walls were plastered with mud. The door was latched from the outside. The window was pasted over with Korean paper and closed from the outside as a precaution against tigers. The house, a simple one-room structure, always faced south to take advantage of sunlight. Ranged against the walls were three *k'ang*, hollow earthen beds which could be heated in cold weather. The family slept on the southern and western *k'ang,* and the servants and slaves occupied the northern *k'ang*. When guests were entertained the master was seated on the southern *k'ang* and the guest on the western *k'ang*. Dogs, chickens, horses, and cattle shared the same room with the human occupants. Fang noticed, however, that some families were beginning to separate the animals, to partition the room with curtains, and to add side buildings. Clothes and furs were kept in a storehouse and grains in a granary. Food was cooked on stoves located on the southern and northern *k'angs*. The house and the outbuildings were surrounded by wooden fences.[22] Household utensils were made of wood. Pottery and ceramic wares were extremely rare [23]

Money was scarce. Silver was used only for the purchase of houses, land, and slaves. Copper coins were traded to tribal people, who used them for personal ornaments. Ordinary trade was conducted through bartering.[24] Every year on the tenth lunar month, a trade expedition was sent to Hoi Ryŏng (Hui-ning in Chinese), a Korean border town, located on the bank of the Tumen River, southeast of Ninguta, where salt, rice, iron, cloth, paper, cattle, and horses were obtained. The Manchus sold the salt at a high price to the Chinese residents; they themselves preferred a condiment made of pickled vegetable.[25]

A traveler could enter any home and receive free food and lodging for himself and his horse.[26] Friends greeted each other by holding hands or embracing. During a feast, the guests were offered tobacco, wine, and buttered tea. Meat was served on oiled cloth, each person cut his own portion with a knife. Men and women of the host family entertained the guests with dances, which were accompanied by singing and clapping.[27]

The frontier Manchus were polygamous. If he could afford it, a man might have as many as ten or more wives.[28] Early marriage was the rule, often when the couple were only ten years old or younger. It was arranged by the parents, whose major consideration was the social status of the opposite family.[29] Divorce was relatively easy. There was no social stigma attached to a woman remarrying many times.[30] Like other Tungus people, the frontier Manchus probably practiced levirate. It was only in 1630 that Abahai publicly prohibited a man marrying his step-mother, wife of his uncle, sister-in-law, or wife of his nephew. Marriage between members of the same clan was also banned in that year.[31] However, the prohibition was violated soon after Abahai's death by his brother, Dorgon, who became the regent of the young Shun-chih emperor. Dorgon married his nephew's wife and was reputed to have married one of Abahai's wives. The Shun-chih emperor himself took as concubine the wife of his younger brother.[32] The Manchus in China eventually gave up such marriage practices, which were considered incestuous according to Chinese law. But the frontier Manchus seemed to have preserved vestiges of these ancestral practices long after they had disappeared among the Manchus in China proper. According to Shirokogoroff, among the Manchus in Aigun, down to the early years of the twentieth century, the younger male members of the family had sexual rights over women of their generation who were wives of the men older than they.[33]

The religious life of the frontier Manchus was dominated by shamanism. The shamanistic dance, called *t'iao-shen* by the Chinese, has been described in various eyewitness accounts, which, although different in minor details, agree in the essential features. The dance could be performed in any season but was performed particularly at the end of the year. It was held to honor ancestors, to exorcise illness, or to divine the future. The central role was always assumed by a woman, either a professional shaman or the mistress of the house. She wore a helmet-like headdress and a skirt festooned with numerous little bells, which jingled merrily as she danced. During the exercise, she chanted incantations and beat on a drum held in her hand. A pig was sacrificed before a long wooden pole erected in the courtyard and believed to be the situs of spirits. The entrails of the pig were read for omen, and the meat was served to invited friends and relatives. Meat was also placed in a container tied to the pole. If crows came to eat the meat, the family was pleased, for it meant that the spirits had come to participate in the feast; otherwise, it would be a sign that the spirits were angry.[34]

The dead were put into dilapidated boats, which served as coffins, and were cremated within three days. According to Fang, when a man died, a concubine was to accompany him in death. The woman destined to be sacrificed was so designated when her master was still alive. She could not refuse to die nor could another woman take her place. As the time for the funeral arrived, she sat on the *k'ang* dressed in her best and refrained from weeping. The mistress led the rest of the household in doing obeisance to her. The victim died by hanging herself with a bowstring. If she refused to die by her own hand, the members of the family would strangle her to death.[35] Fang did not state how widespread was the occurrence of such acts throughout the frontier Manchu society. It was not mentioned in other accounts of early Chinese exiles. We know, however that human sacrifice was practiced by the imperial household down to the end of the Shun-chih reign (1644–1661). Nurhachi's wife and possibly two concubines committed suicide at his death, either voluntarily or forced to do so by his sons, and were buried together with him.[36] A number of eunuchs and palace maids were sacrificed at the death of Empress Hsiao-hsien (1639–1660).[37] It was quite possible that such barbarity was not limited to the imperial household and that influential Manchu families on the frontier merely followed a practice long sanctioned by tradition and that the practices had died out both in China and in Manchuria at the end of the Shun-chih reign. Cremation was officially banned for all bannermen by an imperial decree on December 3, 1735.[38] But the practice continued in Heilungkiang at least down to the early nineteenth century.[39]

The most important Manchu social grouping was the clan or *hala*. A large *hala* would split into a number of branches or *mokun*, whose members generally lived together in a village or *gashen*. During their tribal days, the *hala* and *mokun* were the basic political, military, and economic units of the Manchus. Their members fought and hunted together under the leadership of the clan chiefs, *halada* and *mokunda*. Many of these clan chiefs became hereditary officers under the banner system. A clan chief without military appointment would still retain considerable influence in his own village, serving as village chief or *gashenda*.

Shirokogoroff's study of the Manchu clan as it existed in Aigun in the beginning of the twentieth century could be taken as somewhat approximating the clan system of the earlier centuries, because the Aigun Manchus were the last to be affected by the process of sinicization. According to this study, the Manchu clan was a group of persons united by the recognition of a common ancestor and the worship of a common group of spirits. Descent was patrilineal. Marriage was clan-exogamous. However, the members of the same *hala* might intermarry if it had split into a number of *mokun* whose members did not live in the same locality.[40]

The *mokun* met periodically, usually once a year, and not less than once in three years, to hold clan sacrifices and to choose the *mokunda*. The presence of all members of the *mokun* was obligatory. Men and women met separately. The *mokunda* was chosen for his intelligence, tact, honesty, and education; his wealth and social status in the community were not considered. He presided over clan meetings; acted as the highest authority in resolving clan affairs; supervised clan rituals; maintained clan laws and the moral code; granted permission for marriage, inheritance, and the division of family units; kept up the clan list; and safeguarded the situs of clan spirits. His orders could not be annulled or revised by other authorities. The government referred to the *mokunda* all legal cases concerning the clan members; it acted directly only in very serious cases.[41]

Because of the burdensome character of his functions, few persons were interested in the post. Usually, at clan meetings, members proclaimed someone as candidate and pressed him to accept the honor. Sometimes the *mokunda* served for twenty years or more, and his son often succeeded him after his retirement. The women's meetings were attended by all unmarried women of the clan and the wives of clansmen. A woman clan chief, *hehe mokunda*, was elected by the women with the same rights and functions as the *mokunda* for the men.[42]

The Manchu family, *gargan*, was composed of a couple, their children and grandchildren, the wives of their married sons, and sometimes their aged parents. The family chief was usually the most energetic member of the family. He controlled the economic activities of the household with an autocratic hand. The direction and control of the family law was reserved to the oldest male of the *gargan* as long as he was able to perform his duties. Relationships between family members were regulated by custom. The older generation exercised great influence in the family council until they succumbed to the onset of senility.[43]

Slaves and workmen were also included in the family. After a lapse of time, a slave could be adopted by the clan to which his master belonged; but he would still be considered as the property of the house. Slaves of the first generation and their children were always slaves and were forbidden to marry Manchu girls. However, several generations after their adoption into the clan, their inferior origin was forgotten and they became social equal of other clan members.[44]

There is no doubt that the long centuries of peace had eroded much of the authority and power of the Manchu clan chief, who could no longer aspire to lead his clansmen in military conquest, thus repeating the glorious career of Nurhachi. Still, he presided over a community that was socially cohesive and possessed a large degree of autonomy in village affairs.

The frontier life described above was presumably that which the early Manchu emperors were so anxious to keep untainted by Chinese influence. It was a spartan life, devoid of any intellectual tradition or artistic refinement. By elevating the martial skills of archery and horsemanship as the paramount virtues of the frontier Manchus, the emperors, in effect, ill prepared them to resist the peaceful encroachment of Chinese ideology and material culture.

The Frontier Tribes

With the exception of the Gilyak, who spoke a paleo-Asiastic language, the tribal peoples of the Manchurian frontier were either of Tungus or Mongol stock. The Tungus people, dependent upon their environment, lived by fishing, hunting, or reindeer-breeding. The Mongols were herders of cattle, sheep, and horses. In religion, the Tungus practiced shamanism, and the Mongols followed the teachings of the Lama church.

In the early Ch'ing records, the Tungus tribes were identified by the localities in which they lived. For the purposes of this book, only the large regional groups as they were known to the seventeenth-century frontier administrators will be considered.[45] Among these the most important were the Heje (Goldi) who ranged throughout the Ussuri, Hurka, and the lower Sungari and Amur basins. The Hurka, strongest among the Heje tribes, had engaged in a prolonged struggle with the Manchus, which ended in the absorption of many of their tribesmen into the Manchu banner force. Their homeland was known as Ilan Hala or San-hsing in Chinese. They were the most Manchuized of all the Heje tribes. The Heje who lived along the banks of the Ussuri and its tributaries were known as the Muren and Ch'i-ya Hala. Those who lived along the banks of lower Sungari and the nearby Amur region were known as Shaven Heje in reference to their custom of shaving the forward part of their head and braiding their hair into queues as the Manchus did. The Muren, Ch'i-ya Hala, and Shaven Heje were less Manchuized than the Hurka. The Unshaven Heje (Olcha) knotted their hair and lived along the Amur below the Shaven Heje. The Kile occupied the coastal region of the lower Amur. The Gilyak, known to the frontier administrators as Fiatka, although not Tungus, lived very much like their Tungus neighbors at the mouth of the Amur and in northern Sakhalin. The various Heje tribes and the Gilyak were also known collectively by the Manchus and Chinese as Fishskin Tatars because they wore articles of clothings made of salmon (*tamaha*) skins. The Kiakar (Udekhe), unrelated to the Heje, were found in the Tumen region bordering Korea and along the seacoast in Ussuria. These were all hunting and fishing tribes.

Other Tungus tribes occupied the upper course of the Amur and its tributaries. The Manegir and Birar were found mostly on the left bank of the Amur. The Orochon made their homes in the Khingan ranges along the Amur and Argun rivers. The Solon, who originally lived north of the Amur along the banks of Zeya River and its tributaries, migrated to the Nonni Valley under the pressure of predatory Cossack bands. They submitted to Manchu rule only after having been defeated in a series of skirmishes by the Manchus and harassed by the Russians.[46]

The Dagur, a Mongol tribe, had lived together with the Solon in the Zeya region and migrated with them to the Nonni Valley. In the protracted Manchu campaign against the Russians many Solon and Dagur tribesmen served as Manchu auxiliaries. When peace was restored, some of the Solon and Dagur tribes were absorbed into the banner force. The rest were organized into units called Buteha (hunting) banners under the leadership of their tribal and clan chiefs and supervised by appointed Manchu officers.[47] The Buteha banners were also given jurisdiction over the Orochon, Birar, and Manegir tribes. The Orochon were divided into two groups. Those who had been organized into Buteha banner units were called Moringa (equestrian) Orochon and those who lived in scattered groups deep in the mountains were called Yafahan (pedestrian) Orochon.[48] The Solon, Dagur, and Moringa Orochon became, in the course of time, highly Manchuized. The Birar, Manegir, and Yafahan Orochon had only sporadic contacts with the Manchus and retained much of their original culture.

The strategic Hulun Buir, which bordered on Russian Siberia and Outer Mongolia, was settled by Solon and Dagur banner units transferred from the Nonni region by the frontier authorities and also by various Mongol groups of Barga, Ölöt, and Buriat origin. The Barga Mongols were differentiated into Old and New Barga. The Old Barga were believed to have migrated from Russian territory into Heilungkiang during the K'ang-hsi reign, when the Manchus and Russians were contesting the control of upper Amur region. They were organized into banner units for garrison duties at Tsitsihar, Heilungkiang, and other towns. In 1732, a total of 275 Old Barga soldiers were sent to Hulun Buir, where they were integrated with the Solon banners and settled along the Hailar River. Their descendants had become so thoroughly Solonized that they forsook Lamaism and adopted shamanism as their religion.[49] The New Barga were immigrants who came from Outer Mongolia in 1734. They were organized then into eight banners totaling 2,484 officers and men who occupied the pastures along the I-min River.[50] The Ölöt were also differentiated into Old and New Ölöt. The Old Ölöt were part of the invading Ölöt force captured by the Manchus in 1732. The New Ölöt were Jungar troops who surrendered to the Manchus in 1755 and were brought to Manchuria for resettlement.[51] There were also Buriat Mongols who fled the Russian territory during the Hsien-feng reign (1851–1861) and settled near Lake Hulun.[52] The Mongol nomads of Hulun Buir, thanks to the Lama church, their unique way of life, and a common heritage with their kindred in Outer Mongolia and Inner Mongolia, were able to uphold their cultural tradition until toward the end of the Ch'ing dynasty.

The Aftermath of the Manchu Conquest

The Manchu conquest of the tribal territories had two important consequences: the fragmentation of tribal power and the shifting of tribal population. The Heje are an example:

As among the Manchus, the basic social unit of the Heje was the *hala* or *mokun*. The clan chief, *halada* or *mokunda*, was responsible for the administration of clan affairs and the enforcement of clan rules. A village inhabited by several clans would be governed by a village chief, *gashenda*, elected by the clan chiefs. A large village, containing several thousand inhabitants and protected by an earthen wall, was called a *hoton*. Its chief was called *tsushenda*.[53]

According to Heje legends, an outstanding and ambitious *tsushenda* or *gashenda*, by conquering the neighboring settlements, could become a powerful tribal chief, known as *ejen han* or *han*.[54] This seems to have been the common and traditional process of nation building among the frontier peoples. Nurhachi himself was a humble clan chief who developed into an empire builder. The Heje legends related that the Heje people had been divided in the past into three major tribes living respectively in the Amur, Sungari, and Ussuri districts. The Ussuri tribe had nineteen *hoton* and thirty-six *gashen*; the Sungari tribe, nine *hoton* and twelve *gashen*; and the Amur tribe had an unknown number of settlements.[55]

The *ejen han* governed the tribe with the assistance of a hierarchy of civil and military officials. The tribe itself might be divided into *niru* or sections, each of which was under the rule of a *niru jangin*. The military force was organized into units of various sizes, each led by an officer of designated rank. Soldiers were conscripted for service from each household that had more than one able-bodied male. Punishments of crime included the death penalty for murder, exile, and fines of animals for lesser offenses.[56]

Although these legends, transmitted orally from generation to generation among the Heje of lower Sungari and recorded in the twentieth century, cannot be considered as a completely accurate description of the Heje tribal organization prior to the Manchu conquest, their existence, nevertheless, indicates that the Heje had developed considerable political progress before they succumbed to Manchu rule. As evidence, one may point to the genealogy of the Keike clan, the most prominent of the four powerful Hurka clans in San-hsing. The founder, Ni-ya-hu-t'u, had become a tribal chief during the Wan-li reign (1573–1619) of the Ming dynasty. During the T'ien-ch'i reign (1621–1627), his grandson, So-so-k'u, migrated with his people to the San-hsing region, where he achieved dominance over twenty-two clan or tribal groups. As a paramount chief his power extended from the Hurka River to Wu-cha-la, a village on the north bank of Sungari, which was the site of the battle fought between the Manchus and Russians in 1652.

In 1631, after receiving a Manchu envoy at San-hsing, So-so-k'u personally brought a tribute of sables to Sheng-ching, the Manchu capital, where he was given an audience by Abahai, received a title of nobility, and was married to a princess.[57] In other words, he was being treated as a man of great political significance.

This supposition is borne out by Manchu accounts of battles fought against the Hurka. In 1608 one thousand Hurka invaded Ninguta but were repelled by the Manchu garrison. In 1611 two thousand Manchu troops battered a Hurka village for three days. When the defenders were overcome, one thousand of them were killed and two thousand made captives. In an expedition in 1619, two thousand prisoners were taken by the Manchus. A 1625 campaign resulted in the taking of one thousand five hundred prisoners and the submission of five hundred households.[58] These battles indicated that the Hurka had been organized in a powerful tribal confederation, which succeeded remarkably well in blocking for many years the Manchu expansion toward the Hurka-Sungari-Amur region.

The submission of So-so-k'u signaled the irreversible decline of Hurka power. The Hurka were absorbed into Manchu banners and fought for the Manchus in China proper. (The Kiaker of Tumen Valley and the Heje of Ussuri were similarly defeated by Manchu arms and then absorbed into the Manchu banners.) Their *mokunda* and *gashenda* became hereditary officers in banner units composed of tribal soldiers. In time, their tribal origin became obscured and they were known as New Manchus. Those tribesmen who were not incorporated into the Manchu banners were controlled through the tributary system. Their *mokunda* and *gashenda* were made answerable to the Manchu frontier authorities. Through these devices the tribesmen had been rendered militarily impotent and politically fragmented. The days of *ejen han* and large tribal formations were over. Only memories of them were preserved in the legends.

The shifting of tribal population was the natural outcome of years of warfare involving the tribes, the Manchus, and the Russians and the result of Manchu policy. The southward migration of the Solon and Dagur tribes has already been noted. It is quite possible that similar movements occurred among all Tungus tribes whenever they felt heavy military pressure coming from either the Manchus or Russians. Many of them had followed a nomadic or semi-nomadic way of life, and consequently such migratory movements were easily accomplished.

On the other hand, the peopling of Hulun Buir by refugee and captive Mongol groups was a deliberate move by the Manchu authorities as a defense measure against the Russians and Jungars. The greatest migratory movement occured, however, as the outcome of Manchu recruitment of tribal peoples into their banner system. Entire village and clan groups abandoned their tribal homes and resettled with the Manchus as garrison troops in various parts of the Ch'ing empire. Whether the tribesmen had been killed as enemies or taken in as allies, the frontier population was significantly reduced by the Manchu conquest. The sparsely populated frontier had become emptier still. The resulting population vacuum was not significantly remedied by the reverse movement of banner troops composed of Manchu, Mongol, and Chinese units into the tribal areas.

The Bordering Mongol Tribes of Inner Mongolia

During the Ch'ing dynasty, the Mongols of Inner Mongolia were under the jurisdiction of the Li-fan yüan. Those who lived along the border of Kirin and Heilungkiang belonged to the Front and Rear Gorlos banners, the Jalait banner, and the Dörbet banner of the Jerim League. They were governed directly by a hereditary nobility and the Lama church. Throughout the seventeenth and eighteenth centuries, the administrative relationship between Manchurian frontier authorities and the Mongol princes was limited to the preservation of order along the border areas, for example, in the apprehension of criminals and the settlement of disputes between Mongols and frontier inhabitants. However, geographical proximity created political complications between the two regions in later years.

The Mongols occupied the eastern part of the great Mongolian plateau and the western portion of the Manchurian plain. Across their territory lay a land route to the Manchurian frontier which bypassed southern Manchuria. The early attempts of the Manchus to seal off Kirin from Chinese ginseng poachers, for instance, was frustrated by the latter, who took the Mongol grassland route circumventing the checkpoints along the Willow Palisades. The strategic military route linking Kirin and Heilungkiang also passed through the domain of the Dörbet and Gorlos banners.[59] It was to supply the post stations along this route that government agricultural settlements were first set up in the Mongol lands in Heilungkiang. These settlements, however, were mere hamlets of a hundred or so families composed exclusively of station personnel, who cultivated fodder and grain for the stations' consumption only.[60]

The virgin soils of the Manchurian plain provided the Mongol princes with opportunities to increase their incomes by taking in Chinese farm tenants. The Manchu court, time and again, issued decrees forbidding the cultivation of Mongol lands by Chinese immigrants, but the combination of famine-driven peasants and profit-seeking Mongols continued to frustrate the decrees. In 1791 the ruling Mongol duke of the Front Gorlos banner near Kirin memorialized the throne for permission to open the tribal land for colonization in order to legalize the status of many Shantung and Chihli peasants who had already settled there. In 1799 the government acquiesced to the plea in the face of accomplished fact by setting up the Ch'ang-ch'un sub-prefecture in the settled area to administer the settlers, putting them under the direct jurisdiction of Kirin authority.[61] This was the beginning of the displacement of Mongol herdsmen by Chinese cultivators in the Manchurian frontier and the expansion of Manchurian political control over Mongol banners.

Cultural Autonomy and Imperial Control

Briefly, the geographic and ethnic realities which the Ch'ing rulers had to take into account in the formulation of their Manchurian frontier policy were: a huge undeveloped territory, sparsely populated by relatively backward tribal peoples and frontier Manchus, richly endowed with natural resources especially in arable lands and dependable rainfall, and easily accessible from the population centers of north China. If Chinese immigration were permitted, the region could conceivably overtake or even surpass many parts of China proper in economic and cultural attainment within a not too long period of time. But the early Manchu emperors preferred a policy aiming at the preservation of the frontier political and cultural status quo. The key element in this policy was the prohibition of Chinese immigration.

The Manchu rulers justified their stand on the ground that they wanted to preserve their ancestral homeland and the traditional Manchu values and ways of life from Chinese influences and incidentally to safeguard the exclusive Manchu right to exploit three of Manchuria's most highly valued products: ginseng, furs, and pearls. These were plausible reasons. But they did not go far enough. To understand the

Manchu or Ch'ing policy correctly it must be seen within the context of the long history of imperial China as well as the particular circumstances of the Manchu rise to power.

Because of the constant threat of barbarian invasion and the inadequacy of any system of static frontier defense, strong dynastic rulers of imperial China often attempted to extend political control over the barbarian peoples beyond the Great Wall, and were obliged to devise political forms suitable for the governing of peoples whose geographical environment, economic organization, and cultural orientation differed from that of the Chinese people. The failure of Ming rulers to devise a satisfactory method of political control over the Juchen tribes finally led to the overthrow of the Ming dynasty and the establishment of the Manchu empire in the Far East.

The Manchus had conquered China by forging an alliance composed of themselves, the Mongols, and dissident Chinese. As rulers of China, they were determined not to let such an alliance be formed again. Consequently, one of the basic elements of their frontier policy was to minimize contacts between the different ethnic groups as much as possible. The natural barriers that separated the major ethnic groups of the empire, such as Chinese, Mongols, Uigurs, Tibetans, and Tungusic tribes, were reinforced by legal and political prohibitions. From the administrative viewpoint, the segregation of ethnic blocs eliminated many potential conflicts that might have arisen from the unrestricted intermingling of peoples of different ethnic origin, for example, the struggle for arable lands between peasants and herders and for pasture rights among the nomads themselves. But the overriding concern was to prevent the rise of any frontier power to challenge the imperial rule. For this reason there was an identity as well as a divergence of interests between the Manchu elite in China proper and the frontier Manchus. The elite would have liked to preserve the military strength of the frontier Manchus in support of the dominant position of the Manchu population throughout the empire but not to the extent that it could constitute a danger to the ruling house. In this regard, the material and cultural primitiveness of the frontier region became a political asset rather than a liability. The frontier Manchus, in the eyes of their imperial masters, should be isolated from the corrupting influence of Chinese culture and be content to serve in the frontier banner force all their lives. The privilege of delving into the Chinese classics and becoming members of the civil bureaucracy was to be reserved for the sophisticated Manchus in China proper.

Evidence of this outlook may be seen in the belated establishment of schools for frontier bannermen. The first school in the city of Kirin was opened in 1693, half a century after the enthronement of the first Manchu emperor in Peking; in Ninguta, 1728; in San-hsing, 1734; in Alchuka, 1727; and in Lalin, 1756. The curriculm for all these schools included only the Manchu language, horsemanship, and archery. The first such schools in Heilungkiang were established in 1695 for the children of New Manchus, Sibe, Solon, and Dagur banners. It was only in 1744 that schools for all bannermen children were opened at Mergen, Heilungkiang-ch'eng, and Tsitsihar. Not until 1824 was a Chinese language school opened in Kirin and that only for the purpose of training translators. The first Chinese language school in Heilungkiang, a private school supported by the military governor, was opened in 1796 for the children of bannermen in Tsitsihar.[62]

In retrospect, the policy of isolating the Manchurian frontier culturally from China proper was effective only insofar as it delayed the social and economic development of the frontier. It did not prevent the slow but steady cultural integration of the frontier with China proper. The following reasons may be offered as an explanation for this failure:

The Ch'ing empire was governed as a Chinese empire, ideologically oriented toward Confucianism, administratively patterned after the traditional Chinese bureaucratic state, and culturally nurtured in the mainstream of Chinese civilization. The great majority of the Manchu population lived in China proper where they in time absorbed almost every aspect of Chinese culture. The Manchu emperors and social elite were educated in the Chinese classics and tended progressively to look at the world from a Chinese point of view. It was difficult for the Manchu ruling class in China proper, who enjoyed wholeheartedly the fruits of Chinese civilization, to convince their frontier cousins that they should be content with the comparatively simple life of their forebears. Indeed, among the agents of cultural changes in the frontier region were high Manchu officials sent to the frontier from the capital and frontier Manchus who returned to their home districts after service in China proper.

The confinement of the bannermen to military and agricultural pursuits and the absence of an intellectual tradition combined to inhibit the rise of any vigorous indigenous culture on the frontier that could resist the inroads of Chinese cultural elements. Leadership in frontier Manchu society came from the sophisticated and sinicized bannermen, not from the local residents.

The most important reason was the impossibility of physically isolating the Manchurian frontier from China proper completely. Despite obstacles, Chinese immigrants entered the frontier almost as soon as the dynasty was established. They brought with them their own social values and ways of life and succeeded little by little in engulfing the Manchu population and changing the cultural configuration of the entire frontier region. According to Sa-ying-e, by the end of the eighteenth century, practically everyone in Kirin spoke Chinese. Only those Manchus living in tightly knit clan communities still preserved their ancestral tongue. Because 80 to 90 percent of the town population was Chinese, the local Manchu elite, according to this Manchu observer, had to keep their children off the streets and marry them to girls in the rural settlements in order to preserve a knowledge of the Manchu language among their offspring.[63] In Heilungkiang, Chinese merchants dealing with Solon, Dagur, and Mongol customers often learned to speak the tribal languages, but few of them bothered to learn Manchu as practically all Manchus spoke Chinese.[64] By the end of the dynasty, Shirokogoroff found that only the Manchus of Aigun, the northernmost garrison, still preserved part of their original culture.[65]

The retardation of the frontier Manchus' cultural development facilitated the sinicization of the frontier and the ultimate transfer of the frontier political power from the Manchus to the Chinese. In the following chapters an attempt will be made to trace the course of this historic political and cultural transformation.

2

The Banner System

The banner system was the key Ch'ing instrument for the preservation of the Manchus as a separate ethnic entity and of the frontier as a Manchu stronghold. Because it served different political objectives, the banner force in Manchuria differed from its counterpart in China proper in many significant details.

Origin

Marked arrows had long been used by the Juchen tribes as a means of group and personal identification. In large tribal hunting expeditions, which could involve thousands of men drawn from scores of clans and villages and covering huge territories, discipline was maintained by clan leaders who identified their own groups by their clan arrow marks and the animals slaughtered by the personal marks of the individual hunters. Similar means of maintaining discipline were employed in time of war as the clan leaders led their men into battle. Quite naturally, the term *niru ejen,* master of arrows, came to be applied to clan and village leaders who served as officers during hunting and military expeditions.[1]

By 1584 *niru ejen* had developed into a permanent military rank in the tribal army of Nurhachi. As his army grew, Nurhachi grouped his warriors into larger units, commanded by members of his family and identified by their banners *(gusai)*. In the war against the alliance of nine Juchen and Mongol tribes in 1593, Nurhachi referred to his troops as banner soldiers.[2]

In 1601 Nurhachi carried the development of the banner system a significant step forward by transforming what hitherto had been a confederation of clan and village groups into a more centralized organization. Through aggressive warfare, dating back to 1583, he had conquered some of the neighboring tribes, whose manpower increased his military potential but whose sense of tribal loyalty could become a source of weakness. His solution was to obliterate tribal distinctions without destroying the clan structure of the Juchen society. The entire population, regardless of their tribal background, was divided into four banners, each of which was composed of a number of *niru,* headed by *niru ejen,* who served both as military officers and as administrators of clan and village affairs. Each banner was identified by its color: yellow, white, red, and blue. The *niru ejen* were responsible to the *gusai ejen,* banner master, who in turn was responsible to Nurhachi. As victories brought in more people, more *niru* were created and distributed to the banners. In 1615 four more banners were created, each identified by the colored border of its flag: the yellow, white, and blue flags were bordered with red and the red with white. Five *niru* were combined into a *jalan,* five *jalan* to a banner.[3] These came to be known in a later period as the eight Manchu banners, although within their ranks were tribesmen of non-Manchu origin as well as Mongol, Korean, and Chinese allies and captives. Later, as more Mongol and Chinese soldiers were drawn into the banner system, they were organized into separate banners. The first Mongol *niru* were organized in 1621 and the first Chinese *niru* in 1630. By 1635 there were eight Mongol banners and by 1642 eight Chinese banners. The color of their flags were similar to those of the Manchu banners.[4]

Organization

As a military organization the banners changed little since Nurhachi's days. The number of *jalan* and *niru* increased with the expansion of the banner force, but the number of banners remained the same. Originally, there were three hundred soldiers to each *niru,* but this number varied according to time and local requirements. Ordinarily, an expeditionary force or a garrison command was composed of a varying number of *niru* drawn from all banners. In this regard, the banner was more of an administrative and political instrument rather than an integrated armed force organized for independent military action. For instance, the elite troops, *bayara,* which became the imperial guards, were drawn from the best soldiers of all banners.[5]

The banner was administered by the *gusai ejen,* who was assisted by two *meiren ejen.* The *jalan* and *niru* were administered by the *jalan ejen* and *niru ejen* respectively. In 1634 the term *janggin,* official, was substituted for *ejen* for all ranks except the *gusai ejen,* which retained its original designation. In 1660 standard Chinese equivalents for the Manchu terms were promulgated: *tu-t'ung* (lieutenant general) for *gusai ejen, fu tu-t'ung* (deputy lieutenant general) for *meiren janggin*, *ts'an-ling* (colonel) for *jalan janggin* and *tso-ling* (major) for *niru janggin*. The Chinese banners were translated as *Han-chün* (Chinese army), and the Manchu and Mongol banners were known simply as *Man-chou* (Manchu) and *Meng-ku* (Mongol). In 1724 the *gusai ejen* was renamed *gusai amban* (banner commander).[6] The evolution of the Manchu nomenclature signified the various stages in which the Manchu emperor solidified his control over the banners at the expense of the *hosei beile* (highest ranking imperial princes), who had controlled them jointly with the emperor.

All persons belonging to the banner organization were known as bannermen or *ch'i-jen* in Chinese. Among the bannermen, the *booi* (*pao-i* in Chinese) or bondservants formed a special category. The majority of them were war prisoners enslaved by their Manchu captors and served in the households or fields of their masters. Most of them were Chinese. Others were condemned criminals or persons descended to servile status because of poverty. Unless freed by their masters, they and their descendants remained bondservants all their lives.[7] The great slave-owners were members of the Nurhachi family and high ranking banner officers. Sometime between 1615 and 1620, the bondservants of the emperor and *hosei beile* were organized into *niru* and *jalan*, thus becoming part of the Manchu banners. Other bondservants were not so organized and remained privately owned slaves. The bondservants in the Plain Yellow, Bordered Yellow, and Plain White banners, which came to be known since 1651 as the Three Superior Banners because they were directly controlled by the emperor, became the bannermen of the Office of the Imperial Household (Nei-wu fu); those in the Five Inferior Banners became bannermen of the princely households.[8] Because of their intimacy to the source of political authority, the officers of the bondservant *niru* often attained respectable positions in the civil and military bureaucracy. A bondservant who attained the presidency of one of the Six Boards, one of the highest administrative posts in the empire, could be elevated through imperial dispensation to the status of regular bannerman, a process called *t'ai-ch'i* (banner lifting).[9] The majority of the bondservants, however, worked as serfs on the imperial and princely estates in Liao-tung. A bondservant who served as steward, *chuang-t'ou*, on such an estate often became a prosperous landowner as the estate system disintegrated in the latter part of the dynasty.[10] On the whole, the social status of bondservant progressed from that of personal degradation to a position of equality with the rest of the banner population during the period of Manchu rule.

The political role of the banners could be seen most clearly by examining the composition and responsibilities of the *niru*. The *niru* was originally organized according to the clan or territorial relationship of its members. An entire clan or village (made up usually of two or more clans) was constituted into one or more *niru* or a half *niru*, depending upon the size of its population. When a large clan or village was split into two or more *niru*, the close relatives of the clan or village chief were appointed *niru ejen* of the new *niru*. A half *niru* could be expanded into a full *niru* through natural increase in population or as the result of more clansmen and villagers joining the Manchu cause. When two or more small groups of clansmen were formed into one *niru*, the chiefs of the larger clans could be appointed to administer the *niru* jointly or in rotation. A new *niru* might be formed from the surplus personnel of unrelated *niru*. Because of the clan or village origin of the *niru* no attempt was made to keep the size of the *niru* population uniform throughout the banners, although an upper and a lower limit were roughly set.[11] The major exception to the clan nature of the *niru* were the *niru* of the Chinese banners, which were composed largely of Chinese soldiers who followed their officers in submission to the Manchus. In their case, the officers became hereditary commanders of the *niru* made up of their former soldiers.

As military officer in wartime, civil administrator in peacetime, and enforcer of clan rules and moral code, the *niru janggin* or major occupied a crucial role in the functioning of the banner system. Each majority was classified according to the circumstance of its creation. The *hsün-chiu tso-ling*, meritorious majority, was awarded to the chief who submitted to the Manchus with his people in the time of Nurhachi and Abahai; *yü-i shih-kuan tso-ling*, exemplary hereditary majority, was awarded to the chief who led his people in submission to the Manchus and achieved merits in the banner, and who was rewarded with additional families; *shih-kuan tso-ling*, hereditary majority, was awarded to a chief who led his brothers and clansmen in submission; *hu-kuan tso-ling*, rotational majority, was created for a *niru* made up of two or more clans, the leadership of which was rotated among the clans; *fen-kuan tso-ling*, joint majority, was created for a *niru* composed of two clans of equal size whose chiefs were given a joint command; and *kung-chung tso-ling*, open-selection majority, was created for a *niru* made up of extra men from other *niru* and whose commander was chosen from any qualified person in any *niru* of the banner. The open-selection majority, created in 1674, was the only non-hereditary position among the *niru* commanders.[12] Its number tended to increase in keeping with the increase in banner population.

There were two officers below the rank of major: *fang-yü,* captain, and *hsiao-ch'i-chiao,* lieutenant. The captain was responsible for the military supply of the garrison command and might also be put in charge of a minor post. The lieutenant, always one to a *niru,* was the major's chief aide.[13] Until the Yung-cheng reign the lieutenancy was a hereditary position having been awarded originally to a minor clan or village chief.[14]

The *niru* population could be divided into two broad categories: those who were and those who were not in the military service. An important task of the major was to keep up to date the banner population register. Every three years, census information on each *niru* was sent to the garrison headquarters and included, for each adult male, the names of all persons in his father's, his own, and his children's generation. This information was then forwarded to the Board of War in Peking. In this way, a bannerman, as soon as he reached the age of three, would be listed in the banner register. In the early years of the dynasty, when a bannerman reached the height of five feet and knew how to shoot and ride, he was designated a *hsi-tan (ch'i-ting* in Chinese), able-bodied male, and became eligible to induction as a *ma-chia* (private). At the age of sixty he would be removed from the *hsi-tan* list.[15] The rules were later modified so that a bannerman, if physically qualified, became a *hsi-tan* at sixteen and retired from the list at sixty.

In addition to the privates, a *niru* usually included a number of soldiers who performed specific duties. The *ch'ien-feng* (vanguards) ordinarily the best soldiers in the *niru,* served as personal guards for the military governor and deputy military governor and as executioners. The *ling-ts'ui* (clerks) were literate soldiers in charge of clerical and commissary duties. The *chiang-i* (craftsmen) were responsible for the manufacturing and repairing of weapons and other skilled tasks. The *yang-yü-ping* (supernumeraries) were bannermen who, in Manchuria, worked as military agricultural colonists. A bannerman not in military service was called a *sula* (*hsien-san* in Chinese), man without position.[16] Other non-military personnel in the *niru* were the children, women, and slaves.

The number of soldiers in a *niru* tended to decrease with time. At the formative stage of the banner system, when Nurhachi needed all the manpower he could muster for his small army, the three hundred soldiers contained in each *niru* probably closely approximated the number of adult males in it. During the reign of Abahai, as more people joined the

Manchu cause, the practice was set of taking one able-bodied male for military service from every three in each Manchu or Mongol *niru* and one from every five in each Chinese *niru*. The number of able-bodied males in each *niru* was set at about two hundred in 1634.[17] Because there was no upper limit imposed upon the number of men in a banner force, each military success would follow with an increase in the number of *niru* and soldiers. The soldiers served without pay; their needs were taken care of by those working on the *niru* lands.

With the establishment of the dynasty in China proper, the size of the banner force was gradually stabilized; by 1735 it was practically fixed for the remainder of the dynasty. Though the soldiers now received a monetary stipend, there were fewer of them in each *niru*. In 1665 the number of able-bodied males in each *niru* was set at one hundred thirty to one hundred forty and finally in the eighteenth century at one hundred fifty.[18] As the number of *niru* increased with the natural growth of the banner population, the average number of soldiers for each *niru* declined correspondingly. For instance, during the Chia-hsing reign (1796–1820), the total number of *niru* in the Heilungkiang garrison command was 244 and increased to 266 during the Kuang-hsü reign (1875–1908), but the total number of banner troops remained at about 10,300.[19] An imperial decree of 1727 spoke of a major having, on the average, about forty to fifty families under his care.[20] Because the Manchu extended family tended to be relatively large, the average major would have under his charge anywhere from three to six hundred persons, of whom fifty to sixty would be soldiers. In the nineteenth century, the number of soldiers probably had declined to about forty to fifty in each *niru*.

In a speech to his Chinese officers who complained about their public burdens, Abahai enumerated in 1634 the tasks that a Manchu *niru* had to perform for the government: the contribution of eight frontier guards, three iron miners, six blacksmiths, five silversmiths, four horse herders, and two orderlies for the banner headquarters; the contribution of fourteen families to carry out various duties of the *niru* headquarters; the farming of land to be given to new adherents; the contribution of three women (no specific task was mentioned for them); the making of salt and hunting of wild game; the supplying of post horses for Korean ambassadors; the building and repairing of four frontier cities; the patrolling of frontier walls; the guarding of the residences of the imperial princes; the contribution of one soldier for guarding the Chu-li River; the contribution of two patrol horses; the contribution of several horses, ten *bayara* (best soldiers), and several messengers to the expeditionary force during the campaign against the Warka tribe; care of their horses by the soldiers after the campaign was over; the releasing of houses and villages to new adherents, who were also supplied with grains for food and wine-making, and the construction of new villages for themselves; the transportation of cloth purchased from Korea to frontier towns; the storage of ice in caves (during winter for summer use); the guarding of sable and other skins presented as tribute by new Hurka adherents and the furnishing of firewood and grains for their use; the supplying of water and fodder to Korean and Mongol ambassadors; the harvesting of grass in the summer; the digging of ginseng for sale to Korea; the contribution of one family from each banner to police the Ying-ko region and one family to guard the ferry at Mukden.[21] Thus, during the time of Nurhachi and Abahai, the *niru* as a unit contributed most of the manpower and materials necessary for the running of the state. War loot, trade, and slaves furnished the rest.

After the establishment of the Manchu regime in China, practically all of the tax burden of the *niru* was assumed by the Chinese population. The major task of the *niru* was to maintain the fighting readiness of the banner force and the livelihood and cohesion of the banner communities. This political assignment was entrusted to the *niru* commander, whom the Ch'ien-lung emperor compared to the Chinese magistrate, the parent official of the people. The emperor enjoined him to become intimately acquainted with the behavior of each person in the *niru* and dispense rewards and punishments justly, to be mindful of their livelihood, and to educate them to be good subjects. The emperor also felt it necessary to admonish him not to treat his charges as slaves and servants, which would indicate that the officer was not above using his power arbitrarily.[22]

The great power of the major over his people was derived to a large degree from his position as a hereditary or an usually long-term officer with combined military, political, and clan functions. When a major was promoted to colonel in the same locality, he often retained concurrently his post in the *niru*. The longevity of his command was an advantage no other officer in the banner possessed. Furthermore, his power was reinforced by two prohibitions which limited the occupational and territorial mobility of all bannermen.

The bannerman was forbidden to engage in any other occupation except soldiering and farming. However, he was permitted to enter the civil bureaucracy through the examination process. The first provincial examinations for bannermen were held in 1651 and the candidates were allowed to be examined either in the Manchu or Chinese language. The experiment was discontinued in 1657 and revived in 1667. Thereafter, despite a brief interruption in 1676, it became a major avenue of bannerman political advancement. From 1667 the bannermen had been examined together with the Chinese candidates.[23] Like the Chinese magistrate, the *niru* commander was responsible for the selection of candidates to the prefectural examinations. On the Manchurian frontier, it was in 1800 that a quota for prefectural graduates was set for Kirin and Heilungkiang, which specified that one out of five or six Manchu and Mongol candidates and one out of five or six Chinese bannermen candidates taking the examinations might be granted the *hsiu-ts'ai* degree, provided they passed the examinations.[24] This quota was increased later as the population increased. Because scholarship was generally ignored on the frontier and the candidates had to travel to Fengt'ien for the examinations, only a few from Kirin and practically none from Heilungkiang participated in them. It was only in 1870 that Kirin undertook the holding of prefectural examinations for both the Kirin and Heilungkiang candidates.[25] Like all bannerman candidates for the provincial examinations, the frontier candidates were required to take them at Peking. The quota for all bannerman provincial graduates, after frequent changes, was set at forty-one in 1744.[26] The metropolitan examinations were also taken at Peking together with all candidates throughout the empire. As might be expected the number of bannerman graduates of all levels from the frontier region was extremely few and were found mostly toward the latter half of the nineteenth century.

The restrictions on the territorial mobility of the bannermen were in effect at least as early as 1626 when a *niru* was forbidden to move from its settlement without permission.[27] This meant in effect that no individual from any *niru* could leave his territory without the permission of his commander. In later years this rule came to mean that any bannerman who traveled more than 100 li from his garrison settlement without permission would be prosecuted as a deserter.[28]

The occupational and territorial restrictions served to bind ever more firmly the average bannerman to the authority of the major, who tended to stay on his post until he was promoted to another locality or retired, while his superiors were shifted from one command to another. It was no accident that on the frontier the clan village of the bannerman was very much an autonomous entity not subject to observation by Peking officials and rarely to intervention from regional authorities.

The Disposition of Banner Troops

With the conquest of China proper, the banner forces were divided into *ching-ch'i,* or metropolitan banners, and *chu-fang,* or garrison forces. The garrison forces were distributed among the provinces in China proper, Sinkiang, and Manchuria. The metropolitan banners, which had the responsibility of protecting Peking and its environs as well as the personal safety of the emperor, totaled over 100,000 men. They were made up of 681 Manchu *niru,* 204 Mongol *niru,* and 266 Chinese *niru*. The garrison forces numbered about 107,760 men divided among 840 *niru*.[29] Thus almost half of the banner troops were concentrated in the capital.

The composition of the banner garrisons in Kirin and Heilungkiang revealed highly interesting differences from those of China proper. A major reason for these differences was the desire of the Manchu emperors to bar the entry of non-banner Chinese troops into Manchuria. This decision led to the incorporation of a large number of tribal troops into the garrison forces. For example, in 1736, the banner forces in Heilungkiang totaled 4,500 men, of whom 2,580 were Solon, Dagur, and Barga soldiers. In addition, there were 6,509 Solon, Dagur, Mongol, and Barga auxiliaries in Buteha and Hulun Buir. In contrast, there were only 1,920 Manchu and 400 Chinese banner soldiers. The situation was somewhat different in Kirin where there were 9,682 Manchu and 100 Mongol, and 1,170 Chinese banner soldiers, but no Solon, Dagur, or Barga soldiers.[30] Nevertheless, the importance of tribal troops in frontier defense was indisputable.

The banning of Chinese troops in Manchuria also required modification of the rule governing the disposition of the banner troops. To make this clear, it is necessary to describe the composition of military forces in the Ch'ing dynasty. Prior to the rise of the militia during the T'ai-p'ing Rebellion (1851–1864), the regular armed forces in the Ch'ing empire were composed of the banner forces and the Lü-ying or Green Standard troops. The Lü-ying originated in the desire of the Manchus, after they had entered China proper, to maintain a separately organized Chinese military force. The distribution and control of the Lü-ying troops were modeled after the Ming system but with modifications. The *chen* or military districts in the Ming empire were located along the land and coastal frontiers. In the Ch'ing empire there were fifty-four of these districts located throughout the provinces. They supplemented the provincial banner garrisons in a most revealing manner. Whereas the banner troops were concentrated at strategic and political centers in a given province, the Lü-ying troops were fragmented into many small units throughout each province. In this way a relatively small banner garrison was able to keep watch over the more numerous but less coordinated Lü-ying units. Furthermore, because banner troops were to be employed primarily as combat troops, they were given better pay and equipment. The Lü-ying soldiers were entrusted with a variety of tasks including those ordinarily performed by police units, and inevitably their training and morale as a fighting force were affected.[31]

As to the disposition of the garrison banner troops, the number of garrison posts was stabilized in the reign of Ch'ien-lung (1736–1795) as follows: twenty-six posts in the metropolitan province (Chihli), six in Sinkiang, twenty in the remaining provinces of China proper, forty-three in Manchuria, and twenty along the Manchurian frontier gates. The total number of banner troops was 7,703 (7.5 percent) in the metropolitan province, 45,729 (44.5 percent) in the remaining provinces, 12,492 (12.2 percent) in Sinkiang, and 35,519 (35.7 percent) in Manchuria. There were variations in the number of troops in subsequent years, but the proportion remained about the same.[32]

It can be seen from these figures that in Peking and Chihli province, the garrisons consisted of an overwhelming force of banner troops distributed in many points; the provincial banner garrisons were concentrated in relatively few strategic areas; and the Manchurian garrisons with a lesser number of men were spread out in a great number of posts. In other words, the banner garrisons in Manchuria had to perform both the strategic functions of a defense force and the police and courier duties ordinarily assumed by the Lü-ying in the provinces of China proper. The Manchus, by enlisting Chinese exiles in the banner forces of Manchuria and assigning them to the river patrols, courier stations, and frontier gate posts managed to prevent, to a certain degree, undue dissipation of the fighting strength of the Manchu components in the banner garrisons. This expedient, however, did not completely remedy the basic numerical inadequacy of the garrison force in Manchuria.

The Frontier Garrison

Here, the ethnic composition of the Manchurian frontier garrison force will be described; its organization will be discussed in Chapter 4. According to Sa-ying-e, the bannermen who were brought into the Manchu banners before the conquest of Ming China were known as Fe or Old Manchus.[33] This definition would put all non-Manchu peoples serving in the Manchu banners into the Old Manchu category. As a matter of fact, many Chinese in this group had dropped their Chinese surnames and adopted Manchu names, becoming quite indistinguishable from the Manchus. The Ice or New Manchus were Tungus tribesmen brought into the Manchu banners during the reigns of emperors Shun-chih, K'ang-hsi, and Yung-cheng. Some were identified as Ku-ya-la and others simply as Ice Manchus. The Ku-ya-la were the Kiakar of the Tumen region. The others were the Hurka of the San-hsing region.[34] I have mentioned previously that So-so-k'u, the Hurka chief of the Keike clan, established tributary relations with Abahai in 1631 and apparently led some of his people in the campaign against the Ming force. In 1645 some of the Hurka troops were assigned to the banner garrison in Shantung province, while those who had not yet become immune to smallpox were sent back to San-hsing. In 1652 a number of *niru* were formed among these Hurka tribesmen and brought to Ninguta as part of the frontier garrison force. Subsequently, more of them were recruited into the banner force. In 1714 the San-hsing garrison post was established and the Hurka population was divided into four hereditary *niru* commanded by their clan chiefs. In 1732 six additional *niru* were formed among the Hurka and ten among the Heje population of the Ussuri region.[35] In Heilungkiang, the term New Manchus also came to include the Solon and Dagur tribesmen who were brought into the garrison banners during the K'ang-hsi reign.[36]

Sa-ying-e also divided the Mongol bannermen into Old and New Mongols. Some of the Old Mongols traced their ancestry to the Khalkha and Chahar tribesmen of Inner Mongolia who were incorporated into the banner system by Nurhachi and Abahai.[37] Other Old Mongols were of Guwalca and Sibe origin. The original homes of both these tribes were located in the Petuna region, at the confluence of the Sungari and Nonni. They were among the nine allies defeated by Nurhachi in 1593. According to Sa-ying-e they were conquered by Nurhachi in 1619. There were some ambiguities in his account, which seems to say that some of them were enslaved and served as bondservants for the princely families and others were organized into the earliest Mongol *niru* and distributed among the Mongol banners. In 1692 new Guwalca and Sibe *niru* were formed among the Petuna villagers, apparently from the bondservant population.[38] Yang Pin stated that the Sibe considered themselves of

Manchu origin but became subjects of the Mongols.[39] His assertion was corroborated by other accounts, which maintained that the Guwalca and Sibe were subjects of the Korchin Mongols, who presented them to the K'ang-hsi emperor in 1689; they were then organized into *niru* and sent to garrison posts in Kirin and Heilungkiang.[40] It seems quite possible that some of the Guwalca and Sibe were enslaved by the Manchus and others were conquered by the Korchin, who released them during the K'ang-hsi reign. Some of the Sibe *niru* were eventually settled in the Ili valley after the defeat of the Jungar empire. The New Mongols were the Barga and the descendants of Chief Ayushi of the Törgut tribes.[41]

In 1742 the Ch'ien-lung emperor issued a decree which read in part: "The *Han-chün* were originally Chinese; some of them followed the dragon [sovereign] through the pass [Shan-hai-kuan, gateway from Manchuria to Peking], some of them joined the banners in submission after the founding of the dynasty; there were also those who entered the banners because they had committed crimes or who had been household members of the Three Feudatories; some of them were taken from among the bondservants of the Office of the Imperial Household; in addition, there were musketeers who were recruited [into the banners], persons of different surnames who had been adopted [by banner families], and those who came with their [non-bannermen] mothers."[42] The decree permitted these various categories of Chinese bannermen to leave the banners if they so desired except the descendants of the "dragon-followers," who were known as the Old Chinese bannermen.

The origins of the New Chinese bannermen were clearly stated in the above imperial decree. With the exception of those who became bannermen through adoption or the remarriage of their mothers into banner families, the New Chinese bannermen were found mostly in Manchuria. They were brought into the banner system as part of the preparatory moves against the Russian intruders of the Amur Valley. In order to provide food and fodder for the expeditionary force and the garrison soldiers, government farms were set up in Kirin and Heilungkiang. Those in Kirin were worked by Chinese political exiles and convicts; those in Heilungkiang by former bondservants of the government farms in Liao-tung. Courier stations were set up, staffed by the defeated rebels of the Three Feudatories from the provinces of Yunnan and Kweichow. A river patrol was organized with personnel drawn from the exiles and from Taiwan Islanders who had been recruited into the banners after the collapse of the island kingdom in 1683.[43] The personnel of these government farms, courier stations, and river patrols, although administered as part of the banner garrison were not organized into *niru* and assigned to the existing banners. They were governed by officers who were not chosen from their ranks. It was only in 1884, on the recommendation of the Heilungkiang military governor that the government farm and river patrol personnel were assigned to the Three Superior Banners, which enabled them to be registered in the banner list, a prerequisite to participation in the provincial examinations in Peking. The courier station personnel, however, remained in their semi-bannerman status.[44] In 1733 a battalion of musketeers was organized, drawn from personnel of the courier stations, government farms, and river patrols.[45]

Another group of bannermen who were not organized into *niru* were the personnel of the Kirin Buteha Ula. They belonged to the three banners of the Office of Imperial Household and were of bondservant status; they were probably Ula tribesmen whose homeland was conquered by Nurhachi in 1613.[46] They were governed by a *tsung-kuan* (general superintendent) who was originally responsible to the Office of Imperial Household but was reassigned to the military governor of Kirin in 1748. The Buteha Ula was responsible for supplying local tributes to the emperor. The population was divided into groups of households, each given the task of procuring one type of tribute, such as pearls, furs, wild game and fish, pine nuts, ginseng, wild honey, and birchbark.[47]

The ethnic composition of the Manchurian frontier garrison reveals clearly that it comprised a relatively small percentage of true Manchus and that a large number of garrison soldiers were brought into the banner system only after the conquest of China.

The Frontier Banner Land System

The livelihood of the average bannerman was derived largely from agriculture. It was landownership that held the bannermen together in compact communities. The banner garrisons were in reality self-supporting military agricultural colonies that had been planted at strategic locations throughout the empire. In the Liao-tung region and in China proper the establishment of such colonies resulted in the expropriation of large tracts of cultivated lands from Chinese farmers.[48] On the Manchurian frontier such drastic measures were not required because there was an abundance of virgin soil only sparsely utilized by tribal peoples.

Forms of land distribution changed during the several centuries of

Manchu rule. The land belonging to the banner garrison in the frontier region was divided, in the mature phase, into the following categories: *ch'i-t'ien*, or banner land, was given to the bannermen; *sui-ch'üeh ti*, or emolument land, was given to officers and men on active service in addition to their annual stipends; *kuan-chuang*, or government farms, consisted of public-owned lands cultivated by Chinese bannermen, the proceeds of which went to the government for official use; and *t'un-t'ien*, or military farms, were lands given to Manchu colonists in order to relieve the population pressure among the Peking bannermen or as a measure to improve the livelihood of the frontier Manchus as well as to provide an extra source of income for the military government.

At the time of Nurhachi and Abahai the distribution of land to the banner population seems to have been made on the basis of the number of adult males in each family.[49] The same principle may have been followed on the Manchurian frontier after the establishment of the Ch'ing empire. In any case, according to *Chi-lin wai-chi*, the size of banner land in Kirin in the 1820's totaled 365,092 *shang*.[50] There are no comparable later figures for the whole region; however, *Chi-lin t'ung-chih* gives the figures for the Kirin district in about 1891 as 184,536 *shang*, which is almost twice the figure of 95,134 *shang* given for the same district in about 1820 by *Chi-lin wai-chi*.[51] These figures would indicate that, at least in Kirin, the size of banner land had been doubled from about 1800 to 1900 in accordance with the increase in population. The banner land was not only given free to the cultivators but was also exempted from all taxation.[52]

Emolument land was a later institution which began as a relief measure during the T'ai-p'ing Rebellion when the Imperial Treasury was unable to pay the banner officers and men their full stipends. Because the financial situation of the country never recovered from that disaster, the emolument lands, which were instituted in a piecemeal manner from region to region, became an important adjunct to the incomes of the banner forces.[53]

The size of emolument land was graduated according to the ranks of the recipients. According to the *Chi-lin t'ung-chih*, the military governor received 68 *shang*, deputy military governor 24, colonel 60, major 40, captain 30, lieutenant 30, sergeant 20, corporal 20, and private 16. Clerical personnel, courier station master, and other members of the military government also received proportionate shares of emolument lands. In Heilungkiang, emolument lands were available in Hulan district, but not elsewhere.[54] The comparatively small shares given to the military governor and the deputy military governor indicated that emolument lands were intended merely to supplement the monetary incomes of these high ranking officers, whereas for the lower ranking officers and the soldiers they probably represented a major source of income.

Government farms, called either *kuan-chuang* or *kuan-t'un*, were established during the K'ang-hsi reign (1662–1722) to provide food and other farm products to the military government. Each farm was cultivated by ten *t'un-ting* farm workers, of whom one was appointed *chuang-t'ou* or farm foreman. In the beginning, each man was responsible annually for 12 piculs of grain, 300 bundles of fodder, 100 catties of pork, 100 catties of charcoal, 300 catties of lime, and 100 bundles of reed. Everything in the farm belonged to the government.[55] During the Chia-ch'ing reign (1796–1820), each farm worker in Kirin was responsible for the cultivation of 12 *shang* of land and an annual grain levy of 30 piculs. There were altogether 10,200 *shang* of government farms and an annual income of 25,500 picul of unhusked grain for the government granaries.[56] In later years, the size of the government farms increased to about 40,800 *shang* and the annual grain levy varied from locality to locality, sometimes being commuted into monetary rents.[57] The Heilungkiang government farms were first established at Hulan. The grain produced there was transported by boats to Tsitsihar and Mergen by way of the Sungari and Nonni rivers, and to Aigun by way of the Sungari and the Amur.[58]

There were 40 farms worked by 510 former Chinese bondservants brought over from Sheng-ching. The system functioned so well that more farms were set up later in Hulan as well as in Tsitsihar, Mergen, and Heilungkiang. These were staffed by local bannermen. The government farms were supervised by a *t'un-kuan*, or settlement officer, who was assisted by a number of grain collectors and clerks. The farm workers were subject to an annual levy of 22 piculs of grain; the farm foremen were free of any grain levy.[59]

The military farms were first established in Heilungkiang in 1716 with 350 local banner soldiers as settlers to replenish the depleted granaries. In 1728 the original task was fulfilled and all but 180 soldiers were returned to active service. In 1804 the number of military farms was expanded with 320 soldiers working in Tsitsihar, 180 in Mergen, and 300 in Heilungkiang. They were then referred to as *kung-t'ien* (public farms) and the soldier-colonists were *yang-yü ping* (supernumeraries). Like the government farm worker, each supernumerary was obliged to present to the government granary 22 piculs of grain each year.[60] Unlike the government farm worker, who did not receive any military pay and was not subject to active military service, the supernumerary received an annual stipend of 12 taels and might be called upon for active service.[61]

Another type of military farm originated as a measure to relieve the impecunious Manchu bannermen of Peking. An imperial decree in 1812 instructed officials in Kirin to make a survey of lands available for the settlement of Peking bannermen. Military Governor Fu-chün suggested that the virgin soil near Lalin be used for this purpose and that Kirin and Fengtien bannermen who were not in military service, regardless of their ethnic origin, be recruited to open up the land. These pioneers would be allowed to keep a portion of the cultivated field and the rest would be reserved for Peking Manchu settlers who, as urban residents, were indifferent farmers. The scheme was adopted. However, it was not until 1824 that the first contingent of Peking Manchus arrived at the settlement site, which was named Shuang-cheng pao. Each of the Manchu settlers was given 30 *shang* of land tax free for five years, after which period a grain tax of 20 piculs was levied on each farm.[62] Similar settlements were later established in Petuna and Hulan.[63]

Political Significance of the Banner System

Initially organized as a means of welding together the separate Juchen tribes into an efficient fighting force whose loyalty was directed exclusively to Nurhachi and his family, the banner system, after the conquest of China, became a device for the perpetuation of a military caste made up of hereditary bannermen of Manchu, Mongol, and Chinese extractions, who were expected to be the most staunch supporters of the ruling dynasty. Above all, it served to keep alive the separate identity of the Manchus, a small minority in an ocean of Chinese. They were kept in cohesive communities, supported by their farms, trained as soldiers, administered by their own officers outside the jurisdiction of local civilian governments, and drawn into the highest posts in the civil bureaucracy in numbers highly disproportionate to their population. Thus the bannermen served as watchdogs in both civil and military spheres over the Chinese officialdom and population.

It was hoped that in the Manchurian frontier provinces, the banner population would maintain its numerical superiority. This would help keep the region a Manchu preserve, an emergency retreat if the need arose for the Manchus in China. The banner system would perpetuate Manchu power on the frontier through the regimentation of the banner population into military units, which were then grouped into garrison commands. Under military rule, the bannerman of each command was immobilized within its territorial limits. Not only officers and soldiers but also non-military personnel were forbidden to leave the garrison settlement without the approval of the commanding officers and only for a stated period. This prohibition, together with the restriction on choices of occupation made it possible for the frontier authorities to have under their constant control a permanent pool of manpower that could be pressed into military service whenever necessary. As long as the frontier was populated largely by bannermen and tribal peoples and undisturbed by outside forces the banner system was an efficient instrument of political control which employed a limited number of troops to oversee an expanse of territory as large as several European countries combined.

3

Political Control of the Tribal Peoples

On May 30, 1688, the K'ang-hsi emperor issued the following instructions to So-e-t'u and others who were leaving for Selenginsk to conduct peace negotiations with the Russians:

> The Lo-ch'a [Russians] invaded our frontier territory and fought us at the Heilungkiang [Amur], the Sungari and the Hu-ma-er [Kumar] rivers. They occupied the regions of the Nipchu [Nerchinsk] and Yaksa [Albazin], the territories of our subjects. They harbored our fugitives, including Gantimur. Therefore, our army twice engaged in punitive expeditions to take Yaksa and finally besieged the city. This is the origin of our struggle against the Lo-ch'a.
>
> The territory of Nipchu was originally the camping ground of our subjects, the Mao-ming-an tribe [of Inner Mongolia]; and Yaksa was the old home of Pei-le-er, our Dagur chief. Therefore, the territories which the Lo-ch'a now occupy are not theirs, nor is it a neutral zone between the two countries.
>
> The territory of Heilungkiang is most important. By descending the Heilungkiang, the Lo-ch'a can reach the Sungari, thence to the Nonni and southward to the K'u-er-han River and to Ula and Ninguta and the lands of the Sibe, the Korchin, the Solon and the Dagur tribes. If they descend the Heilungkiang to its mouth, they can reach the sea. Into the Heilungkiang flow the Heng-kun [Argun], the Niu-man [Bureya] and the Ching-hsi-li [Zeya]. Along these rivers live our peoples, the Orochon, the Kile, the Birar, as well as the Heje and the Fiatka [Gilyak]. If we do not recover this entire region, our frontier people will never have peace. Therefore, since Nipchu, Yaksa and both the upper and lower Heilungkiang and all rivers and rivulets flowing into them are ours, it is our opinion that none of them should be abandoned to the Lo-ch'a.
>
> Moreover, our fugitives, the three *tso-ling* of Gantimur and

> others, as well as the few men who deserted after them must be extradited. If the Lo-ch'a agree to all our demands, we shall return their fugitives as well as the prisoners whom our grand army captured, or who surrendered to us. We shall join with them to draw the boundaries, and we shall grant them trade; if they do not agree, we shall not talk peace with them.[1]

The above imperial command revealed clearly one of the reasons why the Ch'ing empire was determined to establish undisputed sovereignty over the peoples and lands of the Amur region: though the tribal peoples by themselves could not menace its security, the empire would face grave potential dangers if the tribal lands and their inhabitants were to fall under the domination of a strong foreign power.

The tribal peoples had been brought under Manchu rule originally as a strategic move to protect the Manchu rear in their war against the Ming Chinese and to draw upon the tribal manpower and resources to strengthen the Manchu military capability. The Russian threat naturally magnified, in the eyes of the Manchu rulers, the importance of putting the tribal lands under their firm control. Because the tribal groups lived in small village communities in a vast region remote from the political center of the empire, it was impractical to govern them through the familiar bureaucratic devices employed in China proper, hence the majority of them were ruled indirectly through the tributary system.

The Tributary System

Under the Ch'ing empire there were several types of tributary relationship, all of which were traceable to precedents created in earlier dynasties. The court, for instance, received tributes from vassal states such as Korea, Annam, and several Southeast Asian countries, from dependencies such as Outer and Inner Mongolia and Tibet, and from tribal enclaves within China proper such as the *t'u-ssu* of southwestern provinces. The types of tribute and the procedures for receiving tribute bearers varied in accordance with the status of the tribute senders vis-à-vis China. In general, tributes from the vassal states and, at times, from foreign lands were freely offered as tokens acknowledging the inferior status of the tribute-bearing peoples in relation to the Chinese empire. On the other hand, tributes from the dependencies and tribal enclaves were compulsory presentations, the contents of which were carefully regulated by statutes. They differed from ordinary taxation in that the tribute senders, unlike taxpayers, were compensated by imperial gifts.

Tributary relations were formed between the Manchus and the tribesmen prior to the founding of the Ch'ing dynasty. At that time, the Manchus looked upon the tribesmen as potential allies against the Ming Chinese; consequently, although they frequently used force to compel the submission of the tribesmen, they were also interested in establishing good relations with them. The forging of marriage ties was one way of accomplishing such objectives. The first instance of marital alliance was concluded sometime after 1600 when Nurhachi ordered the daughters of six high officials to be given in marriage to six Hurka chiefs.[2] Thereafter, the custom continued into the Ch'ing dynasty. In 1698 regulations were promulgated governing the marriage feast to be given by the court in honor of any Heje or Fiatka chief coming to Peking for the wedding ceremony.[3] Some of them apparently obtained their wives on the frontier. According to Chao-lien (Prince Li, 1780–1833), an authority on Manchu history, the K'ang-hsi emperor, in an effort to civilize the uncouth tribesmen, permitted the tribal chiefs to marry Manchu girls of noble birth. When they arrived at Kirin for this purpose, the military governor would deceive them by giving them girls purchased from plebian homes but outfitted with lavish dowries.[4] In the later part of the nineteenth century, Ts'ao T'ing-chieh found, in the villages of Dondon, Adi, Pulo, and Wu-ho-tu, located at the Amur delta, treasured heirlooms of bronze and copper jars which, the natives said, were dowries brought by the wives of their ancestors from China.[5]

The practice of bestowing wives upon tribal chiefs continued sporadically at least into the Ch'ien-lung reign. For instance, an imperial decree was issued on March 6, 1775, instructing the military commanders of Ninguta and San-hsing to notify the Heje, Fiatka, and K'u-yeh (Sakhalin) tribesmen who might be coming to Peking on tributary and marital missions to begin their journey in the fall so that they would be able to return home by early spring thus avoiding the smallpox season at the capital. The decree was received by the military governor of Kirin on March 31 and by the military commander at San-hsing on April 11. A copy of the decree, together with an official communication from the San-hsing authorities, both written in Manchu, were dispatched to the clan chief, surnamed T'ao, of a village in southern Sakhalin. These documents, which had been preserved in the home of another clan chief, surnamed Yang, were discovered in 1792 by a Japanese agent and reported to the Tokugawa government.[6] Thus we have documentary evidence that during the Ch'ien-lung reign tribal chiefs, as far away as Sakhalin, still made regular tributary journeys to Peking where they were married to Manchu girls and were known to the frontier commanders by their Chinese names. When the tribal chiefs were in Peking they were honored with official ranks and given court audiences. Such practices, an integral part of the tributary system, seem to have been ended gradually after the Ch'ien-lung reign.

During the early reigns of the Ch'ing dynasty, the imperial hunting expeditions in Jehol were a source of pleasure for the emperor and his entourage of Manchu nobility and provided an occasion on which the emperor could meet his Mongol vassals in an environment conducive to the display of military might. The hunting tribes of Heilungkiang, according to the regulations of the Bureau of Dependencies were required to send their general superintendents, officers, and expert hunters to assist in the chase.[7] Like the marriage ties and court audiences, these periodic hunts were political devices with which the emperor reminded his frontier subjects of their allegiance to him.

The core of the system was the sable tribute. Its content and manner of presentation had become systematized during the K'ang-hsi reign. According to the Ch'ing statutes, the Heje, Fiatka, and Hurka tribes sent their tributes to the military governor of Ninguta, who, after having them inspected and counted, forwarded the lot to the Board of Revenue in Peking. Gifts for the tribesmen were delivered to the military governor by the Board of Revenue and Board of Works in Sheng-ching. The tribute bearers were entitled to a daily ration of rice, liquor, salt, glutinous rice, and beans. Their horses were given fodder. If Manchu princesses and their consorts came with the tribute missions, they were given special silk clothing, ornaments, and toilet articles.[8]

Wu Chen-ch'en, who was in Ninguta during the 1680's stated that the Hurka, Fiatka, and Heje came annually by boat to Ninguta. The military governor took one sable from each tribute bearer and all his rare black fox pelts. They were permitted to trade the rest of their pelts in the market.[9] Yang Pin, who was in Ninguta a decade later reported that there were eight tribal groups who presented their tribute at Ninguta. They arrived every year from the fourth to the sixth lunar month. The three tribes of Hurka and Sungari, the Muren of Ussuri, the Ch'i-ya Hala of Iman, and the Shaven Heje of Sungari and Amur came once a year. The Unshaven Heje, the Fiatka, and the Kile came once every three years. Those who came annually, in addition to receiving gifts, were invited to a feast. Those who came triennially were feted thrice.[10]

The site for receiving tribute was later shifted to San-hsing, probably in 1732 when a deputy military governor was appointed there as garrison commander. Sa-ying-e, writing in about 1810, stated that all Heje living below Ch'i-chi (Lake Kizi) presented their tribute at San-hsing. The Fiatka who lived beyond Ch'i-chi were met at Deren by officials from San-hsing; and the Kiakar who lived along the coast beyond Hun-ch'un were met at Muren River. All together they presented a total of over 2,600 sables annually to the government.[11]

A Japanese explorer, Mamiya Rinzō (1780–1844), has left a graphic description of the tributary activities in Deren where he visited in 1809 in the company of a group of tribute-bearing Sakhalin Islanders.[12] According to Mamiya, the tributary site was located at the bank of the Amur on uninhabited ground. Surrounding the tribute-receiving station were hundreds of temporary shelters erected by natives who came from all parts of the Manchurian coast, from the Russian territory in the north to the Korean border in the south. He estimated that there were about five to six hundred persons at the site.[13]

The station was surrounded by a log fence about eighty to ninety feet long on each of the four sides. Within the fence there were three trading posts, located on the right, left, and rear of the courtyard. At the center there was another fence, which surrounded the building where tributes were received from the natives.[14]

The Manchu officials left San-hsing annually during the summer, arrived at Deren in the middle of the sixth lunar month, and stayed there until early fall when they closed the station for the year. There were three high-ranking banner officials from San-hsing, a major, a lieutenant, and a clerk.[15] (Judging from their surnames, they were all New Manchus of Hurka origin.) Mamiya estimated that there were about fifty to sixty middle-ranking officials and a large number of lower officials.[16] Mamiya had probably mistaken for officials the soldiers and traders who accompanied the mission. Actually the so-called high officials were low echelon officers in the San-hsing garrison command. Coming from a status-conscious feudal society, Mamiya was impressed by the informality of the Manchu officials who ate and worked together like a big family and mixed amiably with the tribesmen.

As soon as a group of tribesmen arrived at the site, their chief would go directly to the boat where the ranking officials resided. He kowtowed to them and made a customary report, probably a routine statement of conditions in his village. The officials treated him with wine and gave him a pint of polished millet.[17]

During the tribute presentation ceremony, the native clan and village chiefs (*halada* and *gashenda*) gathered outside the inner gate of the station. As his name was called, the chief would enter the gate accompanied by a subordinate official. The three ranking officials sat on chairs placed on a raised platform. The chief knelt before the platform, kowtowed thrice, and presented to them his best black sable pelt. The pelt was taken by a middle official, who in turn brought it before the ranking officials. The tribute bearer was then rewarded with imperial gifts. A clan chief was entitled to a roll of brocade measuring about fourteen yards; a village chief a piece of damask measuring eight yards; the rest of the natives each received a length of coarse cotton cloth, three feet of silk, a piece of gauze, a chain, and a number of combs and needles.[18] Among frontier officials, these imperial gifts were known as *urin* (treasure) and the tributary site was called Mu-ch'eng (Wooden City).

The ceremony over, the natives were permitted to trade for goods brought over by the mission. Mamiya reported that the middle and lower officials fraternized with the natives freely, exchanging tobacco pipes with them, eating and drinking in the native huts, and romping with the native children. Trade was conducted either at the trading posts, in the native huts, or by the roadside. The natives exchanged pelts for wine, tobacco, fabrics, and ironwares. Often a Manchu would be seen taking off the clothes he was wearing in trade for a particularly fine piece of pelt. Loud haggling was the rule and occasional fights broke out. The officials would try to quiet the crowd by hitting pieces of wood together but to no avail. Suddenly, someone would yell out: "The government goods have been stolen!" Cymbals would crash and the gates would slam shut. The natives would swarm over the fences in a frantic effort to flee the compound.[19]

Quietness prevailed, however, when tributes were being presented or when an important order was given by the high officials. Such order was usually quickly given and as quickly executed. Mamiya saw the punishment of a native who wept and cried as he was flogged. After justice was done, the culprit was released and again mingled freely at the site as though nothing had happened.[20]

Altogether it was a disorderly but good-natured occasion as seen through the eyes of the Japanese observer. The only weapon he saw was a single musket. He heard a firework explode on an island in midstream but did not see what sort of firework it was. The major left for San-hsing on the fifteenth day of the seventh month. He astonished Mamiya by embracing everyone regardless of rank while bidding them good-bye.[21]

Several decades later, in 1845, a Jesuit father, M. de la Brunière, in violation of the laws of his host country, undertook a journey to visit and convert the Gilyak of the Amur delta. He, too, witnessed a tribute-collecting mission, which he described in a letter dated April 5, 1846:

> The city of San-sim [San-hsing], the last post of the mandarins in the North is to every Chinese or Manchu traveller the extreme limit which the law allows him to reach. To travel beyond is considered and punished as a great infraction of the laws of the state. About ten merchants protected by imperial passports, which cost each of them one hundred taels or more annually, have the sole privilege of descending the Sungari, entering the Amur, and finally ascending the Usuri, in the forests of which is found the celebrated ginseng root. . . . The Government of San-sim despatches annually three war junks in succession, carrying no guns, and having only a few sabres on board. The first of these goes to Muchem [Mu-ch'eng], on the right bank of the Amur, in 49°13′N. Lat. This Muchem (Dondon of the Tunguzians) is neither a town nor even a hamlet, but simply a building of deal, which during three months serves as court-house for the mandarins of the boat. Their business is to receive the skins and furs which the tribe of the Sham-mao-tze (Long-hair), so called because they never shave the head, furnishes to the Emperor, in exchange for a certain number of pieces of cloth. The second barge collects the same imposts from the Yupitatze (or "Fishskins"), from the skins of fish which they make use of for clothing. The third boat has jurisdiction over the Elle-iao-tze (or "Long-red-hair") [Orochi], a wretched and almost extinct tribe, occupying two or three small inlets of the Usuri, and dwelling under tents made of the bark of trees.
>
> It often happens, however, that the mandarins and soldiers of these boats take more care of their own affairs than of those of the Emperor. Not content with the skins of sable, they exact large sums of money before delivering the promised cloth; and in spite of all the natives may urge, they are no less bound down, under pain of

> being scourged, to this arbitary impost. Many families, on the approach of the boat, leave their huts and fly to the mountains. But even this is of little avail; for during their absence everything belonging to them is pillaged, and the cabin itself burnt down.[22]

According to Ts'ao T'ing-chieh, the natives of the Russian Maritime Province told him that, before the Russian occupation, they and the Sakhalin Islanders went to Mu-ch'eng (Dondon) to present their tribute and to receive gifts of clothing and ornaments, an occasion which was called by them *ch'uan-kuan*. The imperial gifts were later presented by them as tributes to the officials of Hsi-shan (according to Ts'ao a native term for Sahkalin or Japan) in exchange for fox, sable, or sea otter pelts, which, in turn, were sold to the Chinese traders in Mu-ch'eng. This tripartite trade was fondly remembered by the natives, who resented its prohibition by the Russians as much as they did the rule that compelled them to shave off their queues and change their clothing style.[23]

In Heilungkiang, the systematization of the tribute missions probably began with the organization of the Orochon, Solon, and Dagur tribes into Buteha banners in 1689.[24] According to Hsi-ch'ing, a Manchu official in Heilungkiang, all Buteha males who measured five feet or over were required to present an annual tribute of one sable skin.[25] But Ying-ho, who was banished to Tsitsihar in 1828, wrote that only one male of tribute-bearing height from each Buteha household was responsible for the sable tribute.[26] Hsü Tsung-liang, writing around 1890, narrowed the number of tribute senders to include only the officers and soldiers of the Buteha banners.[27]

Every year in the fifth lunar month, the tribal tribute bearers, Chinese traders, and Mongol nomads from Hulun Buir gathered at Tsitsihar. The occasion was called *cūlgan* (great gathering). Prior to 1795, the *cūlgan* was held at a location about forty li northwest of the city. All provisions such as tents, horses, food, and drink of the military governor and his staff were supplied by the Buteha. These exactions became so unbearable under an especially rapacious military governor that a Dagur general superintendent secretly took the case of the tribesmen to the Ch'ien-lung emperor's court in the imperial hunting preserve in Jehol. An investigation followed and resulted in the punishment of the military governor and his staff. Since then, the *cūlgan* was held in the city and its participants camped in the northern suburb.[28] The Buteha and the

Mongol nomads lived in their tents, and Chinese traders constructed temporary shelters of wooden sheds. Horses, cattle, and sheep were let out to graze on the surrounding grassland. A brisk trade usually followed, after the Buteha concluded their tributary obligations and were paid for their services as auxiliary troops.[29]

During the tributary presentation, the military governor and the deputy military governor were seated in the hall of the official mansion, and the colonels of the banner garrison and the Buteha general superintendents sat on both sides of a huge pile of sables. The pelts were graded according to quality and stamped with an official insignia. Those that were not chosen as tribute were released for private trading, but only after one paw was clipped off from each skin. The Solon and Dagur sables were identified by red tags attached to them, the Moringa Orochon sables by green tags, the Yafahan Orochon and Birar sables by yellow tags. If the pelts of an individual did not come up to standard, an extra pelt was chosen from the stock of another individual; and the two owners settled their accounts later by cash. In 1810 the skins chosen as tribute included 42 first class pelts, 140 second class pelts, 280 good third class pelts, and 4,943 average third class pelts, altogether totaling 5,405 skins, which was the average number taken each year. Because the 1808 census reported a total of 4,033 Buteha banner households with a population of 18,933, it seems likely that the tribute was levied on each Buteha household rather than on each Buteha male of tribute-paying height.[30]

The tribute collectors in Heilungkiang like their Kirin counterpart, also indulged in extortion. They sometimes deliberately downgraded good quality pelts in order to release them for trading and then forced the tribesmen to sell them at an arbitrarily set low price. This was one of the malpractices which prompted Ch'i-san, the Dagur general superintendent, to appeal directly to the emperor for redress.[31]

Tribal Auxiliaries

The foregoing account reveals an important distinction between the Kirin and Heilungkiang tribesmen in regard to their tributary obligations. In Kirin, only the non-incorporated tribesmen were required to send in tribute; in Heilungkiang, not only the non-incorporated Yafahan Orochon and Birar tribesmen, but also the incorporated Buteha banner troops had to comply with the tribute requirement. The ambiguous status of the Buteha was related to another aspect of tribal control practiced by the Ch'ing government.

The vastness of the Manchurian frontier, the sparseness of its population, the proximity of Russian power, and the unwillingness of the Manchu rulers to open their ancestral land to Chinese immigration posed for the Ch'ing court the problem of how to safeguard this northern land with their limited Manchu manpower. To a large extent this shortage was made up by the utilization of tribal manpower. The direct incorporation of tribal peoples into the Manchu banners was one of the methods used. The so-called New Manchu bannermen therefore constituted a significant percentage of the frontier Manchu banner troops. According to Hsi-ch'ing, among the Manchu bannermen in Heilungkiang during the early decades of the nineteenth century, the Old Manchus comprised only about one tenth of the total force.[32]

In addition to the New Manchus who had lost their original tribal designations, the frontier banner garrisons also included a large proportion of tribal bannermen. In 1684, a year after the establishment of the regular banner garrison in Heilungkiang, 500 Dagur and Solon tribesmen were recruited into the service. In 1688, 480 of them served in the Mergen garrison and in 1691, a total of 1,000 were in the Pu-k'uei (later renamed Tsitsihar) garrison.[33] Fang Shih-chi (d. 1717), who was exiled to Pu-k'uei in 1713, reported that among the garrison force in Pu-k'uei, there were 581 Manchus, 220 Chinese bannermen, 74 Solon, 240 Barga Mongols, and 925 Dagur. In Aigun, there were 580 Manchus, 120 Chinese bannermen, and 500 Solon and Dagur. In Mergen, there were 900 Solon and Dagur.[34] The 1736 figures for the Heilungkiang garrison forces included 2,580 Solon, Dagur, and Barga Mongol soldiers in contrast to the 1,920 Manchus and 400 Chinese bannermen.[35] Because the number of Manchu soldiers in the above breakdown includes both Old and New Manchus, one can readily perceive the importance of tribal manpower in maintaining the Manchu military strength in the frontier region.

The complete incorporation of the tribesmen into regular banner units would involve not only taking the tribesmen out of their regular occupational and home environment, but also the responsibility for their training and maintenance, with a corresponding drain on the imperial treasury. In view of the undeveloped character of the frontier economy, it was considered unwise to maintain there a large standing army. So it was decided in 1684 to organize the Solon and Dagur tribes into Buteha banners, which functioned as auxiliaries to the regular garrison troops.[36] They were administered by a Solon general superintendent and a Dagur general superintendent, who were assisted by eight deputy superintendents. These officers, originally called *t'ou-mu* (chiefs), were clan or village chiefs who served without pay but whose prestige was enhanced by the conferring of imperial titles. In 1691 a Manchu general superintendent was appointed to command the Buteha banners together with his Dagur and Solon colleagues. In addition, eight more deputy superintendents, ninety-seven majors, ninety-seven lieutenants, and ten clerks were added to the roster of native officers.[37] These moves were probably made in the interest of more efficient control of the tribesmen as well as to facilitate their military training. At that time, although the Russian threat had been removed by the Treaty of Nerchinsk, the Ölöt empire under Galdan was still contesting with the Manchus the control of the Khalkha Mongols of Outer Mongolia. The Heilungkiang garrisons were, in effect, on the first line of the empire defense. In later years the Buteha soldiers were called upon by the Peking court to participate in many of the campaigns that expanded the Ch'ing empire to one of the largest in Chinese history. Hai-lan-ch'a (d. 1793), who was one of the ablest generals of his time and whose portrait hung in the Tzu-kuang-ko (Hall of Military Heroes), was a Buteha Solon.[38] In 1760, an imperial decree fixed the number of Buteha soldiers at 2,000 and gave them a semi-regular military status. They were divided into 47 Solon, 39 Dagur, and 6 Orochon *niru*.[39] The annual stipends of these Buteha men and officers, however, were only half the amount paid to the other banner soldiers.[40] Their tribute obligations remained unchanged.

When the Buteha banners were established in 1684, all the non-incorporated hunting tribes were put under the jurisdiction of the general superintendents of the Buteha. According to Hsi-ch'ing, five Buteha officers, called *anda*, were responsible for overseeing their conduct and collecting tribute from these mountain dwellers. The Birar hunters were similarly supervised by four Buteha lieutenants. When the time for tribute-collecting arrived, these tribesmen would gather at appointed places to meet the officers. As soon as the task was done, they would disperse without a trace to their mountain homes.[41]

Administration of the Hulun Buir Tribes

Hulun Buir was a sparsely populated land when it came under the Ch'ing empire. It was only after the conclusion of the Treaty of Nerchinsk in 1689 and the Treaty of Kiakhta in 1727, which demarcated respectively the Russo-Chinese boundary of Manchuria and of Outer Mongolia, that the Ch'ing court began to set up a permanent administrative structure in this nomadic land. The first step was taken in 1732 when 1,636 Solon, 730 Dagur, 359 Orochon, and 275 Old Barga soldiers, together with 796 tribesmen not in the military service, were sent to Hulun Buir from the Buteha region. Called collectively the Solon tribes, they were organized into fifty *niru*, which were grouped into eight banners. The banners were divided equally into a right and a left wing. The left wing was settled along the Russian border and the right wing was settled along the Khalkha (Outer Mongolia) border. Each *niru* was governed by a major and a lieutenant, each banner by a deputy superintendent, and each wing by a general superintendent. At the same time 100 Ölöt soldiers, brought in from Chahar, were organized into a company supervised by a general superintendent, a deputy superintendent, a major, and a lieutenant.[42] In 1734, 2,484 New Barga soldiers from Outer Mongolia were transferred to Hulun Buir. They were organized into forty *niru*, eight banners, and two wings, and governed by a similar hierarchy of officers as the Solon tribes.[43] In subsequent years, the number of men and officers varied as transfers and additions were made, but the basic settlement pattern remained relatively constant. It was the responsibility of the settlers to occupy the land and to defend it against intruders.

From 1732 to 1742 a high Manchu official was appointed from Peking to Hulun Buir as *t'ung-ling* or commandant of tribal troops. In 1743 a Manchu general superintendent with a rank of deputy military governor took the place of the commandant. The line of authority was placed directly from the military governor to the Manchu general superintendent.[44]

Unlike the Tungusic tribes, the Mongol nomads of Hulun Buir, except for the Old Barga who subscribed to Shamanism, were Lamaists. Because of its political significance, the Ch'ing emperors paid considerable attention to the relationship between the state and the Lama church. Besides posing as patrons of the Dalai Lama and Panchen Lama of

Tibet, the Manchu rulers also laid down broad regulations governing the selection and ordination of the Lamaist hierarchy.[45] In Hulun Buir, the state control of the Lama church was manifested in the following manner: (1) The number and organization of the lamaseries were regulated by the government. There was one lamasery for each wing of the Mongol banners. The highest ranking lama was the *shiregetü* lama, whose status was equivalent to that of the general superintendent. Below him were four *da* lamas, whose status was equivalent to that of the deputy superintendents. The four third ranking lamas, who were in charge of different phases of the church affairs, were equivalent in status to that of the major of each banner. There were also twenty-four non-ranking lama officials, similar in status to the *ling-ts'ui*, or clerk of a banner *niru*. The rest were ordinary lamas, whose number was not specified by regulations. (2) The appointment of lama officials was vested in the hands of government officials. The *shiregetü* lama was appointed by the deputy military governor; the *da* lamas by the wing general superintendents; the third ranking lamas were recommended by the *shiregetü* lama and confirmed by the government. The non-ranking lama officials were recommended by the third ranking lamas and confirmed by the government. (3) In the supervision of religious festivals, on the days when festivals were held, the wing superintendent appointed a major or a higher ranking officer to oversee the proceedings as well as to participate in the rituals.[46]

The Ch'ing Tribal Policy: Period of Establishment (1644–1735)

When the first Ch'ing emperor ascended the Peking throne in 1644 the Ming loyalists were still carrying on the struggle in many parts of China. The last Ming claimant was killed in 1662, but the consolidation of the Manchu control of China proper did not come about until 1681 when the Rebellion of the Three Feudatories ended after eight years of warfare. During this span of almost four decades, the Russians made repeated incursions into the Amur basin. Albazin, the Russian fort on the Amur, was first built in 1651, followed by forts at Kumarsk and Nerchinsk in 1654. The Manchu garrison army was then unable to clear them out of the tribal territories.[47]

At that time, the tribal peoples were in no position to resist the Russian invaders, Their military power had been broken by Nurhachi and Abahai, Their weapons were inferior to those of the Russians and their ranks were depleted by Manchu conquest and recruitment. The bulk of the Manchu banner troops had been sent to China to fight against the Chinese and to garrison the occupied territories, Therefore, the best course for the Ch'ing court to follow at that time was to hold the allegiance of the tribal peoples by containing the Russian threat as much as possible and by treating the tribal subjects as allies of their Manchu conquerors. In this policy the Manchus were aided by the predatory nature of the Russian Cossacks. E. G, Ravenstein commented: "When the Russians first arrived on the Amur, the natives cultivated fields and kept cattle, Ten years afterwards these fields had become deserts; and a country, which formerly exported grain, could not even support its own population."[48] Even so, Gantimur, one of the Dagur chiefs, had gone over to the Russian side while his compatriots fought for the Manchus.[49] Consequently, the K'ang-hsi emperor tried to draw the tribesmen closer to the throne by granting them such favors as court audiences, titles of honor, and wives of noble birth. The tributary system, as it was conducted, offered the tribesmen equal value for their sables as well as providing them with opportunities for profitable trade, The Russians evidently could not compete on the same footing with the Manchus.

When China was completely pacified in 1681, the K'ang-hsi emperor turned his attention to the security of his Manchurian frontier. Reconnaissance parties were sent to investigate the river route from Ninguta to the Amur and troops were sent to the garrison town of Aigun. Albazin was destroyed in 1683. When the Russians rebuilt it after the Manchus left, another seige was laid in 1686, which lasted three months. Finally, the Treaty of Nerchinsk was signed in 1689 and assured the Ch'ing empire of undisputed control over the Amur basin and its tribal inhabitants.[50] New threats, however, had appeared in the previous year, as the Ölöt Mongols, under their great chief, Galdan, invaded Outer Mongolia thus beginning a struggle that lasted until the destruction of the last vestige of Ölöt power in 1757. Down to 1735 when the Khalkha-Ölöt boundary was fixed at the Altai Mountains, Heilungkiang played a strategic role in the contest for Outer Mongolia. For this reason, the removal of the Russian menace was followed by further strengthening, rather than reduction, of the defense capability of the Manchurian frontier.

The reorganization of the Manchurian frontier defense after 1689 affected the tribal peoples in several ways. First, the Manchus showed less inclination to look upon them as allies. Their place was taken over by the Khalkha Mongols, who declared their allegiance to the Ch'ing emperor in 1688 and became strong supporters of the Ch'ing armies in their campaigns against the Ölöt. Second, the headquarters for the administration of the tribal peoples moved closer to the tribal territories, thus bringing the more distant tribes under imperial control. The San-hsing garrison was established in 1715 and a deputy military governor was appointed there in 1732. From San-hsing the power of the military government radiated to the distant fishing villages at the Amur delta. In Heilungkiang, the seat of government was fixed at Tsitsihar in 1699. From there, the administrative arms of the military governor extended to cover all the tribal peoples living along the upper course of the Amur and its tributaries within the boundary of the empire. Third, the organization of the Buteha banners was an imposition of Manchu military forms upon the native clan and village rule. Because Buteha officers were appointed by the government, this move tended to lessen the area of political autonomy within the tribes. Fourth, the resettlement of the tribal peoples from one area to another, as in Hulun Buir, lessened the freedom of tribal movements. The settlement scheme in Hulun Buir was carried out as a military defense measure. Each group of natives was given a definite territory for the pasturage of its livestock and was made responsible for guarding its territory against intruders.[51]

From the foregoing, it is evident that two distinctive types of tribal administration were formed during this period. One was characterized by complete internal autonomy of the tribal peoples, whose relationship with the government was expressed primarily in periodic tributary obligations. The tribal peoples under this type of administration included all the Kirin and Heilungkiang tribes who had not been assimilated into the banner system. The other was characterized by only partial internal autonomy of the tribal peoples. They were organized into banner units. In most cases the banner officers were tribal leaders. But they owed their power and appointment to government authorities. At the apex of the military hierarchy was the Manchu general superintendent or deputy military governor. The tribesmen under this type of administration were, in effect, military reservists. Their regular occupations were the traditional ones of hunting, fishing, and herding. However, they were required to participate in periodic drills, perform certain garrison duties, and were subject to draft for military service away from their homeland. The tribal peoples under this type of administration included the Buteha banners made up predominantly of Solon and Dagur tribes, and the Hulun Buir garrison troops composed mostly of Solon, Dagur, Barga Mongols and Ölöt Mongols. Both types of tribal administration lasted, with little change, almost to the end of the Ch'ing dynasty.

In terms of land area, the tribal territory in the Manchurian frontier zone was far larger than the territory under the direct administration of the military governments of Kirin and Heilungkiang. Down to the end of Yung-cheng reign (1723–35), the garrison towns in Kirin included only Ninguta, Kirin, Petuna, Alchuka, San-hsing, and Hun-ch'un; and in Heilungkiang, only Aigun, Mergen, and Tsitsihar. They were all located along the major rivers of the region: Amur, Nonni, Sungari, Hurka, and Tumen. Away from these settlements were tribal villages and nomad camps scattered thinly over an area of more than half a million square miles. Obviously, unless the imperial government were willing to expend a large amount of manpower and resources, indirect rule was the only feasible means of governing the native inhabitants. The system of control adopted in this period worked so well in terms of the political objectives of the imperial government that it lasted until nearly the end of the dynasty.

The heart of this system of tribal control was the tributary relationship between the imperial government and its tribal subjects. This relationship functioned as tangible evidence of the political allegiance of the tribesmen to the emperor, as a channel through which government officials could keep in touch with tribal leaders and obtain from them information concerning conditions within their own territories; and as a means of inducing tribal loyalty by affording the tribesmen opportunities for profitable trade. The imperial government had the obligations to protect the tribute-bearing peoples from foreign aggression, to settle inter-tribal disputes, and to resolve conflicts arising from questions of intra-tribal succession. The tribesmen, on the other hand, were required to furnish men for the imperial forces whenever called upon to do so. At the same time, the tribal peoples enjoyed full or nearly full internal autonomy. The government seldom, if ever, interfered with their traditional customs. The burden of tribute presentation was slight, except, of course, when unscrupulous officials took advantage of their power to obtain extra-legal exactions. In such cases, the tribesmen could theoretically appeal directly to the regional government for redress over the heads of local officials. In general, the tribesmen could resist undue exactions by hiding from the tribute collectors, refusing to go to the tribute-collecting centers, or in the last resort by migrating to the more inaccessible districts.

Ch'ing Tribal Policy: Period of Laissez-faire (1736–1850)

During this period the Manchurian frontier was the backwater of Chinese history. Its boundaries had been secured from foreign menace and its internal administration ran smoothly in the grooves formed during the previous period. The struggle against the Ölöt empire continued for two more decades, but the scene of conflict had shifted to distant Jungaria in Chinese Turkestan. During the reign of Ch'ien-lung (1736–1795) the empire engaged in a series of extensive campaigns but they were fought over the deserts and oases of the northwest, among the snowy peaks of the Tibetan plateau, and in the jungles of Burma and Annam. So far as the Manchurian tribesmen were concerned, these wars touched upon their lives only when they were called upon to fill the ranks of soldiers. Because only the Buteha and Hulun Buir banner troops were taken for this purpose, the majority of the tribesmen were left alone.

During this period, there was a rapid increase in the population of China. From about 150,000,000 around 1700 or shortly after, it increased to about 275,000,000 in 1779 and 313,000,000 in 1794.[52] In the northern provinces of Chihli, Shantung, and Shansi where rainfall is precarious, droughts periodically devastated large regions, causing an outpouring of hungry migrants seeking sustenance from neighboring lands. Manchuria, with its rich natural resources and low population density was an attractive goal for these famine-driven peoples. Even in the prosperous reigns of K'ang-hsi and Ch'ien-lung and despite stringent government prohibitions, Chinese immigrants were trickling into the forests and valleys of the Manchurian frontier, where they came into contact with the tribal communities, and in the course of time wrought profound changes in the lives of the frontier tribes. However, these preliminary migrations were only dark clouds on the horizon during the period of *laissez-faire*.

In the first half of the nineteenth century, a momentous change also occurred in the history of the Ch'ing empire. This was the deterioration in the international position of China in the Far East. The Opium War of

1839–1842 exposed the weakness of China before the eyes of western colonial powers. Thereafter, foreign pressures against the land and sea frontiers of China were to become increasingly frequent. In 1847 Nicholas Muraviev (1809–1881) was appointed governor-general of Siberia. Three years later the Russians established a settlement, Nikolaevsk, at the mouth of the Amur in the midst of its tribal subjects without encountering retaliation from Peking. The ability of the Ch'ing court to assert its claim as the protector of the tribute peoples had come to an end. The system was on its way to dissolution.

Conclusion

Because the tributary system permitted the tribal peoples a great deal of internal autonomy, its effectiveness as a method of control was due to recognition by the tribal peoples of the inherent military superiority of the suzerain power and its ability to protect them against foreign aggressors as well as the advantages derived from the trading privileges obtained through such a relationship. Since there was a minimum of surveillance by the imperial government over its tribal subjects, the smooth functioning of the tributary system was dependent upon the preservation of the tribal culture, of its characteristic economic and social organization. An upsetting of traditional tribal culture would result in a disturbance of the balance of power among the tribal groups and between the tribal groups and the imperial government, causing the breakdown of the system. An example of such an occurrence was the rise of Manchu power through Manchu borrowing from China and Korea of advanced political concepts and technology during the Ming period. Thus, the Manchu policy of isolating the Manchurian frontier from China proper was conducive to the proper working of the tributary system. Such a policy, however, was tenable only if China and the world around it remained unchanged. By the latter part of the nineteenth century, developments in China proper and other parts of the world soon wrought changes in the Manchurian frontier and brought about the disintegration of the tribal control system.

4

The Establishment of Bureaucratic Administration

Administratively, both the banner organization and the tributary system provided the frontier population with various degrees of local autonomy. Any tendency toward regional autonomy, however, was counteracted by the extension of bureaucratic control in the form of military government for both Kirin and Heilungkiang. The structure of the military government, reflecting both the ethnic characteristics and historical developments of the Manchurian frontier, differed in many ways from the provincial government of China proper and other frontier administrations of the empire such as Outer and Inner Mongolia, Chinese Turkestan, and Tibet. In this regard, an understanding of the organization and functions of the military government is indispensable to our overall knowledge of the political structure of the multi-national Ch'ing empire.

Political Boundaries in Manchuria

When the Manchu court was first established in Peking in 1644, the entire Manchurian frontier region, from Liao-tung in the south to the Amur Basin in the north, from the Mongol lands in the west to the Sea of Japan in the east, was governed by a garrison commander whose troops were deployed around Sheng-ching, originally the Ming city of Shen-yang.[1] Gradually, the name Sheng-ching, chosen by Abahai in 1631, was extended in common usage to cover all of Manchuria. In 1657 a Fengt'ien prefecture was created in southern Manchuria with Sheng-ching as the seat of the prefectural government.[2] Thereafter, Sheng-ching and Fengt'ien were often used interchangeably to denote the same geographical area.

In 1653 an *amban janggin* was installed as the head of the garrison force in Ninguta.[3] The area under his jurisdiction which was carved out of northern Sheng-ching, became known as Ninguta, and Sheng-ching or Fengt'ien became the proper name for a much reduced but more populous area in the south. In 1662 the office of *amban janggin* was abolished and the office of *chiang-chün* or military governor was created. In 1676 the headquarters of the Ninguta military governor were moved to Kirin; hence the origin of the provincial name, Kirin.[4] In 1683 the northwestern part of Kirin was put under the jurisdiction of a newly appointed military governor of Heilungkiang, who was stationed at a site near the present city of Aigun on the bank of Amur.[5] The headquarters of the Heilungkiang military governor were later moved first to Mergen and then to Tsitsihar.[6] However, Heilungkiang remained the proper name for that particular region. Thereafter, the three regions were often known collectively as the Three Eastern Provinces. The term Manchuria or *Man-chou* is a modern invention used mainly by Japanese and Westerners.

To put it briefly, Kirin became an independent regional administrative unit in 1653 and Heilungkiang in 1683. Prior to 1653 the entire frontier region was governed from Sheng-ching, and prior to 1683 Heilungkiang was a part of Kirin. In the study of the military government of the Manchurian frontier, I shall confine myself largely to developments after 1683. Unless specifically stated, the description of government structure and functions is applicable to both Kirin and Heilungkiang.

The Sheng-ching Regional Government

Because the parent administration at Sheng-ching retained certain administrative ties with the frontier authorities, a brief examination of the structure of the Sheng-ching regional government is necessary to a fuller understanding of the frontier administration. When the Manchu court was removed to Peking in 1644, a general of the imperial guards (*nei-ta-ch'en*) was left in charge of all civil and military matters in the Manchurian region. A change was made in 1646 when an *amban janggin* with the title of comptroller-general of Sheng-ching (*chen-shou Sheng-ching tsung-kuan*) was appointed commander of the regional garrison. As the war against the Ming empire was finally coming to an end, Sheng-ching was elevated to the status of an auxillary capital by the establishment of ministerial organs paralleling those in Peking. These were the Board of Rites, founded in 1658; the Board of Revenue and the Board of Works, in 1659; the Board of Punishments, in 1662; and the Board of War in 1691. Only the Board of Civil Appointment was omitted. In 1662 the garrison commander was retitled military governor of Liao-tung; in 1665, military governor of Fengt'ien; and finally in 1747, military governor of Sheng-ching.[7] As the commander-in-chief of the garrison force, the military governor had sole authority over the regional military affairs and through his subordinates over the affairs of all bannermen. As the head of the regional government, he had supervisory power over the five boards and the metropolitan prefecture of Fengt'ien.

The establishment of the five boards with independent prerogatives because of their relations with the corresponding boards in Peking tended to diminish the political power of the military governor. Each of the five boards was headed by a *shih-lang* (vice president), who was a rank below that of the corresponding official in Peking. The Board of Revenue, under the supervision of the Board of Revenue in Peking, took charge of all the revenues and appropriations for the three Manchurian provinces, including the administration of government farms in Sheng-ching, which produced food for the public granaries. In addition, it had the authority to try all civil suits originating among bannermen. The Board of Rites was responsible for all state ceremonies, the most important of which were the annual sacrifices to the imperial tombs, and acted as the official host to Korean envoys. The Board of Works supervised the construction and maintenance of public buildings and government boats and the management of the state forests. Both the Board of Rites and the Board of Works administered government farms, which produced commodities for their needs. The Board of War administered the arsenals, the archery contests, the courier stations, the military personnel records, and the security checks at the frontier gates. The Board of Punishments had jurisdiction over all criminal cases involving bannermen. It tried, in association with the metropolitan prefect of Fengt'ien, all cases involving both bannermen and Chinese and, in association with the Mongol princes, all cases involving both bannermen and Mongols. In criminal cases, where capital punishment was called for, the Board and the metropolitan prefect together referred the case to Peking for final disposition as was done in other provinces.[8]

At first, all board personnel were appointed from the local Manchu candidates. This practice created opportunities for malfeasance as the appointees, often friends and relatives of each other, tended to be chosen from the local influential families. Consequently, in 1727 a ruling was put into effect requiring half of the staff to be appointed from among the bannerman personnel of the six boards in Peking. This ratio was raised in 1732 to 70 percent from Peking and 30 percent from local candidates.[9] In 1730 a Manchu with the rank of president (*shang-shu*) was appointed to preside over the five boards, but the office was soon discontinued. With the exception of the Board of Revenue and the Board of Punishments, the responsibilities of the five boards were related primarily to the affairs of the imperial household and the banner population; much of their work duplicated that of the various bureaus of the *chiang-chün yamen* (office of the military governor). It was another example of the checks-and-balances device that the Manchu rulers employed to prevent the aggrandisement of personal power by high provincial authorities.

At the beginning of the dynasty the non-banner Chinese population of Liao-tung had been greatly decimated by years of warfare. There were extensive tracts of arable lands lying uncultivated. The cultivated areas were populated predominantly by bannermen, who formed separate banner communities of Manchus, Chinese, and Mongols. These banner villages (*ch'i-t'un*) when they came under the jurisdiction of a local banner garrison post, was known collectively as a banner zone (*ch'i-chieh*) and the officers as zonal authorities (*chieh-kuan*). As Chinese peasants, first with the encouragement of Peking and later on their own initiative, emigrated in large numbers to Liao-tung, they formed their own communities, known as civilian villages (*min-t'un*). This civilian population was administered separately by a hierarchy of civilian officials (*min-kuan*). The juxtaposition of banner and civilian villages under separate political authorities was a fruitful source of disputes.[10] The first civilian administration was created in 1653; the entire Liao-tung region was designated the Liao-yang prefecture; it had under its jurisdiction two districts (hsien), Liao-yang and Hai-ch'eng. In 1657 the Liao-yang prefecture was abolished and the Fengt'ien prefecture was created with the prefectural seat located at Sheng-ching (Mukden) and headed by a metropolitan prefect.[11] In later years more prefects and magistrates were appointed to govern the growing civilian population, but the metropolitan prefect of Fengt'ien remained the highest-ranking official, a de facto governor, in the hierarchy of civilian officials.

Thus, early in the dynasty there had been installed in Sheng-ching three parallel administrative structures: the office of the military governor with jurisdiction over the banner population, the five boards with partial jurisdiction over both the banner and the civilian population, and the civil bureaucracy with jurisdiction over the non-banner Chinese population. When the metropolitan prefect was created, the military governor became concurrently commissioner in charge of Fengt'ien prefectural affairs *(chien-kuan Fengt'ien fu-yin shih-wu ta-ch'en)*, indicating that the civil bureaucracy was under his authority. In 1765, possibly because of the Ch'ien-lung emperor's dissatisfaction over the performance of the military government, the military governor was relieved of his concurrent post. The head of the Sheng-ching Board of Revenue became the concurrent commissioner in charge of Fengt'ien prefectural affairs.[12] Thereafter, the prestige and power of the military governor declined relative to that of the five boards, particularly as the civil population had now outstripped the banner population. The divided authority made coordination difficult if not impossible among the separate lines of authority. The system was productive of corruption, inefficiency, and often of miscarriage of justice.[13] In Kirin and Heilungkiang the administrative structure was much less complex, and the prestige and power of the military governor remained unchallenged.

The Powers and Responsibilities of the Military Governor

Chiang-chün was originally a military title conferred temporarily upon the official who had been chosen to direct military campaigns in the field. It was only after the establishment of permanent banner garrisons in various parts of the empire that the office of *chiang-chün* became a regular assignment limited only to bannermen, particularly Manchus.[14] Within China proper, the office of *chiang-chün* possessed the purely military function of a commander-in-chief of banner troops with the rank of general. In frontier regions such as Manchuria, Sinkiang, and Inner Mongolia, because its power extended into civil affairs, it became, in effect, the office of military governor.

The establishment of the office of military governor in the frontier region was primarily a response to military needs arising from the incursion of Russian invaders in the Amur basin. At the beginning of the dynasty, the bulk of the garrison force was stationed in Sheng-ching. The frontier tribes were governed indirectly through the tributary system. In 1653, the year when an *amban janggin* was appointed to head the Ninguta garrison, the number of soldiers under his command totaled only 430 men.[15] At that time the Russians had already crossed the Outer Khingan mountains (Stanovoi) into the Amur basin. From 1643 to 1652 they ravaged the native settlements without encountering any opposition.[16] In 1652, the Ch'ing court finally decided to clear the Russians out of the territory it claimed. At first the Manchu force had very little success against the Russians. It was not until 1658 when the Ninguta *amban janggin,* Sarhuda (1599–1659), intercepted Onufrii Stepanov, the leader of the Cossack plunderers, near the junction of the Amur and Sungari, killing and capturing most of the intruders, that the Amur basin was cleared of large bands of Russians.[17]

In 1665, the Russians again intruded into the Amur territory from bases located at Nerchinsk and Albazin. It was difficult for the Manchus, with their bases at Sheng-ching and Ninguta to defend the upper Amur against the Russian invaders. Consequently, in 1676 the headquarters of the Ninguta military governor was moved from Ninguta at the bank of the Hurka to Kirin at the bank of the Sungari where a dockyard had been erected in 1661 for the building of patrol and transport vessels. After the end of the Rebellion of the Three Feudatories (1673–1680), the K'ang-hsi emperor began in earnest the preparations for the campaign against the Russians in Albazin. In 1683 he ordered the Ninguta Deputy Military Governor Sabsu (d. ca. 1700) to build fortifications on the banks of the Amur and Kumarsk and garrison them with soldiers.[18] Later in the year, Sabsu was promoted to military governor of Heilungkiang with headquarters at Heilungkiang Ch'eng (the city, later called Aigun).[19]

The rationale for the establishment of the permanent garrisons in Heilungkiang was clearly stated by the K'ang-hsi emperor in an imperial rescript of 1687 to the president of the Board of War. The only way to prevent the Russians from raiding the Dagur and Solon settlements was to maintain well-supplied garrison posts in the Heilungkiang region, the emperor averred; otherwise, as soon as the Manchu troops were withdrawn, the Russians would return and build fortifications in the Amur-Sungari territory, which would be extremely difficult for the Manchus to destroy because of the supply problem. On the other hand, the existence of permanent garrisons would discourage the Russians from making petty raids. If they should decide to invade the Amur territories with a large force, they would have difficulty keeping themselves supplied with food.[20]

After the conclusion of the Treaty of Nerchinsk in 1689, which ended the Russian threat, the headquarters of the Heilungkiang military governor were moved south to Mergen, located on the upper course of the Nonni River and separated from Heilungkiang Ch'eng by the Lesser Khingan mountains. The move was probably motivated by a desire to improve the logistical problem involved in maintaining the garrison. The garrison in Heilungkiang Ch'eng had to be supplied either by boats sailing down the Sungari, then up the Amur, or by land across the mountains from Mergen. In 1699 the headquarters were moved further south to Tsitsihar on the lower course of the Nonni and at the terminal of the route leading west to Hulun Buir and the Khalkha territory of Outer Mongolia.[21] The site at Tsitsihar not only further simplified the problem of transportation but also served an important function in the defense of the Manchurian frontier against any invasion attempt by the Ölöt Mongols under Galdan, with whom the Ch'ing empire was engaged in prolonged warfare.[22]

Thus it seems clear that the establishment of the office of military governor in the Manchurian frontier region originated from military necessity. The Amur basin was of such strategic importance to the Ch'ing empire that it had to be defended against the encroachments of a strong foreign power. The military weakness of the tributary tribes compelled the imperial government to establish permanent garrisons at strategic points and those garrisons had to be supervised by military authorities of appropriate rank so that they could exercise independent command in territories located far from the capital.

Prior to 1767 the military governor was accorded full first rank in the hierarchy of military officers. In 1767 the rank was lowered to subordinate first rank. The viceregal duties of the military governor were to keep harmony among the civil and military population, defend the territory under his jurisdiction, and regulate civil and military affairs.[23] Though the official title of the military governor of Heilungkiang remained unchanged from its inception, the official title of the military governor of Ninguta was changed to military governor of Kirin in 1757.[24] Eligibility to the military governorship, according to statutes, was limited to Manchu and Mongol bannermen who had already attained the rank of deputy military governor or lieutenant general.[25] In actual practice, most of the military governors were Manchu bannermen from Peking and among them a good number of imperial clansmen. With the appointment of a Chinese bannerman as military governor of Kirin in 1853, the rule against the eligibility of Chinese bannermen was broken. This was at the time of the T'ai-p'ing Rebellion, when the prestige of the dynasty had sunk to a new low. It was many years later, in 1882 that the first Chinese bannerman was appointed military governor of Heilungkiang. Throughout Ch'ing history, among the military governors (counting those reappointed to non-consecutive terms more than once), there were 44 Manchus, 14 imperial clansmen, 11 Mongols, 3 Chinese, and 7 of unknown ethnic background in Kirin;[26] 40 Manchus, 13 imperial clansmen, 3 Mongols, 3 Chinese, and 6 of unknown ethnic background in Heilungkiang.[27] All the non-Manchus with one exception, a Mongol in Kirin, were appointed in the nineteenth century, most of them in the latter part of the period.

Because military governors of the Manchurian frontier were originally appointed in response to military needs, their primary duties were to assure peace and order within their jurisdictions and to maintain the efficiency of their garrison forces. Specifically, these duties involved the following:

Acting as the representative of the imperial government in dealing with the tribal inhabitants of the frontier region. This meant in effect, the administration of the tributary system.

Prevention of illegal immigration. There were twenty-seven *pien-t'ai*, or frontier posts, located along the Kirin section of the Willow Palisades to check on travelers entering Kirin.[28]

Maintenance of communication and transportation links. Prior to the development of telegraphic and postal services, communications in the frontier area were dependent upon courier stations, which also served as hostels along the land routes. There were thirty-eight courier stations in Kirin[29] and thirty-five in Heilungkiang.[30] The courier routes were also the main land routes. The water transport routes were the Sungari-Nonni route and the Hurka-Sungari-Amur route.

Government transport vessels and ferry boats were maintained along the main river ports of Kirin, Petuna, Alchuka, San-hsing, Tsitsihar, Mergen, Aigun and Hulan.[31] It is interesting that the first dockyard was built in Kirin in 1661, the Kirin river patrol was organized in 1674, and the Heilungkiang river patrol in 1684;[32] but the courier stations in Kirin and Heilungkiang were not established until 1685.[33] The installation of telegraph service in Kirin began two centuries later in 1885 and extended to Heilungkiang in 1887.[34] The courier stations, however, remained in service until 1908.[35]

Preservation of internal order. This involved such responsibilities as apprehension of criminals, custody of exiles, and dispensation of justice. Because an independent police organization did not even exist in China proper until near the end of the dynasty, the garrison troops had to perform all the duties that ordinarily devolve upon a police force. Guard posts (*karum*) were established at strategic points such as road junctions and mountain passes to apprehend illegal ginseng diggers, trespassers in the imperial hunting preserves, escaped convicts, and so on. They were divided into permanent, seasonal, and temporary posts.[36]

Maintenance of border security. The conclusion of the Treaty of Kiakhta in 1727 led to the demarcation of the Russo-Chinese boundary in the Hulun Buir district. In that year, the Ch'ing authorities set up markers called *obo* along the boundary and twelve *karun* along the Argun River, which separated Russian and Chinese territories. In 1733, fifteen additional *karun* were placed some one or two hundred li back of the 1727 *karun*. A year later, sixteen *karun* were erected along the Khalkha or Outer Mongolia border. In 1847 three more *karun* were placed along the Khalkha border. The *karun* set up in 1733 along the Russian border were moved forward in 1857 to about thirty or forty li back of the 1727 *karun*. In 1884, five *karun* were added along the Argun to prevent Russian goldminers from poaching in Chinese territory. In 1907 and 1908 efforts were made to rehabilitate the 1727 *karun* and to add new ones.[37]

The establishment of *karun* made it unnecessary to dispatch troops from Aigun, Mergen, and Tsitsihar for the annual inspection of the Russo-Chinese boundary line, which was done prior to 1727.[38]

Maintenance of public granaries. The frontier granary system comprised a number of *kung-ts'ang*, or government granaries, and *i-ts'ang*, or charity granaries. The government granaries were first erected in Heilungkiang in 1686 and in Kirin in 1689 as part of the military colonization plan. The soldier-colonists were required to contribute annually a stated amount of grain to the government, which was then stored in the government granaries. The amount of public grain stored in each town was set by government regulations. The primary purpose of the government granaries was the storage of food reserves against years of bad harvest. The surplus grain from the government granaries was sold to the population at lower than prevailing market price. The proceeds realized from such sales were used for local government purposes.[39]

Charity granaries seem to have existed only in Kirin. They were organized in 1727 on a *niru* basis without the support of government funds. Each *niru* designated three soldiers to cultivate lands devoted to the charity granaries. Such granaries served primarily as commodity credit agencies. The soldiers of the company could borrow grain from the granary during the season when their food stores were low and repay the loan when their harvests were in. In 1773 the amount of grain stored in the granaries was also regulated by the government. Surplus grain was sold to the soldiers at reduced prices and the proceeds used for the repair and upkeep of the granaries.[40]

Military training. During the Ch'ing dynasty, most of the frontier banner soldiers did not live in barracks and army camps but in villages surrounding their garrison towns. Their daily routine was devoted primarily to farming and hunting. For this reason, the spring and autumn reviews held during the slack farm seasons, when the entire garrison force was called together to participate in drill and competitive contests, and the winter hunts, when the troops were put through manuevers in group formations, were the most important parts of the military training program.[41]

During the T'ai-p'ing Rebellion, when a large number of banner troops were dispatched to China proper and the regional treasuries were nearly empty, the annual winter hunts were suspended. Some efforts were made after the end of the rebellion to revive the custom. But the lack of funds made it a half-hearted and sporadic affair. The last great hunts in Kirin and Heilungkiang were held in 1875. In 1876 the custom was discontinued and the hunting preserves were later thrown open for colonization.[42]

Educational, ceremonial, and tributary functions. During the greater part of the dynasty, only a rudimentary school system existed on the Manchurian frontier. The few government schools were established for the benefit of bannermen children who wished to study the Manchu language. Chinese was taught primarily in schools opened by Chinese exiles. It was only in the Kuang-hsü reign (1875–1908) that public and private schools became more numerous.[43] Ceremonial functions involved the participation of the military governor or his official representative in certain religious rites such as the annual worship at *She-chi-t'an* or Altar of the Gods of Soil and Grains, at the *Hsien-nung-*

t'an or Altar of the God of Agriculture, and at the temple of *Kuan-ti* the God of War. The Kirin military governor had the special responsibility of holding sacrifices to the Ch'ang-pai-shan, the Sungari River, and the Lung-t'an mountains (site of the God of Rains).[44] The tributary presentations involved sending to the court at stated intervals such local products as wild game, fruits, arrow shafts, furs, birchbark, honey, vegetables, and so on.[45] These tributes were in addition to the forwarding of the tribal tribute and the annual local quotas in ginseng, pearls, and sables.

The Organization of the Military Governor's Office

The *chiang-chün yamen* or military governor's office was staffed by a *yin-fang* or secretariat, a *yin-k'u* or treasury, a *hu-ssu* or bureau of revenue, a *ping-ssu* or bureau of punishments, and a *kung-ssu* or bureau of works. These offices were responsible for conducting the routine business of the military governor's administration.

The secretariat was responsible for the drafting of official documents and the custody of the military governor's seal. The chief secretary called *t'ang-chu-shih* or *kuan-tang chu-shih* was the highest secretarial personnel in the administration. The post was first established in Kirin in 1674 and in Heilungkiang in 1694. At first, the chief secretary was chosen from bannermen candidates drawn from the rosters of local clerks, granary officials, and courier station masters. In 1737 it was decided that only clerks serving on the six boards in Peking were eligible for the post. In 1788 it was once more reserved for local candidates. The chief clerk in Heilungkiang was usually a Chinese bannerman.[46]

The bureau of punishments was responsible for the adjudication of civil and criminal cases, the custody and execution of prisoners, and the forwarding to the Board of Punishments in Peking of information relating to the administration of justice and the surveillance of slaves and exiles.[47] The chief administrative official in the bureau was the *li-hsing chu-shih*, judicial secretary, whose post was first created in Kirin in 1737. He was at first appointed from the ranks of Peking government clerks. In 1864, it was decided that instead of a *chu-shih*, who ranked sixth in the nine-ranks civil bureaucracy, the Board of Punishments in Peking should appoint an experienced Chinese official with the next higher rank of *lang-chung* or *yüan-wai-lang* to be the bureau's chief judicial officer and seal-keeper.[48]

In Heilungkiang, the post of judicial secretary, created in 1738, was at first filled by appointees from Peking. In 1880 it was opened to candidates drawn from local clerks. In 1884, the post of *li-hsing yuan-wai-lang*, director of punishments, was created and filled by candidates who had served locally either as chief secretary, treasurer, or judicial secretary.[49] Contrary to the custom in Kirin, the seal of the bureau of punishments was kept by a banner officer, usually with the rank of colonel, whose authority exceeded the judicial official and interfered with his duties. Because military officers were often ignorant of the legal code, the administration of justice in Heilungkiang left much to be desired.[50] The difference in the appointment of judicial officials in Kirin and Heilungkiang reflected not only the heavier concentration of Chinese immigrants in Kirin and the consequent need for more experienced legal personnel but also the more "militaristic" atmosphere of the Heilungkiang administration.

The custody and disbursement of government funds were the responsibilities of the *yin-k'u chu-shih* or treasurer. The post was created in 1738 in Heilungkiang and probably sometime earlier in Kirin. Prior to 1867 it was filled by appointees from Peking; thereafter, local bannermen were chosen instead.[51]

The bureau of revenue was in charge of accounting for government revenues and expenditures. Its duties included the collection of monetary and grain taxes and the receiving of funds from Peking for the payment of officials and troops. It was also responsible for keeping the census register of the banner population, reporting every three months the market price for grain to the Board of Revenue in Sheng-ching, selling surplus granary grain to the public, and checking on the cultivation of public lands by illegal immigrants.[52]

The bureau of military affairs was in charge of keeping the roster of officers and men in service, storing and issuing military weapons, administering the courier stations, issuing road passes, keeping the service records of clerical and military personnel, and sending local tributes to the court.[53]

The bureau of works was responsible for the building and upkeep of official temples, granaries, prisons, yamen, and city walls; the building and repair of ferry boats, grain transports, and pearling vessels; and the manufacture of gun-powder.[54]

The dates for the establishment of the bureaus of revenue, military affairs, and works cannot now be ascertained. Because of their importance in regard to the financial, personnel, and military administration of the military government, their establishment could not have been much later than the creation of the office of the military governor. The presiding official of each bureau, called *kuan-fang-kuan* or seal keeper, was drawn from the roster of local banner officers, usually a person with the rank of colonel or major. These three bureaus were not headed by civil officials as were the other offices.[55]

The statutory number of personnel of the military governor's office was quite small. In addition to the chief secretary, treasurer, judicial secretary, and seal keepers, the Kirin yamen was entitled to only fourteen bannermen clerks distributed to all bureaus and Heilungkiang to only eleven. Among the clerks, there were four Manchu-Chinese translators in the Kirin and Heilungkiang yamens and three Mongol translators in the Heilungkiang yamen.[56] However, additional clerks might be taken into service from the banner force by the presiding officials. The number of these non-statutory personnel undoubtedly increased during the nineteenth century in accordance with the increase in the workload of the military government. Around 1890, for instance, there were twenty such clerks in the Heilungkiang yamen.[57]

From the foregoing it seems clear that whether viewed from the standpoint of the differentiation of governmental functions, or from the number and qualification of the government personnel, the military government operated in a relatively simple manner with the military aspect of the administration receiving the most attention.

Furthermore, given the dates of the establishment of the various official posts, it seems that it was only during the latter part of the K'ang-hsi reign (1662–1722) that the military governor's office began to be transformed from purely a military headquarters to a more complex form of political structure. The change was gradual and involved only the addition of personnel and the source of their recruitment.

Local Governments in the Frontier Region

Local governments in the Manchurian frontier region may be divided into garrison governments and civil governments; the latter appeared relatively late, being completely absent in Heilungkiang until 1863. Garrison governments existed wherever there were garrison towns.

Were it not for the presence of exiles and merchants, the early garrison towns might simply be called fortified army camps. The highest official in a garrison town was usually the *fu tu-t'ung* or lieutenant-general, who, in his administrative capacity, performed the duties of a deputy military governor. The deputy military governors stationed in the capital cities of Kirin and Heilungkiang participated with the military governors in decision making and for that reason possessed greater powers than other deputy military governors who controlled only a single district.[58]

The deputy military governor was accorded full second rank in the military hierarchy of the banner force. Prior to 1762 local banner officers might be promoted to the office of deputy military governor and *ch'eng shou-wei* or commandant of a garrison town. In that year, the Ch'ien-lung emperor made it a rule that only banner officers from China proper were eligible for these posts on the grounds that there had been a deterioration in public order in the Manchurian region, such as illegal ginseng diggers resisting arrest. He blamed the laxity of these high officers, who shielded their local subordinates and colleagues from responsibility for mistakes and malpractices.[59] There had been only two posts of commandant of garrison town on the Manchurian frontier. One, at Mergen, probably created sometime after 1685, was abolished in 1693; the other, at Hulan, was created in 1734 and abolished in 1879.[60] The commandant was accorded full third rank in the military hierarchy. When in sole command of a garrison town, the duties of the commandant were similar to that of the deputy military governor.

The yamen of the deputy military governor or the commandant was composed of the following offices: the secretariat called *t'ang-ssu* or *yin-wu ch'u* was in charge of the flow of documents and the custody of the official seal of the deputy military governor or the commandant. The right bureau, *yu-ssu*, usually combined the functions on a smaller scale of the bureaus of military affairs and punishments in the yamen of the military governor. The left bureau, *tso-ssu*, usually combined the functions of the bureaus of revenue and works.[61] The presiding official of each office was usually a local military officer in charge of several clerks in each office.[62]

Where a garrison town was too small to warrant the appointment of a deputy military governor or commandant, a colonel was usually put in charge of the troops and made responsible to the nearby deputy military governor. For example, the colonel in Hun-ch'un was responsible to the deputy military governor in Ninguta and the colonel in Lalin to the deputy military governor in Alchuka.

Civil government was distinct from garrison government in that the population under its jurisdiction was made up predominantly of Chinese civilians and the officials in charge were drawn from the civil service instead of the military service. The first civil governments on the department (*chou*) and district (*hsien*) levels, in the Manchurian frontier region were established in 1727. They were Yung-chi chou located near Kirin city, T'ai-ning hsien near Ninguta, and Ch'ang-ning hsien near Petuna. They were headed by a department magistrate, *chih-chou* or a district magistrate, *chih-hsien*, respectively.[63] They were at first put under the jurisdiction of the metropolitan prefect of Fengt'ien, although their administrative domains were located within the territory of Kirin.[64] The court seems to have been doubtful of the practicability or desirability of diluting the military character of the frontier administration with civil affairs. For in Sheng-ching, although the military governor had overall jurisdiction over provincial affairs, there was, from the very beginning, a separation between civil and military administration. In 1729, T'ai-ning hsien was abolished and in 1736, Ch'ang-ning was incorporated by Yung-chi chou.[65] In 1747 the Ninguta military governor, Alantai, obtained the approval of the court for the transfer of Yung-chi to his jurisdiction in the interest of greater efficiency and the avoidance of conflicts between Ninguta and Sheng-ching. As a result, Yung-chi chou was reorganized as Kirin t'ing (sub-prefecture).[66]

The organization of the sub-prefectural government in Kirin was similar to that of its counterpart in China proper. The sub-prefect had the responsibility of maintaining law and order among the civilian population under his jurisdiction, collecting taxes, and adjudicating criminal and civil suits involving only civilians. He also presided over cases of fighting and personal injuries involving both civilians and bannermen.[67] Suits involving only bannermen or cases of thievery and robbery involving both civilians and bannermen were remanded to the bureau of punishments of the military governor's office.[68]

After the establishment of Kirin sub-prefecture in 1747, no other civil government was set up until 1802 when a *li-shih t'ung-p'an*, assistant sub-prefect was appointed to take charge of the Chinese immigrant population that had settled on lands of the Mongol Gorlos banner, which later became the site of the city of Ch'ang-ch'un.[69] In 1810 a sub-prefect was appointed for Petuna for similar reasons.[70] Thereafter, for a period of about seventy years no additional civil government was erected in Kirin until the Kuang-hsü reign (1875–1908) when a rapid increase of local civil governments occurred. In Heilungkiang there was no civil government whatsoever until the Hulan sub-prefecture was established in 1875.[71]

Imperial Control of the Frontier Government

The problem of control by the central government of the peripheral regions of the empire has been a constant concern of the dynastic rulers throughout Chinese history. Overcentralization tended to weaken frontier defense and invite barbarian invasions, while over-decentralization tended to enhance the power and prestige of frontier officers at the expense of the court and to invite rebellion. Therefore, it was essential for the central government to devise means of controlling its frontier officers without weakening their ability to deal effectively with the problems of frontier defense and internal security. During the Ch'ing dynasty, the principal means through which the Peking court controlled the governments of the Manchurian frontier were the following:

Internal checks against the aggrandizement of power by the military governor and his chief assistants within the banner organization. As related previously the banner force was composed of a hereditary military caste divided into basic units called *niru*, each of which was headed by a major who was often the clan leader of the men under his control and whose position was often inherited. For this reason, the major possessed a certain autonomous power within his *niru*, exceeding the strictly military functions of his rank. Furthermore, the pyramidal organization of the banner system ultimately vested the control of each banner in the hands of a banner *tu-t'ung* or general who resided in the capital and usually belonged to the imperial clan closely related to the reigning emperor.[72] Thus, the military governor and the deputy military governor, although given full command of the troops in a garrison district, did not possess absolute control over the internal administration of personnel under him.

Administrative devices to curtail the power of the military governor. First of all, the majority of the appointees were Peking Manchu bannermen, and many of them were imperial clansmen. Since they were not natives of the Manchurian frontier region, their personal interests were oriented toward China proper, in contrast to the local officers who lived there for generations and knew very little of the conditions in China proper. Consequently, it was somewhat difficult for officials from Peking and local officers to achieve a complete identity of interests and personal rapport.

Second, the term of office of the military governor was of comparatively short duration. The average term in Kirin lasted 3.8 years and in Heilungkiang 3.5 years. About half of the total number of military governors served only one or two years during their terms of office. The first military governors of Kirin and Heilungkiang, who occupied their posts for 24 and 18 years respectively, were exceptional.[73] It is clear that with such rapid turnover of military governors, it would be very difficult for most of them to develop a personal following on the frontier that could challenge the authority of the central government.

Third, the power and responsibilities of the military governor were shared by the deputy military governor. In particular, the deputy military governors of Kirin and Tsitsihar possessed almost equal authority as the military governors by virtue of their prerogative in countersigning all official communications sent by their superiors to the court.[74] For all these reasons, although the military governor was given vice-regal powers in a region far from the capital, there was never recorded a case of a governor committing insubordinate acts against the court.

Financial dependence of the frontier governments upon subsidies of the central government and the provinces in China proper. Throughout the Ch'ing dynasty the Manchurian frontier governments were never able to finance completely their own expenditures. Prior to 1853 the Kirin and Heilungkiang governments were subsidized directly by the treasury of the central government. The funds allocated to them were sent to the Shengching Board of Revenue where representatives from Kirin and Heilungkiang received their shares according to their need.[75] The importance of the subsidies can be seen from the following accounts: According to Sa-ying-e, chief secretary of the Kirin military governor's office during early years of the Tao-kuang reign (1821–1850), the annual expenditures of the Kirin government totaled 472,700 taels. In addition 74,000 taels were needed for two revolving funds. But the total local revenues, mainly receipts from land and commodity taxes, amounted to only 92,925 taels.[76] According to Hsi-ch'ing, who was the treasurer in the Heilungkiang military governor's yamen, during the early part of the Chia-ch'ing reign (1796–1820) the annual expenditures of the Heilungkiang government was 478,598 taels. The two revolving funds totaled 73,000 taels. But the local revenues consisted of only some 2,000 taels from the livestock tax and some 200 taels from government owned buildings rented to merchants.[77] Thus, in the case of Kirin nearly 80 percent of the expenditures, and in the case of Heilungkiang practically all the expenditures were paid by the central government.

The T'ai-p'ing Rebellion (1850–1864) so disorganized the fiscal system of the empire that the central government could not obtain exact information on the amount of money available for the subsidization of the poorer provinces by the wealthier provinces.[78] Consequently, in 1853 the Peking Board of Revenue assigned to various provinces the responsibility of remitting directly to the Sheng-ching Board of Revenue their own quotas of the subsidies for Kirin and Heilungkiang.[79] Unfortunately for the frontier governments, the provinces assigned to subsidize them often neglectedto honor fully their obligations.[80] As a result the frontier governments were forced to develop their own sources of income. Until then their reliance on outside financial help was an effective check upon their freedom of political action. In this regard, the banning of Chinese immigration and the resulting underdevelopment of the frontier economy was a distinct aid to the central government in exerting control over the frontier governments.

Periodic inspection of the frontier administration by court officials. Beginning in 1723, two censors, a Manchu and a Chinese, were appointed imperial inspectors to Ninguta, and a Manchu censor was appointed imperial inspector to Tsitsihar. They inspected annually, by a tour of the region under their jurisdiction, the administration of the public granaries, fiscal accounts, military supplies, ships, official records, and courier stations of the major garrison towns. In 1729 the post of Chinese imperial inspector was abolished. In 1747 the interval of inspection was lengthened to once every three years. In 1775 it was changed to once every five years. In 1799 the inspectors were drawn from the ministers of five boards in Sheng-ching.[81] Finally in 1818, upon the recommendation of Fu-chün, the military governor of Kirin, the practice was terminated on the grounds that, first, the inspection tours were costly to the garrison towns, which had to strain their resources to accommodate the inspectors and their entourage, and second, they were ineffectual because any malpractice was usually covered up by the time the inspectors arrived.[82]

Bureaucratic control exercised by ministries in the capital over the details of government operations on the frontier. The bureaus of revenue, punishments, military affairs, and works in Kirin and Heilungkiang were required to send annual reports to the corresponding boards in Peking for approval.[83]

General Characteristics of the Frontier Administration

The Manchurian frontier administration was evolved directly from the banner garrison command. Its primary function was the maintenance of frontier security. This was accomplished through its control of a military force composed of hereditary farmer-soldiers and the establishment of local supply bases and communication networks. One of its major defense tasks was the administration of the tributary system through which the tribal peoples were loosely linked to the empire centered at Peking, and the tribal territories formed a buffer zone at the outermost reaches of the frontier lands, between China and Russia.

Structurally, the military government was simply organized with regional authority theoretically centralized in the hands of the military governor but actually diffused among himself and the deputy military governors. Administratively, its power was circumscribed by the central government through a number of bureaucratic devices. Politically, its control over the local banners and tribal population was limited by the semi-autonomous character of the Manchu clan villages and the largely autonomous tribal communities. It was a government autocratic in principle but restrained by internal and external checks in practice.

The military governorship was a prestigious post but the average term of office was so short that it did not provide any opportunity for the display of creative political leadership. No significant collections of memorials and personal writings relating to the frontier have come down to us from the brushes of a long line of military governors until toward the end of the dynasty. No effort was made to explore the unknown parts of the frontier or to seek intelligence across the border until the Russians returned in the last half of the nineteenth century to occupy the left bank of the Amur; by then it was too late. Once the political framework had been set during the K'ang-hsi reign, the succeeding governors seem to have been content to follow precedents strictly. The imperial policy was to keep the frontier unchanged, and the frontier officials were not inclined to disobey the court. Despite official inertia or perhaps because of it, changes did come about which undermined the effectiveness of the military government and caused its downfall.

5

The Sinicization of the Manchurian Frontier

The sinicization of the Manchurian frontier during the Ch'ing dynasty is one of the great enduring events in the history of China. It was a long drawn-out process. Aside from those Manchu and Mongol bannermen who were sent from the capital to govern the frontier population, the agents of sinicization were Chinese immigrants who were scholars, officials, criminal convicts, seekers of quick fortune, famine refugees, traders, and land-hungry peasants. Whether they came to the Manchurian frontier of their own volition or under duress they transformed the land of their adoption as it had never been transformed before. In 1787 the estimated total population for Kirin was 150,000 and in 1850 about 327,000.[1] By 1907 the Kirin Chinese population was stated to be 3,827,762, and the bannerman population 410,101.[2] In Heilungkiang the banner population, including the Buteha and Hulun Buir tribes, according to an 1808 census, was 136,228. In 1887, it was 252,776.[3] By 1907, the total population, including Chinese and bannermen, was estimated to be 1,455,657, of which only 81,247 were in localities where non-Chinese peoples were in the majority.[4] These figures certainly underestimated the actual number of Chinese residents in the frontier region, especially in the early periods when the illegal immigrants could not be counted. Nevertheless, they serve to illustrate vividly the dramatic increase in Chinese population in the frontier region. It was this demographic reality that made the Manchurian frontier culturally an indisputable part of China.

Prior to 1668 the Ch'ing court actually encouraged Chinese colonization to replenish the depleted population of the Liao-tung plain in southern Manchuria, which had long been a battlefield between the Manchus and the Ming armies.[5] During the Shun-chih reign (1644–1661) political and criminal exiles were sent there to supplement the not too successful colonization effort.[6] By 1668, however, the flow of Chinese immigrants to Liao-tung had attained such a volume that the court rescinded its previous decrees to promote colonization and imposed a ban upon further immigration instead.[7]

The first Chinese settlers in the Manchurian frontier region were also political and criminal exiles brought in by the government. In 1676 several thousand families were sent to Kirin.[8] With the establishment of the post of military governor of Heilungkiang in 1684 exiles were also sent to such places as Aigun, Tsitsihar, and Mergen.[9] At about the same time illegal immigrants were already penetrating the Willow Palisades into the ginseng producing areas of Kirin. Yang Pin reported in 1689–1690 that more than ten thousand illegal ginseng diggers went into the mountains every year.[10] Some of them must have stayed on the frontier. Soon illegal peasant settlers were following the footsteps of the ginseng diggers. A 1736 imperial decree specifically prohibited the leasing and selling of land by the bannermen to civilians, which indicates the existence of a sizable Chinese peasant population.[11] The ban against Chinese immigration did not apply to merchants who were already trading with the tribal people in Ninguta in Wu Chen-ch'en's account of life in that city around 1681.[12] Toward the latter part of the eighteenth century, Chinese officials were introduced into the frontier to govern communities formed by peasant immigrants.[13]

Banditry in the Manchurian frontier zone began to be a problem during the T'ai-p'ing Rebellion (1850–1864)[14] and remained to plague the regional authorities until the end of the dynasty. The problem was aggravated by the presence of an aggressive Russian power on the Sino-Russian border. It was to safeguard the border and suppress the bandits that Chinese soldiers from China proper were first introduced into Kirin in 1880.[15] With the reorganization of the regional government in 1907 there was an influx of higher echelon Chinese administrators, army officers, and technical personnel into the frontier region.[16] These were the men who transformed the Manchurian frontier from its historic role as the homeland of "barbarian" invaders into a new regional center of Chinese culture and enterprise.

Chinese Exiles

The first recorded Chinese exile arrived at Ninguta in 1655. He was the scholar-official, Ch'en Ching-yin, who became a prosperous merchant and probably the first resident Chinese trader in the frontier region.[17]

After that time the Manchurian frontier served as a convenient dumping ground for political exiles and criminal convicts down to the nineteenth century. Many of the exiles were unfortunate scholars sentenced in 1658 for irregularities committed at state examinations, victims of literary inquisitions, and luckless participants of the Rebellion of the Three Feudatories (1673–1681). In 1676, in preparation for defense against the incursions of Russian Cossacks in the Amur territory several thousand families of exiles were sent to the dockyard located on the Sungari to build boats and serve as sailors. The dockyard later became the city of Kirin. As garrisons were established in Heilungkiang, exiles were sent to such localities as Tsitsihar, Mergen, Hulan, and Aigun. One account estimated the number of exiles and their descendants at the end of the Yung-cheng reign (1735) in the whole of Manchuria (including Sheng-ching) to be about 100,000.[18]

The treatment received by the exiles at the hands of the authorities varied according to the status and personality of the exiles as well as the existing circumstances at the place of banishment. Some were doomed to servitude in the river patrol, courier stations, and official farms where life was hard and opportunities for improvement were limited. An imperial edict of June 1682 described such exiles in Ninguta and Kirin as deprived of proper shelter, lacking proper means to engage in farming, and burdened with government services. An April 1688 edict reprimanded the official travelers on the Sheng-ching–Ninguta route who made unreasonable demands for carts and horses from the courier stations and frequently struck the station personnel.[19]

The lucky ones were free to make their own living to the best of their ability. This was not too difficult a task for anyone who was willing to make the necessary mental and physical adjustments. The region abounded in natural resources. One could cultivate a small plot of land for vegetables and grain, fish in the bountiful streams, and obtain timber in the forests. There was a shortage of skilled craftsmen among the native population, so a man with some knowledge of a handicraft commanded a good wage. Because the Manchus and the tribal people did not have trained medical doctors, Chinese doctors were accorded the same confidence as the native shamans. Education was rudimentary among the rough frontier bannermen, so educated exiles tutored those who cared to have a knowledge of Chinese language and literature, especially among the children of high officials. Contact with Chinese civilization had stimulated a taste for luxuries, so men with some capital turned to trade. Temples, erected to seek favors from a pantheon of Chinese gods, were staffed by men who sought spiritual release from a cruel fate or by charlatans who found in them a source of ready income.[20]

Some exiles were accompanied by their wives, children, and servants. Relatives were allowed to visit them, and friends were permitted to send them gifts. Occasionally, furloughs were granted for visits to China proper. Although they were under surveillance, the authorities in the early years of the dynasty were often easygoing, and consequently many managed to escape. It was only in 1690 that check posts were established to prevent flights.[21]

It would be misleading, however, to give the impression that the life of the more fortunate exiles was simply an adaptation of the gentry mode of living to the frontier. For those who had never performed manual labor the transition was indeed difficult. An account of Ninguta life around 1659–1660 by Fang Kung-ch'ien stated:

> There is no person of leisure in Ninguta, and women are the busiest of all. The beating of cloth for pasting over the windows in lieu of paper, and the cutting of hemp and mixing it with chaff for lighting are all done by women. Grain is not husked by grinding but by pounding, which goes on day and night. One woman cannot pound enough for the daily needs of two men. Polished grain requires five or six poundings. Recently a mill was built, but the grain has to be carried to the mill. Soon after the pounding of grain comes the task of drawing icy water. The well-site is as slippery as a hill, barefooted and thinly garbed, those who weep and lament while shouldering their burdens are all descendants of the rich and honorable families of China. How heartrending a sight it is![22]

The average bannerman family probably did not enjoy an easier life than the average exile family. There did not seem to be any conscious cruelty on the part of the authorities in the treatment of the political exiles, but the lack of those social and material amenities to which the exiles had been accustomed in China proper made frontier life difficult and bleak for many of them. With the passage of time, improvements were evident and the talented ones soon managed to make themselves comfortable in frontier life. In the late seventeenth century, Yang Pin gave the following description of the exiles in Ninguta:

> It was customary there to esteem wealth and despise poverty, to esteem age and despise youth, and to esteem the Chinese and despise the Manchus. Why? Because all the merchants of the eastern and western boroughs were Chinese. The Manchu officers and soldiers were poor. Their clothing and food were all received on credit from merchant acquaintances whom they paid when their monthly stipends arrived. Consequently, they were extremely diffident in their daily intercourse, being afraid that the merchants might withhold their credits. Furthermore, the merchants were all prominent and scholarly men among the exiles. They associated with the military governor and his staff on a basis of equality. The older ones among them even greeted the military governor and his associates as younger brothers, to say nothing of those with lower ranks. No inhabitant ever starved or suffered from cold. Whoever was hungry or cold was given food and clothing donated by all.[23]

Yang further stated that the rich scholars in exile took up trade, the poor scholars who spoke Manchu served as business managers, and the poor scholars who could not speak Manchu became teachers. It is interesting that he divided the merchants into native and transient residents. The latter were Shantung and Shansi men who were already entering Kirin in pursuit of profits.[24]

In Yang's time it was necessary to know Manchu in order to deal with the bannermen. By the end of the eighteenth century practically everyone spoke Chinese.[25] The ascendancy of the Chinese language in Manchuria was simply one of the many manifestations of the sinicization of the Manchus throughout China. An incident was reported that a member of the imperial clan in an audience with the Ch'ien-lung emperor was unable to converse in Manchu. This prompted the emperor to institute examinations on the Manchu language, as well as on the traditional Manchu accomplishments in archery and horsemanship, as part of the education of the Manchu nobility.[26] This effort to preserve Manchu tradition was ineffective because bureaucratic advancement and social prestige did not come with the mastery of the traditional Manchu arts; rather, the mastery of Chinese classics was the key to government employment and the ability to turn elegant Chinese phrases was a mark of social distinction. So it was not surprising that the high Manchu officials in Kirin and Heilungkiang were eager to be known as patrons of the exiled Chinese men of letters.[27] The social status of the gentry, an educated elite possessing local political influence based upon wealth or bureaucratic connections, was reproduced in a somewhat distorted form on the frontier. It was distorted because the exiled scholar-officials, having been deprived legally of their political privileges, played a purely intellectual, and sometimes commercial role in the frontier society. A true gentry class did not develop in Manchuria until perhaps the latter part of the nineteenth century. By that time the frontier economy was sufficiently developed to produce an educated class who could exercise leadership in the local communities. In 1838 it was recorded that the gentry of Kirin repaired the prefectural school and Confucian temple. The government schools in Ch'ang-ch'un and Petuna were built by the local gentry in 1872 and 1874 respectively.[28] The early scholar exiles promoted the development of a true gentry class insofar as they were the living embodiment of gentry values and personally aided in the development of classical education in a land that was then short of scholars as well as books.

Criminal Convicts

The scholars constituted only a small minority among the exiles. Hsi-ch'ing remarked that with the establishment of military government in Heilungkiang, several hundred convicts were sent there annually. Most of them were kept in Tsitsihar; the especially unruly ones were sent farther north to Mergen and Aigun. He estimated that there were around 3,000 convicts in Tsitsihar and more than a thousand in other settlements. Convicts were placed under surveillance, put to forced labor, or enslaved according to the severity of their sentences. Exiled Manchu bannermen were put to work in their banners, and the Chinese bannermen in the river patrol.[29] The treatment of slaves, as might be expected, varied according to the temperament of their masters. In 1736 the Ch'ien-lung emperor, in order to prevent cruel or undignified treatment in the hands of their masters, decreed that former officials and government students, unless they had actually committed crimes of sedition and robbery, were not to be enslaved.[30]

According to law, slaves were assigned to banner soldiers, including the Buteha auxiliaries, as rewards for their meritorious services or as a means of relieving their poverty. Wives of slaves, unless specifically sentenced by the court, were exempted from enslavement. Clever slaves were often able to redeem themselves and eventually become respected members of the society. Incorrigible convicts frequently engaged in gambling, prostitution, and thievery without any fear of punishment by their masters.[31]

An imperial decree of 1810 admonished the local authorities for irregularities in the supervision of exiled officials and convicts as follows:

> Criminals who were exiled to Kirin as slaves were distributed to the soldiers upon their arrival. Those among them who possessed a certain amount of money, after purchasing their freedom from their masters, were permitted to go wherever they pleased. Some of them settled in localities of their own choice; others escaped in secret. When such cases were discovered during muster, their masters brazenly replied that, since the slaves had redeemed their freedom, the masters were no longer responsible for their actions. Eunuchs who were exiled for criminal causes also lived in freedom after paying their ransoms. Some of them bought business properties. When they were released, they deliberately recommitted crimes in order to be sent back to exile. Thus the intent of the national code for the strict punishment of criminals was being grossly violated through the practice of private redemption, which mitigated the criminals' fear of punishment and encouraged them to look upon the land of exile as paradise. As for officials who were condemned to exile, their offenses must have been of quite serious nature for which they were sentenced to experience personal hardships in partial atonement of their wrongdoings. However, in recent years, there have been instances when the military governor sat and ate in company with condemned officials, repaired their houses, and sent them seasonal gifts. In so doing the officials were indulging in their personal sentiments to the detriment of the law. Following each other's example, they did not realize that such conduct was extraordinary. Thus the exiled officials came to think of life in exile as free and easy without experiencing any feeling of hardship and fear.

The edict ended by instructing the military governor to observe the regulations strictly and to prohibit the purchase of freedom by the exiles.[32] The reason soldiers preferred not to keep slaves was because they could not even support their own families adequately with their meager salaries, let alone slaves. An edict of 1813 took cognizance of this fact and directed the Board of Punishments to suspend the sending of criminals to Manchuria. Another edict sought to lighten the burden of the soldiers by instructing the local authorities to transfer the ownership of slaves from soldiers to officials, who could better afford them, thus legalizing a practice that had been going on locally for some time.[33]

Another reason for the periodic suspension of the sending of criminal convicts to the frontier was their concentration in the cities; they were not permitted to live in the clan villages of the bannermen. When the criminal population of the cities became too large, the local authorities would petition for suspension. In Heilungkiang, the number of convicts, after being reduced during the Chia-ch'ing reign (1796–1820), increased again during the T'ai-p'ing Rebellion. In 1865, the Board of Punishments again suspended the sending of exiles to Heilungkiang, and in 1870 the Criminal Code was revised to make the suspension permanent.[34]

Aside from private redemption, there were also records of slaves being freed by official acts of manumission. In 1779, the military governor of Heilungkiang, because of the increase in the population of household slaves, obtained permission from the court for their release and transfer to government farms. In 1883 a statute provided for the freeing of household slaves.[35]

Some of the slaves were not convicts but individuals brought to the frontier by Buteha bannermen campaigning in China proper. When Ch'eng Te-ch'üan was the acting military governor of Heilungkiang in 1906, he directed the general superintendent of the Buteha to free 476 slave families totaling 1,323 persons from the East Buteha banners. There were such strong objections raised by their owners that it was listed as an impeachable item in a memorial drawn up by a censor in an indictment of Ch'eng's official record. The case was referred to Imperial Commissioner Hsü Shih-ch'ang, who in a 1907 memorial, gave Ch'eng full support on the ground that, because China was preparing for a constitutional government, the existence of slaves would incur the contempt of other powers. Hsü thereby obtained the consent of the court for the freeing of all slaves still in the hands of the Buteha banner troops.[36]

It is noteworthy that the last stronghold of slavery in the Manchurian frontier was among the Buteha bannermen, who were just beginning to take up farming as a major occupation. Perhaps slaves were an asset to a people whose knowledge of agricultural technique was elementary but who possessed relatively abundant virgin lands that could be worked by slaves profitably in a time of expanding market for farm products. By contrast, the ownership of slaves in urban centers appears to have been a definite financial burden to the underpaid banner soldiers.

In any assessment of the role of convicts in the development of the Manchurian frontier, one must perhaps stress their importance as a source of forced labor. They cultivated government farms, built boats, and constructed public works. In the period when free labor was scarce and the economy undeveloped, their work laid the foundation for the latecomers. They were the craftsmen in a region where the economy was as yet unable to attract skilled workers from China. With the increased flow of free immigrants, convict labor was less important and their presence was a source of public disturbance, especially in view of the prevalence of brigandage in the latter part of the nineteenth century.

In the days when convicts and their descendants still constituted a sizable proportion of the resident population in the frontier, they imparted to the frontier communities the rough and untamed spirit that differed greatly from the sedate society of provincial China. The following is a description by Hsi-ch'ing of Heilungkiang in the early nineteenth century:

> The frontier community is not very strict about the segregation of men and women. Out in the open, they bathe in the same stream. At home, they scale the low walls [an euphemism for illicit liaison]. The few women who behave properly often become the targets of profligates who entice them with a hundred temptations until their virtue is compromised. At first only the despised among the exiles, forced by cold and hunger, became prostitutes. Recently, it is heard that the native residents are also losing their self-respect. A foolish man would invite a rascal to his home and seat him publicly with his mother and wife. Women of good families love to make up their faces and put on lavish ornaments. Sallying back and forth in crowded temples and markets, they abandon themselves to the extent of flirting in an outrageous manner. In recent years, a group of women singers dubbed the "cavity troupe," all of them coming from below the Great Wall, suddenly made their appearance in Tsitsihar via Petuna and other towns. They sometimes stayed in the mansions of officials; sometimes hid in the residences of monks. Companions in feasts and in beds, they were sought after by everyone. Although finally driven out of town by a military order, many men had already been ruined because of them.[37]

This loose sexual standard existed together with a passion for gambling. "Everyone gambles in Tsitsihar," wrote Hsi-ch'ing. "The great gamblers play dice for large stakes, and the small gamblers, especially the women, play cards." The exiles opened gambling houses to make fast profits, while shops and temples also served as gambling sites.[38] It seems that by then, the Spartan life of the previous era had given way to the boisterous mode of living characteristic of frontier towns with a gradually expanding economy. An index of the rising level of consumption was the annual importation of several hundred thousand catties of distilled spirits from Petuna to Tsitsihar where the residents could also obtain the local brand of yellow wine and Mongol kumiss (fermented mare's milk).[39]

The Woodsmen

Aside from the political exiles and convicts, there were also those who entered the Manchurian frontier despite government prohibitions and lived in the wilderness outside the protection of the law. These were the ginseng diggers, hunters, pearl fishers, growers of edible fungus, goldminers, and brigands. They went to the frontier almost as early as the exiles and convicts. They were self-reliant because that was the only means of survival. They were often tough and cruel because the only law they knew was the law of the forest. They also knew how to cooperate and organize themselves because they brought with them the knowledge of village and town institutions of China, including that of the secret societies.

The Manchus, who profited enormously in their trade with the Ming, intended after their conquest of China to monopolize the exploitation of the frontier's natural resources.[40] The early measures prohibiting Chinese immigration into Manchuria were certainly adopted also with this view in mind.[41] Among the valuable products of the frontier, the most important was the ginseng, a medicinal plant found in the Manchurian forests. During the Ming dynasty, the consumption of ginseng in China had increased but its production in China proper, largely confined to the T'ai-hang Mountains in Shansi, had been exhausted.[42] The Ming Chinese had come to rely upon Liao-tung and Korea for this valuable commodity. As time went on, the diminishing supply of these two regions necessitated large-scale importation from the Chien-chou Juchen, who possessed the best ginseng grounds. This trade was an important source of income for Nurhachi, and ginseng poaching by Liao-tung Chinese was a constant source of irritation between the Juchen and the Ming authorities. When the Ming government banned trading with the Juchen in 1608, Nurhachi was said to have suffered the loss of over 100,000 catties of ginseng which had rotted during the two years when no trading was done.[43] After their conquest of China, the Manchu rulers imposed strict regulations governing the gathering of ginseng in Sheng-ching, which assured a monopoly of the lucrative trade to the imperial household, the royal clansmen, and certain high-ranking, meritorious officials. This privilege was taken away from the officials in 1648. In 1651 the number of ginseng gatherers for the nobility was fixed according to their ranks, and the localities where ginseng might be gathered were divided among the eight banners. For the imperial household itself, a stipulated amount of ginseng was included in the annual tribute sent to Peking by the Ula Buteha bannermen of Kirin.[44] During the early decades of the K'ang-hsi reign, government financial difficulties led to the adoption of measures for enlarging the source of income derived from ginseng production. These included the extension of the government digging grounds to north Manchuria, the issuance of certificates to the bannerman diggers, the patrolling of the ginseng territory, and the imposition of heavy penalties including capital punishment upon illegal diggers.[45] The economic importance of the ginseng was reflected in its price, which, for the period of 1689–1690, was fifteen taels per catty for the best grade, twelve taels for the second grade, and nine to ten taels for the lowest grade. If an individual piece weighed over an ounce, the price was doubled; and if over a catty, it was worth ten times as much. These were local prices in Ninguta and reflected probably only a fraction of the prices charged in China proper. In comparison a picul of millet in Ninguta in the same period cost one tael, and wheat five taels. A teacher earned between fifteen to thirty taels a year and a shop manager thirty to forty taels.[46] No wonder many men willingly risked punishment and endured privations to become illegal ginseng diggers. Because of the high profits, by 1685 the supply of wild ginseng near Ninguta and Ula (near the city of Kirin) was exhausted and the ginseng lands reserved for the Manchu nobility became quite valueless. Both official and illegal gatherers had to forage in the lands of the Heje tribes.[47]

Most of the illegal ginseng diggers were Shantung and Shansi men called "mountain runners." They started off in the lunar months of March and April and returned in September and October. Usually five men formed a team and elected a leader. By horse and canoe they followed the Sungari to the Nonni where they landed and went into the mountains. The leader chose a camp site where they built birchbark tents for shelter. Each man was equipped with a small knife, flints for firemaking, a four-foot long digging stick, and a leather bag. The leader gave the team instructions and chose the area for digging. They spent the whole day in the forest, eating only in the morning and evening. The day's diggings were given over to the leader, who supervised their washing, boiling, and drying. When the food supply was exhausted, the diggers divided the ginseng and returned home. Every year a large number of diggers went into the mountains and a good many of them died there of hunger and exposure.[48]

As the ginseng diggers spread into the tribal territories, they taught the tribesmen how to find ginseng in exchange for food and clothing. Villages were built, food supplies stored, and trade goods brought in. The tribesmen, particularly the Heje were held in thrall by the lawless elements, called "blackmen," who took over their homes and women. The illegally obtained ginseng was called "black ginseng." In 1811 the military governor of Kirin dispatched troops to clear the "blackmen" off the mountains, going as far as the Iman River below Lake Hinka on the Ussuri. Many of the "blackmen" died, trapped by blizzards as they emerged from the mountains.[49]

As early as 1767, official ginseng digging, which hitherto had been limited to bannermen, was opened to Chinese diggers on license. The change in policy probably was necessitated by competition from illegal diggers and the inefficiency of officially supervised digging. The Board of Revenue decided on the number of licenses to be issued. In the beginning over a thousand licenses were issued, but the number was reduced year after year as the supply of the nearby localities was exhausted. Each licensee was entitled to receive a monetary advance and recruit four helpers. When the season was over, the licensee, in addition to paying back the monetary advance, gave the government a stipulated amount of ginseng. He was permitted to sell, after paying a tax, any ginseng that exceeded the official quota. Because of the difficulty of finding the requisite number of licensees, the government also resorted to assigning a certain number of licenses to the local distillers who would then recruit the diggers.[50] In 1853, the military governor of Kirin petitioned the court to stop the ginseng digging so that the money could be used for paying the troops. It was not until 1880 that digging under license was resumed. Thereafter, it was done periodically, depending on the recommendations of the local authorities.[51]

As wild ginseng grew scarcer, the plant was cultivated by diggers who settled in the mountain vastness.[52] In 1906, V. D. Arseniev, the Russian explorer, found such ginseng gardens deep in the wilderness of the Sinantsa Valley in the upper reaches of the Fudzin River.[53]

Throughout Ussuria, on both sides of the Shihote Alin, Arseniev found Chinese engaging in all sorts of enterprises:

> Some of them hunt wapiti, others ransack the forest for ginseng, others hunt sables, others musk from the musk deer; others collect seaweed, crabs, lobsters, trepang, and others again cultivate poppies for the opium. At every new cabin you come to you find a new trade: pearling, hunting for some sort of vegetable oil and roots, till you lose count. Everywhere they seem to find some source of wealth. The question of labour is to them of secondary importance, if only the supply be inexhaustible.[54]

Ts'ao T'ing-chieh estimated in 1885 that there were about 20,000 Chinese living in the then Russian occupied region between the Ussuri River and the Sea of Japan. They were roughly divided into woodsmen and settlers. The woodsmen made their living by collecting wild ginseng, cultivating ginseng gardens, lumbering, and gathering such forest products as edible fungus. These men lived an almost nomadic life, going from one part of the forest to another in small groups. The settlers lived in mountain valleys and along the coast, half of them with families. They cultivated the land but also hunted for deer in the summer and sables in the winter.[55]

According to Arseniev, these illegal immigrants were expert woodsmen and canoists. Their trails crisscrossed the mountains. On such a trail a traveler could almost be sure to find a cabin of a sort at the end of a day's march. At the top of practically every mountain pass there was a Chinese shrine. There were deer traps with fences that stretched over distances of thirty miles or more and with hundreds of pitfalls.[56] Although Arseniev and Ts'ao were writing about the Chinese woodsmen of Ussuria in the 1880's and 1900's, we may be reasonably sure that they were following approximately the same patterns of activities that the earlier generations of illegal immigrants had pioneered in the forested regions on the other side of the Ussuri River.

The Goldminers

The mountains of the Manchurian frontier were also rich in gold. According to dynastic record, Nurhachi began the mining of gold, silver, and iron in 1599.[57] However, these mining operations seemed to have been discontinued after the establishment of the dynasty in Peking. No reference to them has been left in the accounts of the early frontier residents.

In 1853 a change was made in the government's mining policy. Peking was desperately in need of money to conduct its campaign against the T'ai-p'ing rebels, the Board of Revenue therefore notified the provincial authorities to encourage private mining of gold and silver and to impose a mining tax on such enterprises. In the following year the military governor of Kirin reported that a number of merchants had been given permission to mine gold at the vicinity of Mu-ch'i River at the upper course of the Sungari in southern Kirin.[58] From then on, goldmining attracted an ever increasing number of fortune seekers, fed by the disorders in China proper, to the mountainous districts of Kirin and Heilungkiang. Unlike hunters and ginseng diggers, goldminers tended to congregate in large numbers within a comparatively small area. The unstable conditions in the mining camps populated by men of heterogeneous origin produced a fair amount of violence. The government responded by withdrawing its legal sanction but was powerless to stop the mining activities.[59] The goldminers, now branded gold bandits, organized themselves into armed settlements offering resistance to both government troops and roving bands of mounted bandits. The most famous of these settlements was led by a remarkable man named Han Hsien-tsung, known throughout the region as Han Pien-wai, meaning Han of the Frontier.

There are conflicting accounts of Han's colorful career.[60] His family seems to have migrated from Shantung to Fengt'ien. When Han was still a young man, his peasant father brought the family to Kirin. Han was a passionate gambler who disdained the humdrum life of the farm. After accumulating a heavy gambling debt he left his home to try his luck in goldmining. An initial period of modest success was followed by unfortunate encounters with the government and the bandits and by a spell as a hired farmhand. By the 1860's the rich Chia-p'i-kou gold vein in the present Hua-tien district had been discovered and opened to mining.

Again fleeing from gambling debts, Han joined the throng there and formed a sworn brotherhood with about a dozen miners. It was under his leadership that the miners succeeded in defeating a bandit band that had been preying upon them. Becoming the leader of some twenty mining settlements, Han showed his organizing ability by providing protection to the miners and merchants who flocked to Chia-p'i-kou and the neighboring areas in great numbers. By assuring peace among the miners and keeping out the bandits he was able to effect a "gentleman's agreement" with the provincial authorities, whereby he became nominally loyal to the government but maintained his own independence. The government had sought to entice the miners to give up their illegal activities in favor of farming by issuing land certificates entitling them to cultivate the land around the mining sites. The miners simply surrendered these certificates to Han who became a great landowner by bringing in tenants to work on the land. At the height of his power during the 1890's Han's sphere of influence covered about one third of the Hua-tien district with a population of some fifty thousand. During the Sino-Japanese War of 1894–1895, Han's grandson, Han Teng-chü, led a self-equipped force of some thousand men against the Japanese and was rewarded with an official military appointment, which served to enhance even more the family's political position.

Han Pien-wai died in 1897 leaving his grandson to take over the reins of power. In 1900 Han Teng-chü fought against the Russians during the Boxer Uprising and sustained heavy losses, which undermined much of his influence. His domain was encroached upon by both the government and the bandits. After his death sometime during the early period of the republic, his son finally lost the last stronghold of the Han family by peacefully transferring police functions to the provincial authorities in 1925; thus ended a little forest kingdom founded by an illiterate goldminer, which had endured for more than fifty years.[61]

Han Pien-wai was not alone among leaders of the goldminers who dared to defy the legal authorities, but none possessed his political and diplomatic acumen. For instance, during the T'ung-chih reign (1862–1874), large numbers of miners congregated in the mountains around San-hsing. They were organized into bands of several scores of men, each led by a chief. There were dozens of such chiefs who took custody of the gold yield and divided it among their followers at the end of each month. In 1875 the Kirin authorities, fearing their growing number, attempted to destroy a potential source of danger by a single stroke.

They blockaded the mountain passes with troops and killed anyone who tried to escape. The goldminers, incensed by the death of their comrades and the cruelty of the government, followed the leadership of Kung Kuang-ts'ai, who had formerly worked in Chia-p'i-kou, into open rebellion. They broke through the military encirclement and sacked the villages around San-hsing, Ninguta, and Hulan. Lacking any political program, the rebellion did not rise above its destructive fury; it was eventually suppressed in 1889.[62]

The woodsmen and goldminers played an important role as pioneers in the development of the frontier. Their trails were found in the most inaccessible regions. Their clearings and camps became the sites of villages and towns as traders and cultivators followed their footsteps. As they wandered in the wilderness they developed means of confronting the many difficulties and found new sources of wealth. The scarce products they brought to market stimulated trade and attracted more immigrants. As a group they flaunted the law of the government whose discriminatory policy served only to undermine its own authority. Branded as bandits, they relied on their own strength and resources to survive and multiply. The government, facing opponents whose resilience and courage were equal and often superior to those of its own soldiers, compromised by granting them tacit recognition. In so doing, the weakness of the government was exposed and a spirit of lawlessness flourished. There was no insuperable psychological barrier for a law-abiding man engaged in an "outlawed" profession to become a full-fledged brigand, especially when the successful brigand was often pacified by being accepted into the ranks of the government forces with a suitable title.

The Brigands

Brigandage was quite rare in the early years of the frontier's history. Articles found in the streets were turned over to the authorities until they were claimed by the owners. It often happened that a lost animal would be found and returned to its owner even after a lapse of five or six months.[63] Later on, ginseng diggers sometimes stole horses for their journey to the mountains; otherwise, outright robbery was confined to the route across the Mongol territory where the traveler did not have the protection of the military governor.[64] However, as more convicts and famine refugees settled in the region, the incidence of crime increased. Beginning in the middle of the nineteenth century, when civil wars ravaged China proper, driving more and more destitute people into the frontier, banditry became the scourge of Manchuria. The situation was aggravated by the draining of the military manpower from Manchuria for service in China proper and by the demoralization of the garrison forces, who were underpaid and underequipped. The dilemma of the government is described vividly in a report on the local military situation. The bannermen were dismissed in the report as useless because of their antiquated training and demoralized state. The newly formed battalions were also considered worthless because the recruits were taken in only if they brought along their own horses and weapons, thus admitting many unsavory characters. There was really no great difference between bandits and soldiers, for the personnel of both camps changed allegiance almost at will.[65]

Manchurian bandits were called *hung-hu-tzu* (red beards) by the frontier residents. This sobriquet was supposed to have originated in the early days of banditry when local bullies in the towns and marketplaces ran gambling dens and fought each other in gang fights. Highway robberies were often committed by such gamblers, who wore theatrical masks with red beards to avoid identification.[66] Eventually, the gangs became bigger and bolder and the masks were discarded but the name stuck. They were also known as *ma-tse* (mounted bandits), because without a horse a Manchurian bandit would be degraded to the status of a common thief.

The bandits worked in bands. They kidnapped wealthy men for ransom, robbed mercantile establishments, attacked armed caravans, sacked villages and towns. Small bands coalesced into a formidable guerrilla army that fought from one region to another. In 1865, Ma the Crazy led his men in a rampage that resulted in the destruction of scores of towns from Kirin to Fengt'ien, the death of several thousand persons, and the threatened invasion of Sheng-ching.[67] They were finally suppressed in 1866 by Grand Secretary Wen-hsiang, who commanded an imperial army of 4,000 men including the newly formed (1861) *shen-chi-ying,* Peking banner troops trained in modern firearms.[68]

Bandits had to have guns and their leaders were usually reputed to be good shots. These guns could be hired. The imperial government hired them to be soldiers; the Russians and Japanese hired them during the Russo-Japanese War as irregulars. During the revolution of 1911, the T'ung-meng hui wanted to make revolutionaries out of them.[69] Two of the powerful warlords of the republican era, Chang Tso-lin and Chang Tsung-ch'ang, emerged out of their ranks. They preyed upon the people, yet posed as their protectors in territories they controlled. The Manchurians feared them and were fascinated by them.

The bandits needed bases from which they could go forth in raiding expeditions. Such bases were located in the mountain fastness or more profitably in cultivable areas, particularly those where opium could be grown. It is difficult to ascertain the exact date when the cultivation of opium poppies began in the Manchurian frontier.[70] The tax on native opium was first levied in Kirin and Heilungkiang in 1885, whereas it was taxed in China proper in 1859. In 1891 a survey was made of the lands devoted to the cultivation of poppies in Kirin and was found to total 7,043 *shang,* with an estimated production of about 63,000 catties of opium per year. In Heilungkiang opium was first cultivated mostly in the Hulan district in patches of several *shang* or more by individual peasant households.[71] In 1906 the Ch'ing court decided to eliminate poppy cultivation within a period of ten years throughout the Chinese empire and planned complete eradication in Kirin and Heilungkiang by 1909.[72] But opium, because of its small bulk and high value, was an attractive product in the frontier region. Bandits, therefore, protected the opium growers from the law and sometimes cultivated the poppy themselves. In the course of time legal settlements reached and incorporated the opium villages. While many of the old villagers remained and some of the bandits made terms with the new settlers, others moved on and founded new communities. There are reports of outlaw opium villages along the Ussuri that governed and defended themselves, admitting no officials and paying no taxes.[73] Owen Lattimore concluded from his description of Manchurian banditry that more villages were probably founded there by outlaws than anywhere else in the world.[74]

Banditry was responsible for one of the most unique business enterprises in China—the *piao-chü,* an escort service that flourished in the latter part of the nineteenth century, when roads were dangerous for travelers. The *piao-chü* provided expert fighters who had an intimate knowledge of the route and who took complete charge of the merchandise-laden carts. The service guaranteed the complete safety of the goods in transit and would pay for any losses incurred while they were under the protection of its agents. The reputation of these *piao-chü* was so great that the government relied on them for the safe delivery of government funds.[75] Perhaps the *piao-chü* and the local bandit bands worked out some sort of agreement in which the latter refrained from molesting the escorted caravan in return for a monetary payment. Regardless of the real situation, the armed escorts of the *piao-chü* attained, in the popular folklore of the Chinese people, the same type of romantic coloration that surrounds the gunmen and cowboys of the American West. The *piao-chü* eventually faded away when Shansi banks and railways made their appearance in Manchuria during the closing decades of the nineteenth century and rendered obsolete the services performed by the *piao-chü*.

Traders and Trading Firms

Prior to the Manchu conquest of the Ming empire, the traditional exports of the Manchurian frontier consisted of such luxury goods as ginseng, furs, deer antlers-in-velvet, and pearls. Because trading between the Manchus and the Ming Chinese was conducted under tributary regulations, it was a political as well as a commercial relationship. The privilege of trading with the Ming became, for the Manchus, a monopoly of the nobility.[76] The efforts of the Ch'ing court to prohibit illegal trading in ginseng and sables may be considered as a continuation of this monopolistic tradition. After the Manchu conquest, the Ch'ing court, for political reasons, prohibited bannermen from engaging in trade. The collection of ginseng, sables, pearls, and other frontier products was supervised by government agencies in the form of regional tribute. When the tribute quota was filled, the surplus was then bought up by Chinese merchants for distribution on the commercial market. The government apparently realized the economic importance of frontier trade, because unlike the peasants the merchants were not prohibited from entering the frontier region.

Thus, in the early years of the dynasty, in addition to the exiles who turned to trade, there were already a number of Chinese merchants in such garrison and tributary centers as Ninguta and Tsitsihar.[77] The merchants dealt in the exchange of commodities and also acted as sources of credit to private individuals and the local governments.[78] As time went on, they began to penetrate the tribal areas in search of native products. M. Brunière reported that in 1845 there were about ten merchants in San-hsing who held government permits, which cost each of them 100 taels or more annually for the privilege of trading in the Heje territories.[79] M. Venault in 1846 discovered a great number of merchants in the lower Amur region who had evaded the authorities in San-hsing and were trading with natives as far north as Sakhalin Island.[80] Ts'ao T'ing-chieh noted in 1885 that there were about a thousand Chinese traders who went annually from San-hsing to the lower Amur and the Ussuri regions to barter with the tribesmen.[81]

As the frontier lands began to produce a surplus of grains, transportation problems and the consumption habit of local residents led to the mushrooming of distilleries which specialized in the production of a strong alcoholic beverage using kaoliang, a sorghum native to China, as the raw material. These distilleries soon became the most important commercial enterprises in the frontier agricultural districts, doing a major share of the business in grain trade, milling, oil-pressing, money-lending, and the issuance of currency scrips.[82] Some of the distilleries were built like fortresses to withstand the assaults of Manchurian bandits. H. E. M. James described them as follows:

> The distilleries were really formidable places, with strong brick walls, eighteen feet high, surmounted by terre-plein and parapet all complete, the gate fortified, and at each angle flanking towers armed with small carronades, which are protected from the weather by picturesque cupolas or pavillions. The doors and doorframes are of sheet iron, ornamented with massive studs, and strengthened with heavy lock and bars. Groups of buildings in the inside are often gaily ornamented, a proof that the trade is flourishing, and the lofty chimney reminds one of an English factory. These distilleries represent the capital and wealth of the district, which can only export its surplus grain in the form of liquor, owing to its distance from the sea and badness of the roads.[83]

Another commodity that could surmount the transportation difficulties was opium. James averred that in 1886 opium was already an important export from Manchuria to China proper. It went by land, carried in light swift carts, which evaded the customs barriers at the palisades, and conveyed it to various trade centers in north and central China. Some of it went to Canton by sea, packed up like Indian opium to deceive the southerners.[84]

When the Russians began to colonize their Far Eastern possessions and work started on the Chinese Eastern Railway, the export of cattle to feed the beef-eating Russians became an important business in Heilungkiang.[85] The building of railroads in turn stimulated the export of grain and soybeans to the outside world. More immigrants poured in and settled along the routes that the railroads traversed. Grasping the opportunity for profits, the merchants organized land companies, bought up virgin lands from the government and from Mongol princes, and then attracted settlers to their holdings or waited until land values shot up to make a financial gain.[86]

Big trading firms played an important role in the development of the frontier. These firms, with their headquarters generally in Shansi and Chihli, were often very old establishments, for only large trading firms could supply their agents with credit and goods as they fanned out into tribal territories to establish collecting and distributing networks. In the areas of colonization, as villages appeared in the wilderness, branch stores of these trading firms were set up, catering to the immediate needs of the settlers for such things as groceries, cloth, and medicines and performing such services as money exchange, issuance of bills of credit, and postal facilities. As time went on, large stores appeared performing even more varied services and catering to a wider locality. Located in communication centers, these stores often gave their names to towns that gradually grew up around them.[87]

A distinctive feature of the frontier trading firms was the near monopoly of certain provincial houses over the regional trade. The Shansi merchants, for instance, occupied a predominant position in Heilungkiang. This situation may be attributed partly to the financial affluence of Shansi bankers and partly to their long tradition in carrying on a frontier trade that ranged all over the Mongolian steppe and into Sinkiang and Chinghai. However, an important factor which enabled them to entrench themselves in Heilungkiang was the patronage of the local elite. Hsü Tsung-liang reported how their favored position was first established: When the city of Tsitsihar was first built as a military town, the area within the town wall was allocated to the different banners. As the town became the commercial center of north Manchuria, the bannermen rented their houses to Chinese shopkeepers. After a year or two, the bannerman landlords would come and "sweep the street," (evict their tenants by force) as a means of extortion. A Chinese bannerman, who had served as a high official in Shansi and who belonged to the Ts'ui clan, which had long been prominent in Heilungkiang, complained to the military governor, who put a stop to this act of harassment. This happened sometime in the beginning of the Tao-kuang reign (1821–1850). Ts'ui thereupon invited twenty-four firms which he had known in

Shansi to Tsitsihar and gave them his personal protection. The firms prospered. They took over all government contracts and acted as guarantors for new immigrants.[88] This story emphasizes the legal handicaps of the Chinese settlers in the frontier and the importance of official protection for the merchants.

In addition to the big trading firms, Shansi merchants also controlled many of the smaller enterprises. Their success was due in great measure to hard work and their system of training apprentices. According to Liu Wen-feng who traveled in Heilungkiang in 1896, the Shansi firms usually began as a partnership of several persons. Those who contributed capital were called "money-share owners"; those who contributed experience and work were called "body-share owners." At the beginning every effort was made to economize; when the business was on a firmer basis, steps were taken toward expansion. Young men who knew how to read and calculate were taken in as apprentices. After a few years, when they had proven themselves, they were given a number of body-shares. Instead of salaries, they received a small amount of spending money. After three years, the accounts were settled and the young clerks were entitled to profits accrued to their shares. For this reason, everyone worked hard in order to make the business prosper. The number of shares also increased with the increase in business. When a founder or a person who had been with the firm for many years died, a number of body-shares would be given to his family, and his descendants, if qualified, would also be accepted into the firm. An apprentice was not allowed to return to his home district before he had earned the right to body-shares. Anyone who committed an unpardonable act would be immediately dismissed and none of the neighboring firms would hire the culprit. Consequently, there were very few cases of fraud. The apprentices of firms trading along the Amur all studied Russian, those in Hulan Buir studied Mongol, and those in Buteha and Mergen studied the Dagur and Orochon languages. In the evening, Liu said, the shops sounded like schools.[89]

The most affluent of the Shansi mercantile houses were the *p'iao-hao* or banks. The first Shansi bank appeared on the Chinese commercial scene in 1831 in response to the growing demand for a safer and more convenient means of settling inter-regional accounts than the cumbersome transfer of silver bullions from one province to another over unsafe roads. In the beginning, the bulk of the banking business came from commercial houses, who made use of the draft to pay their distant suppliers. Gradually the transfer of government funds came to overshadow the commercial transactions. The Shansi banks acted as agents of provincial governments in delivering tax receipts to the Board of Revenue in Peking and in dispersing appropriations to local civil and military offices. Government funds were also entrusted to the banks for safekeeping so that they had large amounts of cash for lending purposes. In addition, the banks were accustomed to issue notes in denominations varying from 10 to 1,000 taels.[90]

Not long after their establishment in China proper, branches of the Shansi banks were set up in the Manchurian cities. The heyday of their prosperity was during the T'ung-chih and Kuang-hsü reigns (1862–1874, 1875–1908). They monopolized the annual delivery of several million taels of government funds from China proper to Manchuria and an equally large amount of commercial and private remittance from Manchuria to China proper.[91]

As a newly developed region, Manchuria as a whole and the frontier in particular was perpetually short of cash, and the value of money was driven upward. It was under such conditions that opium became a favorite medium of exchange. Seasonal or migrant workers in the north preferred to be paid in opium, which was less bulky than silver and copper coins and certainly less conspicuous to prying eyes. As the workers traveled southward to their homes in Chihli and Shantung, the value of their opium increased while the worth of money declined in proportion to the distances covered.[92] The shortage of cash was also responsible for the multitude of scrips, *t'ieh-tzu,* issued by commercial houses of every size and description. Since there were no government regulations governing the issuance of these scrips, their acceptance was dependent entirely upon the confidence of the local population. A typical scrip bore the name of the issuing firm, the date of its issuance, and the serial number printed on the best local paper stock. In the center were the words *p'ing t'ieh ch'u ch'ien,* meaning roughly "pay the scrip-holder." The face value of the scrip was not printed but written in ink, each firm using its own style of calligraphy to prevent forgery. Substantial firms such as distilleries, wholesale houses, and pawnshops issued scrips with denominations from one to a hundred strings of cash; others from one to ten strings (one string contains 1,000 coins). Before a firm was allowed to issue scrips, the local merchant association made an investigation of its books and assessed the total value of the owner's property. The firm itself had to obtain the consent of the important commercial houses in neighboring towns and markets to honor its scrips; otherwise, they could not be circulated outside the firm's locality.[93] No one, however, knew how much cash the scrip-issuing firm had on hand to redeem its notes. If the firm failed, the scrip holders suffered total loss. As might be expected, the temptation to overissue was great and many frontier towns suffered from chronic currency inflation.[94]

The merchants played an indispensable role in the development of the frontier. They opened up trade outlets for the remote settlements and the tribal territories, thereby aiding the exploitation of the natural wealth of the region and integrating its economy with the rest of the empire. They were active agents in spreading the material culture of China throughout the frontier territories. Operating in a society where merchants as a class lacked strong political power, they sought alliance with the officials, often through unethical means, in order to promote their interests, thus contributing much to the deterioration of the moral standard of the government. However, this was a weakness of the Chinese social structure as a whole and the merchants should not be held solely responsible. The dependence of the mercantile class upon officials in power was detrimental to the development of industries, as merchants could never be sure how long their official patronage would last. Consequently, they tended to invest only in enterprises which required relatively little capital but brought quick returns, for example distilleries and flour mills, or in such speculative ventures as land companies. The officials themselves were unable to sustain industrial enterprises which they organized with government funds, such as the Moho Gold Mines.[95] Ultimately, the industrialization of the Manchurian frontier was undertaken by foreign capitalists backed by their governments.

Chinese Colonization

The exiles, woodsmen, goldminers, brigands, and traders, penetrating into the Manchurian frontier, gradually brought back first-hand reports which changed its fearful image into that of a land of opportunities. The most enticing of these reports probably described the abundance of fertile lands. The first Chinese agriculturists, as we have noted, were the exiles and convicts who were incorporated into the banner system and assigned to work on government farms. Non-incorporated exiles who preferred to stay on the frontier after serving their sentences were permitted to settle as freemen on the land. They constituted the tiny nucleus of *min-jen* or the civilian population in the frontier settlements.[96] As time went on, men who sought land trickled into the frontier in increasing numbers. This immigration prompted the Manchu court to prohibit the entrance of Chinese to the new lands on the grounds that the home of the imperial ancestors must be protected from desecration by the immigrants, the livelihood of the frontier bannermen from illegal ginseng diggers and hunters, and the imperial hunting preserve from trespassers. So the Willow Palisades were erected to control illegal entrance. But there were not enough men to guard a frontier hundreds of miles long. By 1736 the Willow Palisades were breached at will. In 1740 an imperial decree directed all illegal residents of the frontier, with the exception of merchants, craftsmen, and servants whose services were needed by the bannermen, to be expelled within ten years. The decree was clearly directed against the peasants. But it could not arrest the flow of tens of thousands of hungry men driven by a series of great famines in the eighteenth century to seek a living on the frontier.[97] The government simply could not drive them out without making other provision for their livelihood. As a result, although the decrees were never revoked, the squatters were permitted to stay on their land. These and other illegal entrants were called *liu-min* or wanderers; they were not considered regular inhabitants of the localities in which they resided. At the same time, the experiment of resettling Peking bannermen on the virgin lands of Lalin and Alchuka was a failure. The urbanized Manchus could not cope with the rigors of a pioneering agricultural life. Most of them ultimately leased or sold their holdings to the Chinese immigrants.[98] Thus, by squatting and by leasing and buying lands, the immigrant peasants were putting the Manchurian plains to the plow. Their persistence and hard work earned them the right to stake a permanent claim to the Manchurian soil. The official recognition of such claims was completed when the government enrolled the cultivators in the population register and taxed them accordingly. The first of such enrollments was made in Kirin in 1726.[99] The first census of Heilungkiang *min-hu,* or civilian households, was made in 1771 and showed a total of 20,508 households or 35,284 persons.[100] The small number of individuals to each household revealed in the census indicates that most of the Chinese population there was made up of resident exiles and transient merchants without families. In any case, it was not until 1860 that a land tax was levied on Chinese immigrants in conjunction with the opening of the Hulan district to Chinese colonization.[101] However, as early as 1810, Hsi-ch'ing had noted that there was a great number of illegal immigrants in Tsitsihar.[102] Some of these immigrants probably made their living on the land but their status had not yet been given official notice by the government.

During the latter part of the nineteenth century, as the European powers were carving out spheres of interest in China, the imperial government finally realized that the preservation of the Manchurian frontier as part of the Ch'ing empire should take precedence over the preservation of Manchu interests in the frontier. The case became urgent after the ceding of the areas north of the Amur and east of the Ussuri to the Russians in 1858 and 1860. It was plain that any successful defense of the frontier would depend upon manpower and material resources that the Manchurian authorities could draw upon in case of emergency. The military governor of Heilungkiang, Te-p'u-ch'in, memorialized the court in 1860 requesting that the Hulan district be opened to Chinese settlement. He pleaded the immediate need for new sources of revenue to reduce accumulated arrears of over 600,000 taels in payments to the men and officers of the banner forces and the urgency of filling the population vacuum on the frontier to discourage further Russian encroachments.[103] The T'ung-kẹn valley was opened in 1896, a year after the first Sino-Japanese War. The entire province was opened in 1904 as a reaction to the Russo-Japanese War, which was fought on Manchurian soil.[104] Similarly, the Lalin district in Kirin was opened in 1860, the upper Hurka valley in 1878, the Tumen valley in 1881, the upper Ussuri in 1882, and the entire province in 1902.[105] The resultant population movement was aided in the twentieth century by the building of railroads, which facilitated the transportation of immigrants and the marketing of their produce. Large numbers of laborers recruited for railroad construction also tended to settle on the land after their contracts were completed.[106] Thus, the exclusion policy of the Manchu court broke down in the face of foreign threat and population pressure from China proper.

"Occasionally we meet a melancholy procession of emigrants, driven by poverty or floods from their homes to seek fresh and cheap land in the north—their carts piled with furniture and boxes and covered with extempore awnings, inside which the wives and infants huddle together out of the cold, while the young and stalwart walk bravely on, though sometimes driven by hunger to ask for a meal."[107] Such description was a common sight in the Manchuria of the 1880's. The emigrants were mostly Chihli and Shantung men who undertook the wearisome trek not in high spirits but in the realization that they had been defeated in the struggle for survival in their overcrowded ancestral hamlets. Often men of the same clan or from the same home district migrated together. Upon arriving at their destination, they set to work building temporary shelters called *wo-p'eng*. As the new village gradually took shape, they gave it their common surname or the name of their home district.[108] On the virgin land, these villages were sited miles apart, each village containing from a few to several scores of households. Villages of over a hundred families were seldom seen. The houses, too, were located far apart, each surrounded by the land that the occupants tilled, an arrangement differing markedly from the village pattern of old China where the farmlands enclosed an island of closely grouped cottages and gardens.[109] Having erected a roof over his family, the pioneer settler burned away the matted vegetation to prepare the land for cultivation. The first crop was usually buckwheat; the next, kao-liang and millet.[110] It took three or four years for the land to become "ripened" and to return the settler a fair surplus for his backbreaking toil.

Children were an asset in the pioneering family, which had to be as self-sufficient as possible; weaving its own cloth, making its own tools and carts, and defending its own farms and animals. Because land was easily obtained a family could stay together and expand. The people married young and multiplied. Large extended families were the rule, often numbering from thirty to fifty persons, sometimes even over a hundred.[111] Such a family required a household head *(tang-chia-ti)* with more than the ordinary managerial talent. When the grandfather was alive and capable he usually occupied such a position; otherwise it was entrusted to the most qualified person in the family. In order to hold the family together and minimize dissent, the head of the household had to consult the family council on matters pertaining to the general welfare such as the planting of different crops, the rotation of the lands, the purchase of draft animals, the building and repairing of houses, the assignment of handicraft chores, the distribution of cloths, soaps, and other necessities, and the marriage of the teenagers. Formal education for the young was rudimentary. Children attended the village school, if any was available, for a couple years or more, until they could keep simple accounts and read the money scrips. If a bright boy wanted to continue schooling, his own parents, not the family as a whole, would have to support him from their own savings.[112] Eventually, such a large family might break up for personal or economic reasons. As the new saplings from the old immigrant stock took root elsewhere on the land, they were joined by an unending stream of transplants from the ancestral provinces. The wilderness was transformed, in ever faster tempo, into a blossoming plain of men and crops.

The frontier had at last become a bastion of Chinese culture. Only the peasant cultivators could give permanency to the occupation of the land. Prior to their arrival the regional economy, dependent upon the exploitation of wildlife and forest growth, could not sustain a large population or nourish a high standard of culture. The administrative and military expenses of holding this enormous region under the empire were provided by the central government and the wealthier provinces. The production of ginseng and furs tended to fall as the years went by, and the number of people who depended on them for a living decreased correspondingly. The forest settlements which grew up to serve the diggers and hunters would, in due time, wither and die. The frontier would have been easily infiltrated and incorporated into the expanding Russian empire.

The Government of Fugitive Settlements

The clandestine immigrants who filtered into the frontier may be divided roughly into two broad categories: peasants who leased or bought lands from the bannermen for cultivation, thus settling in areas where government authorities had been fully established; ginseng diggers, hunters, goldminers, and a minority of cultivators who settled in the more inaccessible regions and founded their own communities where the legal arm of the established government did not penetrate. The political structure of these fugitive settlements is worth consideration because it represents efforts at self-government within the traditional Chinese pattern.

The following is an account by H. E. M. James, who discovered in 1886 well-organized governing bodies in the Ch'ang-pai-shan:

> The colonists form themselves into associations or guilds, with presidents, vice-presidents, and councils, who legislate for the community, and exercise powers of life and death. The existence of these guilds is known to the authorities in Kirin, who occasionally call on them, and not unsuccessfully, for assistance in hunting robbers. On such occasions the headman of the guild sends a circular around, and

a hunter told us that, even if a man had got a deer in every pit, he must shoulder his matchlock and go; yet theoretically, as I have said, there is no taxation, except what the settlers impose upon themselves. Some items in their legislation are peculiar, but practical. We saw one proclamation warning people not to harbor certain characters, whose names were given. A second forbade Coreans to fish. The Coreans, be it noted, are employed in large numbers as agricultural labourers by the settlers, who want them, so they said, to labour in the fields, and not waste their time in sport. A third was for regulating the trade in ginseng, and forbade any person buying or selling it before a certain date. The penalty for transgression of that law was, in the case of a rich person, a fine to the guild of one pound of rice (a luxury in the hills), ten taels in money, and two pigs weighing at least seventy-five pounds each. If the offender were an outsider, and therefore moneyless and unable to pay the fine, he was to be beaten to death with sticks. This law was for the protection of zealous ginseng seekers, who sought the more remote valleys, and occasionally found the market forestalled by less venturesome hunters returning before the season was fairly over. The guilds are most efficient institutions, and the only place within Manchuria where life and property may be said to be really secure is within their limits; although, from the configuration of the country, and the vast area of forests with which it is covered, robbers would, under ordinary circumstances, find there a safe refuge. In fact, it is a boast of the settlers that, even if a man drops a knife or a handkerchief, he is perfectly sure of getting it back again. The members collect at headquarters in the winter, when their huts or homesteads are snowed up, to pass the time and discuss regulations for the public weal. The guild-house has, therefore, extensive accommodation, and it also serves as a store for supplies of grain and groceries, which are brought during winter along the frozen Sungari on sledges from Kirin. Till quite recently these little republics were looked on as dangerous, and the head of the guild next to T'ang-ho-k'ou was proclaimed at Kirin as an outlaw. A Governor, however, of more sense than usual sent an emissary in disguise to find out the real state of the case. His report was so favourable that the Governor invited the outlaw to Kirin; and he went there, leaving the spy as a hostage. He half expected his head would be taken off, but he was well treated, presents were made him, and he was told to go back and behave himself.

The T'ang-ho-k'ou guild, according to James, had a membership of a thousand men.[113]

Ts'ao T'ing-chieh found similar organizations in Ussuria in about the same period. The Chinese settlers in the region between Ussuri and the Sea of Japan, Ts'ao reported, congregated in mountain valleys and along the coast, making a living by hunting and cultivation. The settlements in each valley were headed by a chief, and several valleys together elected a paramount chief. When a meeting was to be held, the members were notified by wooden tallies and got together in a matter of days. The laws of the valley were few and simple: the death penalty for the killer and banishment for the trouble maker. No favoritism was permitted in the execution of the code. Ts'ao was told that these laws were bequeathed to the settlers by an old chief. There was no thievery in these settlements, and the traveler could find hospitality everywhere.[114]

V. K. Arseniev described such a chief, whom he met on one of his explorative trips:

> Chan Bao was a tall man of about forty-five years. He was wearing the same kind of blue costume as ordinary Chinamen, only rather cleaner and better than usual. On his mobile face I read the impression of much privation endured. He had the usual drooping black moustache of the Chinese, already touched with grey. Through his black eyes shone the light of his intelligence, and a faint smile hovered constantly upon his lips, though not for one moment did his expression lose its seriousness. Before speaking he always considered his answer, and spoke quietly, unhurriedly. I had not before had occasion to meet a man in whom were so perfectly blended seriousness, good nature, energy, judgment, firmness, and diplomatic talent. From the personality of Chan Bao, from his movements and gestures, from his whole poise, there radiated intelligence. His wisdom, his self-respect, and his power of dominating the crowd, all showed that he was no ordinary John Chinaman. Most probably he was a political offender who had escaped from China.
>
> Throughout the district, from Kusun to the Olga Bay [a stretch of coastal area along the Sea of Japan, from about 43°N to about 45°N], Chan Bao was regarded as the most influential personage. Chinese and aborigines alike turned to him for counsel, and if there were ever need for reconciling two irreconcilable enemies the

> Chinese always referred to him. He often took the side of the oppressed, and on this ground had many enemies. He had a particular hatred for all brigands, and by his action against them he inspired them with such respect that they never ventured beyond the Iodzyhe.[115]

Official reports of these fugitive governments, commonly called *hui-fang* (guild) in Chinese, were much less flattering than the reports of the travelers. In 1908, Li T'ing-yü, a Kirin official, made an inspection trip in the Ch'ang-pai-shan region in preparation for bringing the whole area under government administration. His description of one of the *hui-fang* located in the T'ang-ho district, perhaps the very one described by James, was most revealing. The first Chinese immigration to T'ang-ho, Li stated, began in 1801. The immigrants at first engaged in the gathering of ginseng, medicinal herbs, and fragrant plants and later, also in hunting and pearling. The illegal cultivation of land did not begin until 1862. The first guild was organized in 1858. From then on to the time of Li's visit, a span of fifty years, there had been four guild heads. The guild was organized with the following personnel: a *cheng tang-chia* or guild head, a *pang tang-chia* or deputy head, four *p'ao-tou* or sergeants, forty gunmen, four cooks, two watchmen, eight servants, a gardener, two millers, and two grooms. The annual income of the guild came from the following taxes: 6,000 taels from ginseng gardens; 600 taels from *pei-mu*, a medical herb; 500 taels from *hsi-hsin*, also an herb; 1,500 taels from opium; 3,000 taels from lumbering; and more than 400 taels from peasant settlers, who were divided into three grades for taxing purposes.[116]

Li reported that the inhabitants were ruled by terror. Every settler must obey the command of the guild head. When a call arrived from him, each man must bring along his gun and meet at the guild house, no matter at what time of day. The absentee was punished according to the will of the guild head who had absolute control over their life and death. Punishments included severing the ears, breaking the legs, and death by burying alive, drowning, or the firing squad. Li averred that there was no clear distinction between the activities of the guild and the bandits. It might appease a strong bandit band and bully a small one. In 1897 an official in charge of colonization, the seven persons in his retinue, and two soldier escorts were murdered by the guild residents in connivance with bandits. As a result, the official colonization efforts in the district were effectively blocked. Li, however, suggested that after the establishment of an official administration in that district and the dissolution of the guild, the incumbent guild head should be made an officer in the bandit-suppressing corps as a means of isolating him from his followers.[117] The facts that the residents were armed individually, that they hated officials, and that Li saw the need to isolate the leader from his followers seem to show that he may have exaggerated the despotic nature of the guild.

The guilds of the Ch'ang-pai-shan and the valley governments of Ussuria were variations of the type of self-government based upon kinship, geographic origin, or secret fraternities that the Chinese were apt to set up whenever there was a need to ensure a measure of security in a strange or hostile environment. They were fairly common, for example, among overseas Chinese communities in Southeast Asia prior to the establishment of stable colonial rules. They were not democratic institutions in the Western sense of the term. In most cases they operated on a patriarchal principle with experienced elders assuming the role of lawgivers and arbitrators of disputes. Once in power the leadership tended to perpetuate itself. There was seldom any formal check against the exercise of absolute power by the leaders except the realization that their own safety resided in the loyalty of the group, and that loyalty in the wilderness could be gained more by fair dealing and persuasion than by force.

We can perhaps reconstruct, from the information we have gathered so far, the formation of such a self-governing unit as follows: Most of the illegal settlers were Shantung and Chihli men. They were driven to make a living in the wilderness because of poverty or to escape the vengeance of the law. They had no previous experience in woodcraft, for their home provinces were in the most thickly settled regions in China where the mountains were generally denuded of trees. In their minds the forest was the haunt of spirits where dangers lurked behind every stone and tree and where natural elements conspired against all men. Outside the forest, officials and soldiers watched every opportunity to persecute them. So for safety's sake, they banded together in small groups of relatives or friends. Mutual trust was essential, for there was no recourse from deeds of robbery and murder committed in the mountains except that of personal vendetta. Many men died in the early years from violence inflicted by the elements and by fellow men. Gradually, valuable experiences were accumulated and taught them how best to survive in the wilderness. At first they went into the mountains only during the hunting or digging seasons. As the pioneers grew older they brought with them younger men who learned from them the indispensable knowledge of the woods. A code gradually grew up among them, and they maintained it with simple vigor in order to assure safety for all. As they came to understand the forest more thoroughly and discovered means with which to sustain life in all seasons, they began to build semi-permanent cabins along the trails and in the valleys. As the diggers and hunters went deeper and deeper into the forest, it became necessary to have supply bases located conveniently in the mountains. Soon small hamlets appeared in the more accessible valleys where small patches of vegetables and such staples as corn and millet could be cultivated. The forest code, upheld by the strength of a nuclear group became in the course of time the law of the valley obeyed by hundreds of men. The leader was a man who could command the loyalty of the people by his knowledge and experience and who could take decisive action in defense of their interests. The lives of the settlers were never entirely free from danger. Many men who ventured out into the wilderness where the legal arm of society did not exist were often individuals of strong character with a questionable past; they would not hesitate to prey upon their fellow beings. In a lonely trail or clearing a handful of ginseng or a few sables could be the cause of murder and robbery. Bands of brigands roamed the forest to raid and kill. So, an alliance was formed by several valleys to deal more effectively with these human scourges.

As settlements became strong and prosperous they became centers of power with recognized territorial limits. The original inhabitants came to consider themselves masters of little forest kingdoms where outsiders were permitted only on terms set by the old timers. Those Koreans brought into the Ch'ang-pai-shan to cultivate the land were barred from hunting and ginseng digging. The Heje of Ussuria were practically enslaved through their debts to the settlers, who exchanged guns, ammunition, liquor, and opium for furs and ginseng and who enforced their payments by whipping and murder.[118]

Eventually, the government began to take notice of the nearest of these illegal settlements. Any policy of force in dealing with them would certainly provoke an outbreak of violence and drive the woodsmen into the ranks of brigands. Thus an accommodation was made in which the government legalized the positions of the settlement chiefs and their officers in return for the observance of government laws and regulations. An example of such an accommodation was found in Lin-chiang located on the bank of the Yalu River in a region set aside for the imperial preserve. According to an official account, Lin-chiang was first inhabited in 1875. Up to 1901 the inhabitants had no formal relations with the government. In that year a *hsiang-yüeh* (village association) was organized, and it brought the inhabitants indirectly under the jurisdiction of a newly formed district government. The village association was evolved out of the existing local political structure. The chief of the association, called *hui-shou*, was elected by the villagers with or without the nominal consent of the county magistrate. He was aided by a *p'ai-t'ou* (warden) in each of the subdivisions of the village and four to eight clerks. The association was responsible for the arbitration of disputes, the arrest and extradition of criminals, the collection of taxes, the execution of government orders, and the taking of a village land survey and population census. The expenses of the association were shared by all families in the village. The assessment could be paid in cash or in grain, tobacco, and domestic animals. In addition, land taxes were collected and remitted to the district government. The authorities found that the association officers often exercised arbitrary power over the villages, even to the extent of administering illegal punishments and levying extra taxation.[119] The accusations of the authorities pointed out the frustration of the government in not being able to govern the villagers directly. It also demonstrated clearly that, when the government extended its power over such villages, the inhabitants often had to pay both the local assessment and government taxation because the village leadership would not give up the privileges they were accustomed to enjoy. Furthermore, once their status was legalized, the leaders were to a certain extent less dependent upon the consent of the inhabitants for the exercise of their power and consequently more prone to despotism. The final evolution of these villages would be for the government to assume direct control, which the villagers might come to regard as the lesser of two evils.

The Sinicization of the Manchurian Frontier—A Summary

An important consideration in the study of early Manchurian frontier history was the existence of a virtual population vacuum north of the Willow Palisades. Into this population vacuum came the probings of Russian Cossacks. The Manchu court was apprehensive of those excellent fighters equipped with firearms. The Russian threat had to be met. However, Manchu expeditions against the Russians were not always successful because of the difficulty of transportation and the consequent lack of adequate provisions for an expeditionary force. For this reason, prior to the campaign against Albasin (Yaksa) in 1685, the K'ang-hsi emperor spent several years in establishing both a water and a land route across the length of Manchuria to the Amur. In addition, military agricultural colonies were introduced in Aigun. All these measures were accomplished with the compulsory labor of Chinese exiles. The reasons were quite apparent. The Tungusic peoples were not accustomed to building and navigating large vessels to transport grain and other bulk cargoes. There were two types of native watercraft: a canoe made of a tree trunk or birch bark, seating several persons, and a larger boat seating a dozen or more men, made of five planks nailed together with wooden pegs and without caulking, seepage being stopped by moss stuffed into the crevices.[120] Consequently, Chinese exiles from the southern provinces were drafted into the river patrol for the building and sailing of large ships. As to farming, the Chinese were certainly much superior to the Tungusic tribes. Besides, the Manchus could not spare their limited banner forces in the frontier for these auxiliary functions. Thus, for strategic reasons, the Manchu authorities had to bring in the Chinese to help in the defense of the Manchurian frontier.

Another salient fact in the history of the Manchurian frontier was the inability of the Manchu court to prevent illegal Chinese immigration. The impossibility of patrolling the huge frontier region was certainly an important reason for the ease with which Chinese immigrants evaded the law. The banner garrison forces attained their greatest strength in 1738, totalling 11,573 men in Kirin and 6,498 men in Heilungkiang. These forces, which included non-Manchu bannermen, were scattered in sixteen garrison points, four frontier gates, and four river patrol headquarters.[121] We can imagine how thinly guarded Manchuria was against determined attempts at penetration. Moreover, we have reason to believe that the local authorities welcomed the immigrants, for they provided additional sources of local revenues through the development of the economic resources of the frontier. In 1821, the revenue from land tax in Kirin totaled 85,369 taels. Taxes on domestic animals, tobacco, hemp, liquor, lumber, fishnets, sables, and pawnshops totaled 7,460 taels.[122] Since all salaries for the military and administrative staff and for the garrison soldiers were paid from the imperial treasury,[123] these taxes represented a welcome source of income for local expenditures and the possible enrichment of local officials.

With the coming of Chinese immigrants, there followed a number of material and social changes. First, there was the change in the settlement pattern. We have noted that early Manchurian frontier towns originated as garrison sites surrounded by wooden palisades or mud walls. The agricultural settlements of the soldiers and government farms were located in the surrounding countryside. Later, as more Chinese exiles and merchants took up residence, these garrison centers became trade centers and Chinese became the common spoken language. A new relationship was established between the town and the countryside as Chinese shops became sources of credit to the soldiers and peasants. Finally as Chinese temples, schools, and amusement troupes made their appearance, the towns became centers of Chinese culture, rather uncouth in appearance, but not differing greatly from the common northern Chinese provincial towns.

In the forests and mountains where the woodsmen congregated, fugitive settlements appeared, completely outside the jurisdiction of the Manchu authorities. The number of these settlements were later augmented by illegal mining and lumbering camps. In the valleys and plains, Shantung and Chihli peasants organized their villages according to their traditional patterns. All these rural settlements were completely Chinese in character, differing from the Manchu clan villages.

There were also changes in the daily mode of living. The early inhabitants lived in wooden houses plastered with mud. These gradually gave way to brick and tile structures, at first, among temples and public buildings, later, among urban dwellings.[124] Wooden utensils of all kinds were gradually replaced by ceramic wares.[125] Clothing made of hemp cloth and animal pelts were supplanted by cotton cloth and silks.[126] The traveler of an earlier era camped out in the open or found shelter in private homes where food and bed were offered in the traditional spirit of hospitality.[127] In later years, he was lodged in inns that dotted the main thoroughfares.[128]

The increase in amenities was made possible only with the increase in trade, which in turn was dependent upon the evolution of the frontier economy from that of hunting, fishing, gathering, and subsistence agriculture to that of commercial agriculture and small industries. In this process of economic transformation, the Manchus were largely bystanders. The Chinese settlers assumed the risks and carried out the hard work of taming the wilderness. Trade and industry in the frontier, however, manifested some colonial traits. Capital and managerial talents were imported from the outside and much of the wealth was also drained away in the profits of trading firms located elsewhere in China proper and in the remittances of the immigrants to relatives in the home provinces. On the other hand, the military and administrative expenses of the region were subsidized throughout the dynasty by the treasury of the central government and the contribution of other provinces.

Economic and cultural changes of such magnitude inevitably caused constant readjustments in social relationships. The early Manchurian frontier society was characterized by an apparently rigid social hierarchy. At the apex was the military elite, composed of Manchu, Mongol, Chinese, Solon, and Dagur banner officers, with the highest offices gravitating into the hands of Manchus from Peking. Below them, also included in the governing class but looked upon with considerable condescension by the "civilized" population as a whole, were the tribal chiefs, who had been given official ranks and titles by the imperial government. The plebian class was composed of ordinary bannermen, merchants, craftsmen, and exiled officials. At the bottom were convicts, slaves, and servants. Outside the pale of the lawful society were the fugitive hunters, ginseng diggers, goldminers, and brigands.

The division of social classes was softened, although not elminated, by the intrusion of wealth and education as measures of social prestige. Thus, exiled officials, although legally degraded, could associate on terms of equality with the military elite, while convicts and slaves could become respectable merchants through the amassing of wealth.

As the frontier became increasingly Chinese in population, economy, and culture, the relationships between Manchus and Chinese underwent changes. The Manchus with the help of their banner organization dominated the political scene almost to the end of the nineteenth century. This dominance was aided by Manchu statesmanship in neutralizing the Mongol power in the west and the Russian power in the north. Internal challenge to Manchu power, except for organized brigandage, was nonexistent because of the smallness of the population and the presence of the wilderness acting as a safety valve for the dissatisfied elements of the society. However, by the latter half of the nineteenth century the military strength underpinning the Manchu political power had become largely an empty shell. There were symptoms of political disintegration with the increase of lawlessness and the appearance of clandestine political units which effectively challenged the authority of the military government. Organized banditry took on menacing proportions as bands numbering several hundreds and even a thousand men sacked villages and towns.[129] It was entirely conceivable that without outside interference these bandit bands might have coalesced into an effective military organization able to overthrow the legal government of the frontier region. Banditry was finally brought somewhat under control by army units composed largely of Chinese soldiers. Thus, Manchu military power on the frontier was supplanted by Chinese military power.

The colonization of the Manchurian frontier by Chinese immigrants necessitated the extension of administrative control over the immigrant settlements. There was a need for administrators versed in Chinese laws and administrative practices which the frontier Manchus were unable to supply. The dearth of Manchu talents was especially acute in such spheres as foreign relations, modern education, and economic development, in which the regional government began to take a serious interest after the Russo-Japanese War. Meanwhile, the pressure of revolutionary and reformist movements in China proper also forced the Ch'ing court to abandon gradually the barriers separating the Manchus and Chinese, which had existed since the earlier years of the dynasty. Thus, for various reasons, more and more Chinese officials were brought into all levels of the frontier administrative system, effecting a profound shift in the balance of political power in the Manchurian frontier.

The Manchurian economy was dominated by the Chinese immigrants. This was in strong contrast to the pauperization of many Manchu bannermen. Since wealth not only enhanced the social status of the owner but also made it possible for him to gain entrée into official circles, the rise of a rich Chinese mercantile and landlord class in the Manchurian frontier was another manifestation of the rising political power of the Chinese immigrants vis-à-vis the Manchus.

6

The Frontier Government in Transition

Historical Background

The period of transition (1851–1907) spanned some of the most fateful years in the history of modern China. I can only indicate here some aspects of the history of that period which affected most deeply the frontier political organization. The year 1851 is chosen as the beginning of the period because it was the first year of a new reign and the second year of the T'ai-p'ing Rebellion. In the wake of the T'ai-p'ing, came the Nien and Moslem rebellions. These rebellions occurred at a time when the Ch'ing empire had experienced a prolonged period of population growth that greatly overstrained its economic resources and produced widespread poverty.[1] The population pressure was especially intense in Chihli and Shantung, the two northern provinces nearest to the Manchurian frontier. And it was toward the frontier that the land-hungry peasants of these provinces moved, although the restriction against Chinese immigration was still in force.

The rebellions affected the development of the frontier in the following ways: first, they caused a general breakdown in the financial administration of the empire. The wealthy provinces of the northern plain and the Yangtse delta were devastated by years of warfare. They had hitherto contributed their surplus revenues to the less favorably endowed provinces. When these subsidies were reduced or withheld altogether, such income-deficit provinces as Kirin and Heilungkiang experienced acute financial crisis. It was up to the military governors to find new sources of revenue to sustain their governments. Because land was the most abundant natural resource on the frontier and there were many eager hands ready to work on the land, the opening of the frontier to immigrant peasants, reasoned the frontier authorities, would contribute substantial sums of money to the local treasuries both by the sale of land and by taxation of the cultivated acreage. Second, the rebellions also affected the strength and morale of the garrison troops as a substantial number of them were dispatched to the battlefield. In Kirin, according to an 1865 memorial by the military governor, over 10,000 banner troops had died in the campaigns, and of those who returned almost half were disabled.[2] In Heilungkiang, according to the *Heilungkiang chih kao* (Draft gazetteer of Heilungkiang), during the Hsien-feng (1851–1861) and T'ung-chih (1862–1874) reigns, the number of troops sent to China proper totaled about 67,730 men; of these only about 10 to 20 percent survived.[3] The banner soldiers who were left behind did not receive adequate pay or equipment. They could neither stop the entry of illegal immigrants nor maintain order within their territories. In the end, it seemed to the authorities that it would be far better to legalize immigration and reap the benefits to be derived from it than to try to enforce an unenforceable policy.

The domestic rebellions exposed the military weakness of China to all imperialistic powers. In 1847 Nicholas I of Russia appointed Nikolai Muraviev as governor-general of Eastern Siberia. From then on, Muraviev, with the able assistance of Admiral Nevelsky, explored the mouth of the Amur and the nearby coastal area and established in Chinese territory a series of bases along the lower course of the Amur. In 1854 and again in 1855, he sailed down the Amur River without encountering any opposition from the Manchu garrison. In 1858, he was able to impose the Aigun Treaty upon the Ch'ing court, which was still fighting the T'ai-p'ing rebels and engaging in a serious dispute with Britain and France over the revision of the Treaty of Tientsin. Two years later, the Ch'ing court concluded the Treaty of Peking with Russia. As the result of these treaties, the Ch'ing empire lost all the lands north of the Amur and east of the Ussuri. These treaties had two immediate consequences. They undermined the historic tributary relationship between the Ch'ing court and the Amur tribes. Those tribes who lived in the lost territories were, of course, excluded from the court's jurisdiction and those who remained on Chinese territory were confronted with a loss of good hunting grounds. The treaties also deprived China of a vast buffer zone and provided the Russians with easy access to the heart of Manchuria, a situation the K'ang-hsi emperor had tried resolutely to avoid in the seventeenth century. From then on, the defense of Manchuria was an overriding concern to the frontier officials.

The task of suppressing the domestic rebellions also brought forth a group of practical statesmen who perceived the internal weakness of China, appreciated the strength of the western powers, and possessed the prestige and courage to advocate and carry forward projects designed to revitalize the empire. Foremost among these men were Tseng Kuo-fan,

Li Hung-chang, and Tso Tsung-t'ang. It is beside the point to argue that they did not really understand the spirit that animates Western advances in science and industry. It is important that these men, who had rescued the dynasty from the brink of total disaster, assumed leadership in the introduction of Western learning to China.[4] Their example influenced a later generation of officials who were to bring about changes in various parts of the nation. Thus, Li Hung-chang, who began his career under the tutelage of Tseng Kuo-fan was the political patron of Yüan Shih-k'ai. Yüan, in turn, was responsible for the promotion of the career of Hsü Shih-ch'ang. Hsü, as the first governor-general of the Three Eastern Provinces, brought with him to Manchuria a group of energetic officials who pushed forward a program of reform and modernization in the frontier that compared favorably with the program in the more progressive provinces of China proper.

The years of internal turmoil also altered the balance of political power within the empire. The military props of the Manchu ruling house, the banner force and the Lü-ying, were utterly discredited as fighting forces. More and more, Chinese officials took over the leadership in such crucial matters as foreign policy, economic development, and the modernization of the armed forces. They were appointed to important frontier posts in Sinkiang, Tibet, and Manchuria where no Chinese officials had been sent before.

There was also a shift of political power from the central government to the provincial governments. In order to suppress the rebels, the local governors and governors-general were given wide latitude in the recruitment, training, and command of local troops, which became in effect their private armies.[5] They disrupted entirely the checks-and-balances system in the provincial government by centralizing the military, fiscal, and executive powers in their hands. This trend was to be reflected in the pattern of political reorganization in the Manchurian frontier region.

At about the same time that China was reeling under the impact of Western imperialism and domestic rebellions, Japan began a program of modernization which ultimately made her the strongest power in the Far East and propelled her across the Korean Strait to the continent of Asia. In the Sino-Japanese War of 1894–1895 China lost the buffer state of Korea. Japanese power was extended to the border of the Yalu River. From then on, the rivalry between Russia and Japan over the control of Manchuria and Korea resulted in the steady undermining of Chinese sovereignty over the Manchurian frontier. In the secret Sino-Russian Treaty of 1896, concluded by Li Hung-chang in Moscow, China granted Russia the right to build the Chinese Eastern Railway across Heilungkiang and Kirin. Two years later, Russia obtained a twenty-five year lease of Dairen and Port Arthur. Through these concessions, Russia penetrated into the heart of Manchuria.

The Sino-Japanese War and the following scramble for concessions on Chinese soil by foreign powers produced strong demands by thinking Chinese for changes in the body politic. The anti-Manchu slogans of the T'ai-p'ing rebels were taken over by the revolutionaries, who called for the overthrow of the dynasty and the establishment of a republic, while the reformers advocated the adoption of a constitutional monarchy. The reactionaries pinned their hopes on the blind antiforeignism of the Boxer movement, which brought on the capture of Peking in 1900 by eight foreign powers. Russia took advantage of the occasion to send her troops across the entire length of Manchuria and delayed their withdrawal even after the signing of the Boxer Protocol in 1901. Russian ambitions aroused Japanese apprehensions and led to the Russo-Japanese War of 1904–1905, which was fought on Manchurian soil. The Treaty of Portsmouth obligated Russia to return Russian-occupied Manchuria to Chinese administration and to cede the Liao-tung leasehold to the Japanese together with the South Manchuria Railway. Thus on the eve of administrative reforms in Manchuria, north Manchuria, traversed by the Chinese Eastern Railway, was under the sphere of Russian influence, while south Manchuria, bisected by the South Manchuria Railway, was dominated by the Japanese from their base in the Liao-tung Peninsula.

Tribal Societies under Pressure

The tribal peoples, as we have seen, enjoyed a large measure of internal autonomy under the Ch'ing system of tribal control. They could have preserved their traditional cultural patterns with few changes if the ethnic balance had not been upset by the steady flow of Chinese immigration. During the period of transition the flow had become a disastrous flood for many of the tribal communities. It was during this period that the ban against Chinese immigration was lifted to permit settlement on tribal lands. In Kirin, the upper Hurka Valley was opened in 1878, the Tumen Valley in 1881, the upper Ussuri in 1882, and the entire province in 1902. In Heilungkiang, the Hulan basin was opened in 1862 and the entire province in 1906.[6]

The flood of Chinese settlers meant for the tribal peoples the shrinkage of their hunting and fishing grounds, the competition of Chinese hunters and fishermen, and the undermining of their traditional values. These effects were most noticeable among the Heje of Kirin. Even in Russian occupied Ussuria, the appearance of Chinese settlers produced disturbing consequences. Arseniev reported:

> After a short rest I went to have a look at the home of a family of natives near the Chinese. The aborigines of Ussuria, inhabiting the central part of the mountain district of the Sihote-Alin and the coast to the north of Cape Uspenika, call themselves Ude-he. Those who used to live in the southern part of the country have in the course of time become assimilated with the Chinese, and cannot now be distinguished from them. Chinese call them *da-tsy* (*t'a-tzu*), which means foreigners, that is neither Russian, Korean, nor Chinese, which has been corrupted by the Russians into *tazi*, the name our people generally know them by. The characteristics of these assimilated natives are poverty and slovenliness, poverty in their homes, poverty in their clothing, poverty in their food.
>
> When I walked up towards their cabin, an old *tazi* came out to meet me. Clad in tatters, with swimming eyes and sores on his head, he greeted me, and in his voice I could hear fear and submissiveness. Near the cabin some children were playing with the dogs. Their bodies were completely unclothed.
>
> The cabin was old and tumbledown; here and there the clay had peeled off the walls; the old paper on the window, yellow with age, was torn; on the dusty *k'angs* lay a few fragments of matting, and on the wall hung smoke-begrimed, discolored rags. On every side neglect, dirt and squalor.
>
> Formerly I had thought that all this was from sloth, but I have since come to the conclusion that the poverty of the natives is due to other causes, in particular their position among the Chinese settlers. From what I heard on inquiry, I learnt that the owner of the Chinese farm of Iolaiza was a *tsaidun* (*ts'ai-tung*), that is lord of the river, in other words a capitalist. All the natives living on the Fudzin get things from him on credit, opium, spirit, provisions, and clothing. In return they are obliged to pay him in the proceeds of their hunting, sables, antlers, ginseng, and so on. The result is the natives have fallen into a bottomless debt, they have lost their wives and

> daughters, and it has happened that they have sold themselves into other hands. These aborigines having adopted Chinese culture could not absorb it, and succumbed to the influence of the Chinese themselves. As farmers and tillers of the soil they could not live, and they forgot the arts of the hunter and trapper. The Chinese have taken advantage of their spiritual poverty and made themselves indispensable to them. From that moment the natives lost all independence and become converted into slaves.[7]

Because the Heje were in close contact with the Chinese immigrants for a longer period than the Udehe of Ussuria, there is little reason to doubt that their contact with the Chinese settlers was anything less than catastrophic. The Heje of lower Sungari were incorporated into the banners in 1882—a move intended to strengthen the defense of the exposed Amur frontier against the Russians. In 1902, following the aftermath of the Boxer Uprising and the Russian invasion of Manchuria, the lower Sungari and Ussuri regions were opened to agricultural settlement. The Heje villages, located along river banks, were particularly desirable. An arrangement was made by the provincial authorities according to which strips of land adjoining the Heje villages were allotted to the inhabitants. These grants were made proportionate to the size of the village and were divided among individual villagers by the clan and village chiefs. Unfortunately for the Heje, they were unable to compete with the Chinese as farmers and almost all their lands later passed into the hands of the newcomers. So the Heje remained dependent upon hunting and ginseng gathering for their livelihood. The money they earned was spent quickly in drink and opium. The Chinese, who were short of women, outbid the Heje themselves for their women as wives. The Heje were demoralized and their number shrank. A Russian investigator estimated that from 1897 to 1915 the Heje population declined by 25 percent.[8]

Prior to the official opening of Heilungkiang to unrestricted settlement, the presence of Chinese settlers among the Solon, Dagur, and Orochon tribes was much less disturbing than among the Heje. The upper Amur Valley and the Nonni Valley were considered strategic regions where troublesome settlers were kept out more effectively than in the Ussuri-Sungari region. Furthermore, many of the tribesmen had been brought into the regional military and administrative structure, and being so organized they were able to deal more effectively with any attempt at forceful subjugation by illegal immigrants. The institution of *cūlgan*, which gave the Buteha and Orochon opportunities to trade with Chinese merchants under official supervision also reduced the chances of undue exploitation by Chinese traders. Consequently, Chinese influence among the Solon and the Dagur was greatest, not among the hunters and herders, but among the officers and men of the garrison force, who were much more sophisticated and could be more selective in their assimilation of Chinese cultural elements.

During the campaigns against the T'ai-p'ing and other rebels, forty-four contingents of Solon and Dagur troops were sent to the battlefields in China proper. Among those who returned, many won high-ranking commissions, which greatly enhanced their social status.[9] However, their military glory did not compensate for the social and economic ills that beset them after the rebellions. Many veterans acquired the opium habit, which rendered them unfit for productive life. At the same time, the government was unable to pay them because of financial difficulties.[10] But the worse blow was the ceding of the left bank of the Amur to the Russians in 1858 and the opening of Hulan to Chinese settlement in 1862, which deprived them of some of the best hunting grounds in Heilungkiang. When the entire province was opened in 1906, the Buteha were forced to turn from herding and hunting to other means of livelihood such as farming, fishing, and lumbering.[11]

The Orochon were less affected by Chinese immigrants. They were, however, much influenced by the proximity of the Russians across the Amur. A government report stated that the Orochon found it more convenient to trade with the Russians than with the Chinese; and because of the decrease in wild game, many of them sought work in Russian settlements. Consequently, a large number became naturalized Russian subjects. Even those who remained on Chinese territory were often found wearing Russian clothes and taking Russian names.[12]

The construction of the Chinese Eastern Railway (1896–1903), which brought Hulun Buir closer to Tsitsihar and Harbin, also brought Russian influence into this strategic nomad land. The apprehensive Heilungkiang authorities were determined to strengthen the frontier defense by bringing in Chinese colonists and by reorganizing the existing administrative and military structure. In 1908 a Frontier Agricultural Settlement Bureau was established in preparation for large-scale colonization.[13] Measures such as this provoked widespread Mongol and Dagur resentment and was an important factor in the Hulun Buir independence movement of 1911.[14]

As for the Mongols of the Jerim League, whose land lay adjacent to that of the Manchurian frontier, their princes had permitted Chinese settlements in their midst as early as the late eighteenth century. As time went on and immigration continued, conflicts between Mongol herdsmen and Chinese cultivators became more and more serious. At the beginning, colonization had proceeded at the discretion of Mongol princes, who, although attracted by the extra income brought by the settlers, were mindful of the effect of the shrinkage of pastures upon the livelihood of the Mongol commoners. In 1902 the imperial government took over the promotion of the colonization program for defense and financial reasons. Thereafter, the expropriation of Mongol lands became a matter of national policy. The Mongol reaction was the spontaneous outbreak of violence and banditry along the line between agricultural settlements and pastoral lands and eventually the growth of separatist sentiments in the latter years of the dynasty.[15]

The Decline of Manchu Military Power

As early as the K'ang-hsi reign, poverty among the bannermen had become a serious government concern. Twice during the reign government funds totaling about 12 million taels were used to repay debts incurred by the bannermen. Other measures of relief included the distribution of government grains, the issuance of government loans, and in the Yung-cheng reign the redemption of banner lands sold to the Chinese.[16] None of these measures succeeded in solving the problem of bannerman livelihood throughout the dynasty.

The basic cause of poverty was the severe restriction on economic opportunities for the average bannerman due to the immobilization of the bannermen within the area of each military command and the limitation on their choices of occupation. In China proper, the contributing causes were the increase in bannerman population, the inability of the average bannerman to become a successful farmer, and the tendency of the bannermen to live above their means. Because of the abundance of virgin soil and the generally rustic mode of life, the frontier bannermen were able to stave off the threat of poverty much longer than their intramural cousins. They seemed to have felt the pinch of economic necessity only in the wake of the T'ai-p'ing and other rebellions. The rebellions forced the government to fall into arrears in its payment to the banner forces. Governor-general Hsü Shih-ch'ang stated that from the Hsien-feng reign (1851–1861) to 1906 the imperial treasury owed the Heilungkiang banner soldiers a total of about four million taels. In Kirin, the officers and men constantly received only half of their stipends, the buying power of which had deteriorated with the rise of commodity prices.[17]

Because the frontier bannermen had depended on their farms for a living, the reduction in government stipends should not have brought undue hardships on them. However, like their counterparts in China proper, the frontier bannermen by this time were also losing most of their lands to the Chinese immigrants. It usually began with bannermen hiring the cheap labor of the immigrants to work on their lands and ended with them leasing and eventually selling their lands to the immigrants. Hsü Shih-ch'ang observed that, in Petuna, all the emolument lands of the banner garrison were being cultivated by Chinese tenants.[18] Much of the Hulan banner lands had been lost through the above process to the immigrants.[19]

Another blow to the bannermen's income resulted from the Boxer Uprising. As punishment for that tragic event, the victorious allies imposed upon China a staggering indemnity of 450,000,000 taels (or a total value of U.S.$333,900,000) to be paid with 4 percent interest in 40 years. To meet the annual payment each province was allocated by the Peking government a share of the indemnity. The military governor of Kirin, unable to raise the necessary funds through the existing sources of revenue, obtained permission in 1902 to levy a tax on all banner lands.[20] In Heilungkiang, government farms and post station farms were put on the tax rolls in 1906;[21] other banner lands seem to have preserved their tax-exempted status.

Equal in importance to the pauperization of the banner population was the steady deterioration of the fighting power of the banner forces as a factor responsible for the decline of the prestige of the bannermen in general and of the Manchus in particular. The frontier banner forces, aside from their responsibilities in guarding the frontier, functioned also as a reservoir of military manpower completely committed to the dynastic interest. During the T'ai-p'ing Rebellion they were drawn upon extensively for campaigns in China proper where they generally gave a better account of themselves than their intramural counterparts. Many of the officers, especially those from Heilungkiang attained high rank. The most famous of them was To-lung-a.[22] But the T'ai-p'ing were suppressed mainly by the strength of Chinese militia trained and organized by Chinese officials. The standing armies of the empire, both the banner forces and the Chinese Lü-ying, were powerless to resist by themselves the onslaught of the rebels. When the remnants of the banner forces returned to their frontier posts, the frontier governments greeted, not contingents of disciplined veterans hardened by battlefield experience, but dispirited soldiers weakened by years of hardship, many of whom were opium addicts.[23]

In a scathing report to the Grand Council in 1904, Ch'eng Te-ch'üan, the military governor of Heilungkiang, characterized the banner soldiers as ignorant of everything except living on their stipends. The banner officers, he reported, were content to follow the routine of their jobs, adept in covering up the mistakes and corruptions of each other, and determined to resist any innovation that might deprive them of their entrenched privileges.[24]

The court itself recognized the weaknesses of the banner forces. In 1880 the first attempt was made to modernize its antique training method. Groups of soldiers were taken from their units and given intensive training in the use of modern firearms. The result was disappointing. The officials and instructors sent from Peking could not overcome the vested interests and age-old inertia of the local banner commanders, who were suspicious of the outsiders.[25] After 1890 new army units, which took in an increasing number of Chinese recruits, were organized. Thus, the defense of the Manchu homeland was being consciously abdicated by the Manchus to the Chinese.

Dissolution of the Tributary System

In 1886, following a seven-month trip in Russian territories gathering intelligence for the military governor of Kirin, Ts'ao T'ing-chieh, while in Peking for an imperial audience, reported to Prince Ch'ing, presiding member of the Tsungli Yamen, that the tributary system, as it was functioning in Kirin, existed in name only. According to Ts'ao, the tribes living between San-hsing and the lower Ussuri, having been incorporated into the banners, were no longer obligated to send tribute. Those living in Russian territory came to San-hsing in groups of a hundred or less, accompanied by Chinese traders, ostensibly as tribute-bearers, but actually only to trade for Chinese goods. The sables were really bought from Chinese traders on credit. But the fiction of tribute presentation was maintained by the military government. The same amount of imperial gifts was sent to San-hsing as in the past and a great deal of money was spent in assembling and transporting them. Since the tributary quota had been fixed by statute at about 2,600 pelts and the tribesmen did not bring along the requisite number, the San-hsing authorities made up the full quota by buying them from the market, probably from the same Chinese traders who accompanied the tribesmen. Ts'ao, therefore, recommended the termination of the sending of imperial gifts, using the money so saved to buy sables in the Fengt'ien market for the imperial household. The tribesmen who came to San-hsing to trade would be rewarded by the local authorities and their actual number registered with the Board of Revenue.[26] Ts'ao's recommendation had the merit of ending the tributary fiction while still maintaining a tenuous tie with the tribesmen in Russian Manchuria for whatever political benefit it would bring.

Ts'ao's proposal was taken up later by the military governors of Sheng-ching (Fengt'ien) and Kirin, who suggested that the imperial gifts should be sold on the market so that sables might be purchased to fill up the tribute quota. Finally, in 1899, even this pretense was done away with. Instead, the Board of Revenue appropriated annually a sum of money to the San-hsing authorities for the purchase of sable pelts.[27] Thus ended the tributary system in Kirin. Ironically, the corruption that characterized the tribute-collecting agency in the latter part of the dynasty seems to have taken a turn for the worse with the change of policy. Te-hsing, the acting deputy military governor of San-hsing, for instance, was censured in 1909 for his practice of purchasing 4,000 to 5,000 skins in the market at an arbitrarily set price of about 8 taels each, while the official quota was 2,600 skins and the prevailing market price was from 20 to 30 taels each. To assure himself a good supply of skins at below the market price he limited private trading in sables to a number of assigned firms which had to register the skins they had on hand with the Tax Bureau.[28]

The situation in Heilungkiang was similar to that in Kirin. In 1882, the number of tribute sables was set at 4,200 skins, about a thousand less than in 1810. Later on it was reduced to 3,155. Even so it was a heavy burden to the Buteha tribesmen, who had lost part of their population and the best hunting ground to the Russians in the Aigun Treaty of 1858. Consequently, they often had to make up the quota by buying the skins from the open market.[29] The situation became much worse after 1900. From 1902 to the end of the dynasty the Heilungkiang authorities had to request every year the suspension of the annual tribute.[30] Thus the system died in fact if not in name.

The tributary sables, however, were mere symbols of a political relationship. The ending of the tributary system was caused not so much by the disappearance of the fur-bearing animals as by the changing political concepts regarding the proper relationship between China proper and the Manchurian frontier. The old policy of isolating the frontier from the rest of the empire and of upholding the traditional social and economic structure of the frontier peoples had been upset beyond repair by the influx of Chinese immigrants, rapid economic development, and the presence of a foreign menace. The overriding necessity of the time was not to preserve the distinctive characteristics of the frontier but to integrate it more closely with China proper. The laissez-faire attitude inherent in the tributary system was no longer in accord with reality.

Official inertia, however, delayed the reorganization of the frontier administrative system until 1907. When reorganization came, the hitherto tribal areas were hastily thrown open to Chinese colonization and subdivided into regular administrative units. With these changes, the autonomous status of the tribal areas came to a definite end and so did the usefulness of the tributary system.

Furthermore, the traditional policy of regarding the tribal peoples as guardians of the imperial frontier could no longer be sustained in an era of modern armies. The martial reputation of the tribesmen had been seriously tarnished by the deterioration in the fighting quality of the banner force, of which the tribal auxiliaries had been an important component. What the government needed were well trained professional soldiers and officers capable of fighting on Western terms, not just weapon-wielding hunters, fishermen, and herders. Thus, the approaching end of the frontier military government was accompanied by the dissolution of the tributary system and the tribal enclaves.

Frontier Settlement under Government Sponsorship

Nothing illustrates better than the changing official concept regarding the proper relationship between the Manchurian frontier and China proper than the frontier settlement program sponsored by the government. Prior to the latter part of the nineteenth century, some government efforts had been made to resettle indigent bannermen on frontier lands. The purpose of those efforts was to relieve the poverty-stricken bannermen of Peking, whose number had grown too large to be adequately provided for by the banner organization. The settlement programs in the latter part of the nineteenth century were carried out under the slogan of *i min shih pien* (to strengthen the frontier by settling it with people). The purpose was directed outward against potential invaders and the settlers involved were Chinese.

The settlement projects in Heilungkiang may be used to illustrate the procedure and machinery developed by the frontier authorities for the realization of this new policy. In 1860 the military governor of Heilungkiang, T'e-p'u-ch'in, memorialized the throne for the opening of the Hulan district. At that time there were already over 2,500 Chinese peasants cultivating more than 8,000 *shang* of land in Hulan. They had acquired their holdings surreptitiously from bannermen, who sold them the public lands originally reserved for military colonization, courier stations, and government farms. T'e-p'u-ch'in believed that because Chinese settlement was an accomplished fact, it would be a better policy to legalize and encourage immigration and reap the financial benefits from it rather than to let the land remain idle and attract the coveteous gaze of the Russians. Under his proposal the virgin lands were sold to the immigrants at parcels of 45 *shang* each. The price of each parcel was figured at 70 percent of its actual size (31 *shang*, 5 *mou*) to allow for uncultivable land and land reserved for farm buildings, roads, and wells. Each *shang* was sold for two strings of cash and one hundred copper coins. The provincial treasury received the two strings of cash and the settlement project received the one hundred coins to defray administrative expenses. The settlers began to pay land tax to the government in the sixth year. The tax was fixed at 600 copper coins per *shang* for the provincial government and sixty coins for the local government. The task of getting the immigrants to the project was relegated to speculators, who bought up the land from the government then resold it to individual immigrants. From 1860 to 1868 the total acreage of land sold by the government exceeded 200,000 *shang*.[31]

The increase in Chinese population, prompted T'e-p'u-ch'in to request the appointment of a Hulan subprefect in 1863 to take charge of the financial and legal matters involving Chinese settlers. At first, the sub-prefect was stationed at Hulan where the commandant had his headquarters. The move aroused the antagonism of the commandant who, although being the superior of the sub-prefect, preferred not to have the latter in the same city. So the next year, the sub-prefect was shifted to nearby Bayensusu. The jurisdiction between the two officials was divided along territorial lines.[32] In 1872 the commandant established a *min-wu t'ing* (bureau of civil affairs) to take charge of the settlement program, tax collection, and public security in the areas of Chinese settlement. The officials of the bureau were all banner officers.[33] The Hulan sub-prefect was the first local civil magistrate appointed to Heilungkiang. The post was theoretically opened to both Chinese and banner candidates, but up to its abolition in 1905, no Chinese was ever appointed.[34]

In 1896 more districts in Heilungkiang were released for settlement. According to the *Heilungkiang chih kao,* the regulations promulgated at that time were used as a model in many subsequent projects. A colonization bureau was established in Tsitsihar and branch bureaus were located at project sites. The virgin lands were surveyed and divided into individual sections of six square li. Each section is called a *ching,* a modern term for "well" but one having long historic connotations as a system for land distribution and settlement. Each "well" was subdivided into nine fields. Each field contained four parcels and each parcel measured 45 *shang*. Each "well," therefore, contained 36 parcels totaling 1,620 *shang*. The settlers were permitted to purchase the 32 parcels at the edge of the "well." The four parcels in the center were reserved for the village site. For each parcel of land purchased by the settler, he was entitled to 5 *shang* of land at the village site. Consequently, of the 180 *shang* of land put aside for the village, 160 *shang* would be owned by the individual settlers. The remaining 20 *shang* would be public land, the proceeds from which would be accumulated for the building of a public village school and a public granary. The management of the public land would be entrusted to a village chief elected by the villagers. The public land was given free to the village and exempted from taxation. The village chief was required to turn over to the village one picul of grain from each *shang* of public land. When sufficient grain had been accumulated, it would be sold for the construction of the school and granary and for their operating expenses.[35]

The above plan was designed to correct the situation in Hulan, where the settlers occupied scattered parcels of land and lived far away from each other and thereby opened themselves to attack by bandits. The regulations also provided for the self-defense of the villagers by specifying that each village should be organized according to the *pao-chia* system.[36] The village was to be divided into three *chia*. Each *chia*, containing ten to eleven households was commanded by a *chia* chief. The *chia* chiefs were in turn, commanded by a *pao-cheng* elected by the whole village. The *pao-cheng* would be responsible to the local magistrate for the behavior of the villagers.[37]

This symmetrical scheme of landholding, devised by Military Governor Yen-mao, was an effort to establish on the frontier an ideal type of village structure that had a long antecedent in the writings of Confucian scholars. It failed to accomplish its objectives because the settlers preferred to build their houses on their farms instead on the designated village site. The public land that had been set aside was later purchased by influential villagers and the provision for the building and maintenance of village schools and granary was never put into effect.[38]

In Hulan, the necessity for self-defense prompted the villagers to organize from 1887 to 1906 militia units called *lien-hui* (drilling association). Each drilling association was a cooperative undertaking of several villages. The villagers elected a commander, who received official appointment from the banner garrison officers. The financing of the association was apportioned according to the size of the individual landholdings, and each family was required to contribute one recruit to the association.[39]

In 1898 the Peking court called for the formation of *hsiang t'uan* or village battalions, which were organized as follows: one *p'ai* or squad consisted of ten men, one *chia* or company consisted of five squads and two companies made up one *t'uan* or battalion. A commander and a deputy commander were appointed over every five battalions. The officers and men were unpaid and had to supply their own uniforms and arms. Later, the system of financial apportionment was reinstituted and the members of the militia were paid for their services. In 1906 the militia gave way to a police force. Aside from the special training that the officers received from police schools, the organization and financing of the police did not differ too greatly from the militia principle.[40] The significance of the militia and police force in the rural areas derived from the fact that, among the districts settled by immigrants, the banner force had lost its role as guardian of public order. The immigrant leaders responsible for the organization of the local militia or police force became important personalities in local politics.

The career of Chang Tso-lin illustrates most vividly the dramatic rise of such local personalities.[41] Although Chang made his first impact on the Chinese political scene in south Manchuria, the process through which he attained power was peculiarly a frontier phenomenon. During the Sino-Japanese War, villagers living along the route of the retreating Ch'ing army in the western Liao plain, captured a large quantity of firearms from the demoralized and ill-disciplined soldiers. The availability of these weapons was responsible, on the one hand, for the appearance of a large crop of mounted bandits and, on the other hand, the formation of village militia in defense against them. Unlike the traditional pattern in China proper where the local gentry usually assumed the leadership for such task, the Manchurian militia leaders were often illiterate or semi-illiterate men with a shadowy background. There was no deeply rooted rural gentry class in the new Manchurian settlements. The conduct of these militia leaders naturally left much to be desired especially from the point of view of the legally constituted local authorities, who considered them not much better than the bandit chiefs. It was as militia leaders that Chang Tso-lin (1873–1928) and such of his associates as Chang Tso-hsiang, Chang Ching-hui, and T'ang Yü-lin first achieved their status as prominent local figures.[42]

The disturbed situation in the Liao plain was seriously aggravated by the Boxer Uprising and the Russian invasion. Again, government troops, retreating from the Russians, pillaged the countryside; again, villagers rose in self-defense. Within a year or two, fortified villages patrolled by armed peasants dotted the countryside. Neighboring villages formed federations, *lien-chuang-hui*, for more effective protection. Such federations were presided over by a commander who levied land tax, conscripted men, and ruled with autocratic power over his domain. Again, some of the federation commanders had the reputation of being both protector and oppressor of the people.[43]

Two commanders achieved regional fame: one was Chang Tso-lin and the other, Feng Lin-ko.[44] By that time, Chang's militia was in possession of over one thousand guns. During the Russo-Japanese War, both Chang and Feng fought for the Japanese as irregular allies against the Russians. They emerged after the war with enhanced strength.[45] In order to prevent the further undermining of government authority, the Ch'ing court told the local prefects and magistrates to bring all the privately armed groups, including known bandits, into the ranks of the regular army. It was under such circumstances that both men were appointed battalion commanders of the reorganized provincial army. Thereafter, Chang distinguished himself as an effective bandit suppressor. On the eve of the 1911 Revolution he had already become one of the five route commanders of the provincial army with a force of seven mixed infantry and cavalry battalions.[46] This was the initial military capital with which Chang staked his way into national fame as one of modern China's most powerful warlords.

The Increasing Complexity of Governmental Affairs

Following the growth of immigrant villages, there was a corresponding growth of civil governments on the levels of the *hsien* or district, *chou* or department, *t'ing* or sub-prefecture, and *fu* or prefecture. In Kirin two sub-prefectures were established in 1880; one district, one department, two sub-prefectures, and one prefecture in 1882; one prefecture and one district in 1888; two districts and three sub-prefectures in 1902; and one department and two prefectures in 1905. In Heilungkiang, Hulan sub-prefecture was established in 1875 and Sui-hua in 1885. In 1904 Hulan and Sui-hua were elevated to prefectural status; in addition, four districts, one department, and three sub-prefectures were founded. In 1905 two districts and in 1906 one district and two sub-prefectures were added to the list.[47] These new governmental units were located primarily in the fertile plains of western Kirin and eastern Heilungkiang where good transportation was provided by the Sungari River, the Chinese Eastern Railway, and the South Manchuria Railway.

Paralleling the growth of towns and villages was the multiplication of governmental functions. In contrast to the early days when the major functions of the military governor were related to the routine administration of the banner forces and the garrison towns, many difficult tasks arose during the latter part of the nineteenth century demanding his attention. Among these tasks, the most important were the following:

Reorganization of the armed forces. The deterioration of the banner force necessitated the training and formation of new army units outside the banner organization for the purpose of eradicating banditry and protecting the exposed frontier lands. The program started in Kirin in 1867 and in Heilungkiang in 1880.[48] It was in 1880 that a Chinese official, Wu Ta-ch'eng, was entrusted with the task of organizing a new military force called the Ching-pien chün or Border Pacification Army. Wu was also instrumental in establishing a modern arsenal at Kirin in 1883, probably the most imposing single industrial enterprise in the frontier region at that time.[49] Thereafter, army reorganization occupied the constant attention of frontier authorities down to the very end of the dynasty.

The search for new revenues. This search was conducted on two fronts. One was taxation. In 1855 a tax bureau was established in Kirin which collected taxes on thirty-three local consumer products. In 1879 likin was introduced into Kirin, and in 1885 an opium tax.[50] The first tax bureau in Heilungkiang was established in 1885 in Hulan, although local taxes had been levied on the local population since 1737.[51] Afterwards various taxes were levied on local products.[52] The land tax, of course, remained one of the most important sources of revenue.

The other method of increasing revenue was the development of new sources of wealth. In this regard, the selling of public lands to the immigrants was most fruitful in its long term effects. Once the lands were developed, taxes could then be levied on the cultivated acreage, their products, and the commercial transactions that arose from them. Also important was the effort to develop mining enterprises. Permission to legalize goldmining was obtained in 1854 by the military governor of Kirin.[53] The famous Mo-ho goldmines in Heilungkiang were first exploited clandestinely by Russians in 1884. After the Russians were expelled through diplomatic representations, a mining company was formed in 1888 with private capital but official supervision.[54] In 1890 the military governor of Kirin memorialized the throne for the exploitation of the San-hsing goldmines. However, the result was disappointing and the mines were abandoned after a year.[55] Coalmining was first started in Kirin in 1815, primarily as a means of relieving the shortage of firewood in the city area. Five small shafts were opened and permission to open additional shafts was denied until 1821, when four new shafts were opened to replace the four that had collapsed. In 1880 permission was granted for the opening of new mines upon the entreaty of the military governor, who stressed the necessity for more fuel as well as the prospect of increasing tax revenues.[56]

The conduct of foreign affairs. It was a peculiar feature of Ch'ing diplomacy that the provincial authorities had to carry the burden of negotiating with foreign powers on matters which impinged upon territories under their jurisdiction. After the conclusion of the secret Sino-Russian Treaty of 1896, which granted the Russians the right to construct the Chinese Eastern Railway, Russian demands for land concessions along the railway and for lumbering and mining rights had to be skillfully parried by the local negotiators. The occupation of Manchuria by the Russians during the Boxer Uprising and the delay in the withdrawal of Russian troops also taxed the diplomatic skill of the military governors and their subordinates. The Sino-Japanese Treaty of 1905, which provided for the opening of Harbin, Hun-ch'un, Kirin, Ch'ang-ch'un, Ninguta, and San-hsing in Kirin; and Tsitsihar, Aigun, Hailar, and

Manchouli in Heilungkiang as treaty ports, brought with it a long train of problems that had to be solved by negotiations.[57]

The problem of Korean immigration. The fertile Tumen Valley, enclosed by the Ch'ang-pai-shan, was a part of the imperial preserve. It was only during the Tao-kuang reign (1821–1850) that illegal Chinese settlers began to penetrate into its wilderness. With the conclusion of the Russo-Chinese Treaty of 1860, in which China ceded Ussuria to Russia, it became a strategic area where Russian, Korean, and Chinese boundaries met. To forestall possible Russian encroachment, the imperial government repealed the ban against its settlement. Because of the difficulty in crossing the mountain ranges and the availability of land elsewhere, Chinese immigrants were slow in taking up these empty lands. Korean peasants, however, found it comparatively easy to cross over the Tumen into Chinese territory. In 1875 local authorities reported that Koreans were found in great numbers on the Chinese side of the river. Because Korea was a vassal state of China, the court did not raise immediate objection against the entry of the Koreans. In 1881 the Korean settlers were put under local Chinese jurisdiction. In 1885 special bureaus were established for their supervision and lands were designated for their settlement. In 1890 they were given title deeds to the lands they cultivated and made liable to land tax as full Chinese citizens.[58]

The Chinese local authorities interfered very little with the affairs of the Korean immigrants. The Koreans formed their own communities and established their own schools where only the Korean language was taught to the children. They came under the jurisdiction of Chinese courts; but Chinese officials, following age-old practices, often remanded Korean criminals to Korean authorities across the river for punishment. It was only in 1890 that the military-governor of Kirin ruled that only those Koreans who had adopted the dress and hair style of the Chinese would be permitted to enjoy the privilege of citizenship. However, the Sino-Japanese War of 1894–1895 broke out soon after. The prestige of defeated China sank in the eyes of the Koreans and the ruling was completely ignored.[59]

As a result of the war, Korea came under the domination of Japan. The existence of the Korean communities in the Manchurian frontier now became a cause for concern among the military authorities. In 1899, a Sino-Korean Treaty was concluded, each party prohibiting immigration into the other's territory. Unfortunately, as soon as Japan established her protectorate over Korea in 1905, the Korean minority in

Manchuria immediately became the target of solicitude on the part of the Japanese government. The Sino-Korean boundary became a cause of dispute as the Japanese attempted, on dubious evidence, to extend a claim over the entire region where the sources of the Tumen, Yalu, and Sungari originated, an area equal to the Japanese island of Kyushu, as part of Korea.[60] The aggressive intent of Japan spurred the Manchurian authorities to find means of integrating the Koreans more closely into Chinese society. These efforts were largely frustrated by Japanese countermeasures. Thus the problem of Korean immigration and boundary dispute became one of the thorny diplomatic issues between China and Japan.

The settlement of Mongol affairs. During the period of transition the Mongol problem became of great importance to the frontier administration. The Inner Mongolia lands adjoining Manchuria consisted of the following banners of the Jerem League: The front, center, and rear banners of the Korchin Left Wing; the front, center, and rear banners of the Korchin Right Wing; the Gorlos front and rear banners; the Dörbet banner, and the Jalait banner. Of these ten banners, the three Korchin Left-Wing banners situated just north of Fengt'ien were customarily dealt with by the Fengt'ien government. The Gorlos front banner, separated from Kirin by the Willow Palisades and the Sungari River, came under the attention of the Kirin government. The Gorlos rear banner and the Dörbet banner, located north of the Sungari and east of the Nonni River, and the Jalait banner, located west of the Nonni River, were considered to come under the jurisdiction of the Heilungkiang government. The three Korchin Right-Wing banners, surrounded by the Korchin Left-Wing center and rear banners, the Jalait banner, and the Gorlos front banner, came under the supervision of the Fengt'ien government although they were located near Hulun Buir in Heilungkiang.[61] Properly speaking, none of these banners was under the legal jurisdiction of the three Manchurian governments. They were formally but loosely administered by the Bureau of Dependencies in Peking. Throughout the greater part of Ch'ing history, their relationship with the regional authorities in Manchuria consisted primarily of the settlement of disputes between the subjects of the Mongol princes and the military governments on adjoining territories. The gradual encroachment by the military governments upon the Mongol banner authorities was the result of two historical trends: the settlement of Chinese immigrants on the Mongol lands and the penetration of Russian and Japanese influence among the Mongol population. I shall discuss here only the relationships between the Kirin and Heilungkiang governments and their neighboring Mongol banners.

The Dörbet, Jalait, and the two Gorlos banners are located at the lower course of the Nonni River where it joins the Sungari. The soil is rich and water adequate. The land and water routes connecting Kirin with Tsitsihar, and Tsitsihar with Hulan either paralleled the boundaries of these banners or traversed their territories. Because both Kirin and Heilungkiang were entrusted with the maintenance of courier stations and river transport along these routes they came to have certain administrative interest in the territories of these banners. During the Ch'ien-lung reign, Chinese settlers, with the encouragement of the Mongol princes, began to settle in the region of the Gorlos front banner. In 1799 upon the suggestion of the military governor of Kirin, the area of Chinese settlements was organized into the Ch'ang-ch'un sub-prefecture, which was elevated to prefectural status in 1889.[62] Three districts were carved from its territories; Nung-an in 1889, Ch'ang-ling in 1907, and Te-hui in 1910.[63] In Heilungkiang the Jalait banner region was opened to Chinese settlement in 1902, and those of the Gorlos rear banner and the Dörbet banner in 1905.[64] Since these settlement projects were organized by the regional governments under imperial sanction, the net effect was the extension of the political boundaries of the military governments of Heilungkiang and Kirin into the neighboring Mongol lands.

The building of the Chinese Eastern and the South Manchuria railways also compelled the regional governments to extend their control over the Mongol lands which the railways traversed. The railways brought with them foreign political, economic, and military (railway guards) influences into the Mongol territories and the frontier governments could not ignore them. During the Boxer Uprising and the Russo-Japanese War, Russian troops penetrated the areas of the Mongol banners and obtained food and fodder supplies from the Mongols. The Japanese, too, infiltrated agents among the Mongols to seek information and allies.[65] The centuries' old policy of the Ch'ing court to isolate the Mongols from outside influences was no longer workable in view of the changing situation. Because military governors were given the responsibility for frontier defense and the routine conduct of diplomatic relations, the political supervision of the Mongol territories gradually gravitated into the hands of the military governors.

Meanwhile, Mongol reactions to the intrusion of Chinese immigrants into their lands under official sponsorship became a cause for anxiety among the frontier officials. In general, the Mongols were unhappy over this development. The ordinary herders were faced with the shrinkage of their traditional pastures, which was a threat to their livelihood. The opinions of the Mongol aristocracy were divided. Some of them were willing collaborators of the settlement schemes because they shared with the military governments proceeds from the sale of the lands and the land taxes.[66] Some of them were against the imperial policy, either because they were out of power and did not share in the benefits resulting from the alienation of land rights or from a genuine concern over the fate of the Mongol herders, who had either to change their way of life and become cultivators themselves or to try to carry on in less desirable pasture lands. The apprehension and anger of the displaced Mongols found outward expression in the growth of violence within the Mongol territories. There were raids against the immigrant settlements as well as fighting among Mongol factions.[67] Thus, solutions to the problems of restoring peace in the Mongol banners, of preventing the Russians and Japanese from gaining political influence among the Mongols, and of implementing the settlement policy of the court all demanded a high degree of political knowledge and administrative ability from the frontier officials.

The major tasks outlined above were interrelated with each other. They also cut across regional lines and had to be approached with national objectives clearly in mind and by governmental machinery capable of carrying out whatever policies might be adopted by the court. It was clear that the traditional military government staffed primarily by local bannermen with their limited training and cultural horizon would be unequal to the responsibilities that the rapidly changing national and international situation had placed upon them. The time for reorganization had arrived.

7

Reorganization of the Frontier Government

The Boxer Uprising provided the Russians with a perfect excuse to invade Manchuria. Within three months, from July to September 1900, they had occupied all strategic areas from Heilungkiang to Fengt'ien. The Russians intended to remain in Manchuria even after the withdrawal of the allies from Peking. In order to accomplish this end, they tried to force the Peking government to sign treaties that would transform all of Manchuria into a Russian protectorate. The aggressive aims of the Russians aroused strong opposition both among the Chinese and the rival foreign powers, particularly Japan. On March 26, 1902, after intense negotiations and the death of the pro-Russian Li Hung-chang, a Sino-Russian agreement was finally concluded providing for the complete withdrawal of the Russians in three stages within eighteen months. In April 1903, when the second stage of withdrawal was due, the Russians not only reneged on their promise but dispatched more troops into Manchuria and reoccupied Mukden. The intransigent attitude of the Russians ultimately led to the outbreak of the Russo-Japanese War in 1904.

A Letter from Prince Konoe

In May 1901, while the Russians were applying almost unbearable pressure on the Chinese negotiators, with Li Hung-chang in favor of their demands, Prince Konoe Atsumaro, the speaker of the Japanese House of Peers, wrote an identical letter to governors-general Chang Chih-tung and Liu K'un-i, who were leading the opposition to the Russians.

Konoe had toured China in 1898 and had met Liu in Nanking and Chang in Wuchang, making a favorable impression on both men by stressing the cultural ties between China and Japan and the importance of mutual assistance between the two countries.[1] In the 1901 letter,

Konoe stressed the strategic and historic importance of Manchuria to China, the expansionism of Russia, and the danger of China being partitioned by the powers if Russia were permitted to take over Manchuria. In order to forestall the Russians, Konoe advised the adoption of a two-pronged policy: the opening of Manchuria to international trade and development so that Russian influence would be equalized and balanced by other powers; and the reorganization of the existing Manchurian political structure as a means of strengthening the ability of the imperial government to uphold its interest there. The Japanese statesman then outlined a practical program to help achieve the above aims. The following were some of the steps suggested by him, which were incorporated later into the official reorganization plan: amalgamation of the three Manchurian provinces into a single regional authority under the jurisdiction of a governor-general; separate administration of military, civil, financial, and judicial affairs in the provincial government; establishment of an advisory organ in the provincial government for legislative purposes; and employment of Chinese personnel without discrimination.

Konoe also suggested the revision of Chinese laws to conform with international standards and the employment of foreigners as government advisers and court judges, the opening of Manchuria to foreign residence and commerce without restrictions, and the designation of Ying-kow (New-chwang) in South Manchuria as a free port.[2]

In a joint memorial to the throne, dated October 6, 1901, Chang Chih-tung and Liu K'un-i argued strongly against signing a bilateral agreement with Russia under pressure. Adopting Konoe's suggestion, they advocated an open-door policy for Manchuria so as to involve all great powers in its defense against Russia. Furthermore, they strongly endorsed Konoe's program in its entirety and submitted his letter for court perusal together with their own memorial. The court rejected the memorial on the ground that its suggestions would aggravate the difficulties encountered in negotiating with the Russians without any compensating assurance that other powers would come to Chinese aid if the Russians were provoked into occupying Manchuria permanently. The court, however, did not comment directly upon Konoe's plan for political reorganization in Manchuria.[3] Judging from subsequent events, one would have to conclude that the Konoe letter made a deep impression among the policy makers.

The Recommendations of Ch'eng Te-ch'üan

It was during this trying period of Russian occupation that a young Chinese official, Ch'eng Te-ch'üan, distinguished himself in Manchurian affairs.[4] A Szechwanese, Ch'eng joined the staff of Heilungkiang Deputy Military Governor Wen-ch'üan in 1891 as an assistant in charge of diplomatic affairs. During the Sino-Japanese War of 1894–1895 he volunteered to serve at the front under the command of Military Governor I-ke-t'ang-a, who was favorably impressed by his talents. After the end of the war he was awarded the rank of expectant district magistrate and returned to Szechwan for a visit with his parents. In 1897 the new military governor of Heilungkiang, En-che, and the deputy military governor, Shou-shan, asked the court for Ch'eng's return to Heilungkiang. While Ch'eng was passing through Fengt'ien on his way to the frontier, the military governor of Fengt'ien, Tseng-ch'i, sought permission to keep him on his staff. The request was refused by the court and Ch'eng proceeded to Tsitsihar where he was put in charge of the silver mint. In 1900 Shou-shan, a Chinese bannerman and native of Heilungkiang, was promoted to military governor. When the Boxer Uprising reached its peak and the Russians were sending troops to guard the railroads, Shou-shan appointed Ch'eng to coordinate the defense of Aigun, Hulun Buir, and T'ung-ken. The Russians, after routing the garrison forces, surrounded Tsitsihar. Shou-shan, unable to save the city, shot himself to death after entrusting Ch'eng with the task of seeking a truce with the Russians and protecting the lives of thousands of refugees who had congregated in the vicinity of the regional capital. Ch'eng succeeded in convincing the suspicious Russians of the sincerity of his truce proposal. At one point, he even tried to bar with his own body a Russian cannon that was shooting at the troops withdrawing from Tsitsihar. When the Russians discovered the death of Shou-shan, they tried to force Ch'eng to act as military governor. Ch'eng threw himself into the river rather than compromise himself by accepting the Russian proposal. He was rescued and sent to Russian-occupied Hulun Buir as a prisoner. While in Hulun Buir the Russian Red Cross team discovered his plight and secured his release. The Heilungkiang population was so grateful for his role during the conflict that they petitioned the government for his stay to help in the rehabilitation of the region. Upon the recommendation of Acting Military Governor Sa-pao, Ch'eng was promoted to subprefect. In the following years, he was able to revive the local economy by several adroit trade deals. In 1902 he assisted the military governor of Kirin, Ch'ang-shun, in rehabilitating the city of San-hsing. Ch'ang-shun was so impressed by Ch'eng's ability that he recommended the appointment of Ch'eng to a position of greater responsibility. In 1903 Ch'eng was recalled to Peking for an audience with the Kuang-hsü emperor and the Empress Dowager.[5] In 1904, Ch'eng was appointed deputy military governor of Tsitsihar, the first non-bannerman Chinese to attain such a post. In 1906 he was promoted to military governor of Heilungkiang, also an unprecedented appointment. We have outlined Ch'eng's career at some length here because his prestige and knowledge of the frontier affairs made it possible for him to initiate the first steps toward the reorganization of the frontier government in the face of opposition from the local banner population.

The proposals Ch'eng Te-ch'üan submitted to the court in 1903 for dealing with the Manchurian situation contained strong indictments against the state of bureaucratic rule in the frontier. Ch'eng was openly critical of the ability and integrity of the personnel of the military government. He condemned the bureau of military affairs for hamstringing civil authorities in Hulan and Sui-hua so that nothing could be done to improve the administration in the districts of Chinese settlement. As an example of official malfeasance, he cited the fact that village chiefs were known to pay local authorities bribes of several thousand strings of cash in order to be appointed to their posts, which exercised authority over areas as large as districts or departments in China proper. These village chiefs publicly installed instruments of punishment in their homes, levied taxes and other exactions upon the villagers, and obtained annual incomes exceeding ten thousand strings of cash. Similarly, local officials in Hulan enriched themselves by pocketing much of the taxes paid into the local treasury.[6]

Ch'eng was concerned with the lack of civil officials in such districts as Aigun, Mergen, Buteha, and Hulun Buir, where, except for traders, all settlers were looked upon with antagonism by the local population and officials. He recommended the installation of civil authorities in such strategic areas as Aigun, Hulun Buir, San-hsing, Ninguta, and Hun-ch'un, where railroad and waterways converged; and where it was not possible to do so, he urged the selection of well-educated and qualified men as deputy military governors for these areas rather than such persons as the Aigun deputy military governor, who was illiterate in both Chinese and Manchu, and the Hulun Buir deputy military governor, who was appointed despite having been previously censured for official misconduct.[7]

As for the settlement projects, Ch'eng reported that the banner officials in the military governor's office had taken over the best lands, which they leased to settlers who were required to pay for the land as well as all improvements. When the virgin soil began to yield good harvests, these bannermen landlords levied a rent of six piculs of grain per *shang* on the tenants while they themselves paid only 660 copper coins in land tax to the state.[8]

Ch'eng remarked to the court that officialdom in China traditionally avoided taking initiatives that might upset the established order. He stressed that officials must now break this habit of the past and really try to achieve an orderly program of progress. He did not believe that Russia was ready to take over Manchuria entirely but was waiting to see how determined China would be in recovering the occupied territories. Japan's demand for the withdrawal of Russian troops, Ch'eng warned, was not due to its friendship for China but only to assure its share of spoils. He, therefore, recommended that the government press for the withdrawal of Russian troops through all diplomatic means available while undertaking a program of development for Manchuria to reassure the population that the government would not abandon the land.[9]

After his appointments as deputy military governor, Ch'eng wrote a letter to the Grand Council in the autumn of 1904 in which he urged the abolition of military government in Manchuria and the establishment of civil rule. The following were the major arguments he used in presenting his case:[10]

Lack of qualifications among local bannermen as administrators. Local bannermen and tribes, out of touch with the modern world, clung to their prejudices against outsiders. They considered the land their own property, refusing to countenance changes that might injure their immediate interests. Their traditional education, limited to the Manchu language and the traditional military arts, did not provide them with the necessary training to meet contemporary administrative requirements. Appointments and promotions in the military government followed age-old precedents without any regard to the qualifications of the appointees. The habit of shifting responsibility was too deeply ingrained among the officers to expect them to accomplish anything worthwhile.

Factionalism among local bannermen. The local bannermen were accustomed to cover up each other's wrongdoings. If the military governor and the deputy military governor acted against their interests, the local bannermen would retaliate either by ignoring orders or by initiating a campaign of slander. Since they outnumbered their superiors from the capital, they inevitably won out in the end, forcing the latter to seek compromise.

The distrustful nature of local bannermen. Any effort to explain the precarious situation of the frontier to the local banner officers and to win their support for a program of long-range development would be met initially with incomprehension, followed by suspicion, which would turn finally into covert resistance.

The necessity for reorganizing the frontier into provinces. Since the local banner officers could not be relied upon to carry out a program of modernization, the only recourse would be to utilize outside talents and replace the military government with a civil administration. However, the reorganization would proceed in gradual stages because of the lack of funds and the inevitable obstruction of the bannermen. It would be best to follow the Kirin example of installing civil governments in areas where the size of the population justified them. The magistrates would be chosen from men experienced in frontier affairs. They would be responsible directly to the military governor and the deputy military governor and the local banner organization would be forbidden to interfere with their work.

Ch'eng clearly realized how much opposition he would encounter when he tried to change the *status quo* in Heilungkiang, but he felt compelled to make a start because China was racing against time and the ultimate fate of the frontier depended upon how much effort he and others like him could put into a program of local development. For this reason he was willing to step on the toes of the local bannermen and risked intrigues directed against himself.

Ch'eng's suggestion for the overhauling of the frontier government coincided with the contrite mood of the court. The Boxer Uprising had totally discredited the diehard conservatives who gambled the fate of the nation upon the strength of a superstitious mass movement. On January 29, 1901, the Empress Dowager, bowing to the inevitable, announced the court's intention of instituting political reforms. From 1901 to 1905 some beginnings were made in the direction of revamping the government bureaucracy but no drastic changes occurred.[11] In 1906 after the conclusion of the Russo-Japanese War, China was forced to cede to Japan all the rights that the Russians had enjoyed in South Manchuria as well as additional privileges.[12] The Manchurian situation was becoming more precarious than ever, for it was now surrounded on three sides by two aggressive neighbors.

Meanwhile the half-hearted attempts at reform by the court disappointed and alienated large segments of the public. The revolutionary movement was gaining momentum. The T'ung-meng hui, an alliance of various revolutionary groups led by Sun Yat-sen, was formed in Tokyo in 1905. The reform movement led by K'ang Yu-wei and Liang Ch'i-ch'ao, which had been temporarily suppressed by the Empress Dowager in 1905, regained its strength and demanded the immediate establishment of a constitutional monarchy. The defeat of Russia by Japan, argued the reformers, proved the superiority of a constitutional government over an absolute monarchy. Unable to go against the tide any longer, the court dispatched a government mission to investigate the various forms of constitutional governments abroad. Upon the return of the mission in 1906, the court announced its intention to prepare for the establishment of a constitutional government. A decision was made to eliminate appointments to the bureaucracy based upon ethnic distinction. In other words, Chinese were made eligible to posts hitherto held exclusively by Manchus.[13] It was in this atmosphere that Ch'eng Te-ch'üan, now acting military governor, submitted his memorial dated December 3, 1905, on the rehabilitation of Heilungkiang. On January 13, 1906, he received the approval of the court to carry out his program. The following were proposals related to governmental reform:[14]

The elimination of the supernumeraries and craftsmen from the banner force. The supernumeraries, who were part reservists and part military colonists, and the craftsmen, who manufactured such articles as bows, arrows and saddles, were no longer necessary adjuncts to the banner force. Their maintenance, Ch'eng told the court, cost more to the government than their contributions.

The elimination of the firearm battalions and the river patrol from the banner force. Both of these services were outdated by the development of modern arms and transport.

The reduction of the number of personnel in the bureau of punishments.

This proposal was made because the bureau's work had been increasingly taken over by civil magistrates as the areas of settlement expanded.

The reduction of the number of personnel in the office of the T'ung-ken deputy military governor. The office was originally established to take charge of the settlement of bannermen on the virgin lands of T'ung-ken. Since only a small number of bannermen had settled there in contrast to the large number of Chinese, a civil government was then instituted. Consequently, the office of the deputy military governor was overstaffed.

The elimination of banner granaries, military colonists, and courier stations. Most of the granaries had been destroyed by the Russians in 1900 and had not been rebuilt. The courier stations were outdated by the development of modern communications and transport. The military colonists contributed only a small part of their harvest to the state while occupying a large expanse of land. The government would benefit more by changing the status of the military colonists to civilian colonists.

Broadening of the eligibility of candidates to various banner posts. Hitherto the banner posts were divided into Manchu, Mongol, and Chinese bannermen posts as well as unrestricted and restricted posts. (Restricted posts, *chuan ch'üeh*, were usually those set aside for tribal peoples in Hulun Buir and Buteha, while unrestricted posts, *kung-ch'üeh,* were opened to any qualified bannerman.) These limitations tended to bar the advancement of talented persons who happened to fall into categories with limited openings. Thereafter, with the exception of posts reserved to tribal peoples, all posts were to be opened to all qualified candidates.

The opening of Hulun Buir to agricultural settlement as a precautionary measure against the Russians.

Although Ch'eng's proposals did not constitute a frontal assault upon the military government, their combined effect would be the whittling down of the entrenched influence of the local bannerman elite by providing more opportunities for the employment of Chinese talents and by the outright elimination of some military posts which would eventually be replaced by civilian posts. It was no wonder that he aroused the ire of the local elite. In 1907 he was impeached for malfeasance in office on the charges that he wrongly disciplined a number of banner officers, changed the rules of land sale in T'ung-ken, emancipated the slaves of the Buteha tribes, and misappropriated funds. These charges were investigated by Imperial Commissioner Hsü Shih-ch'ang, who absolved Ch'eng of any wrongdoing but stated significantly that his land policy had incurred the anger of the local bannermen. Hsü recommended that the court accede to Ch'eng's desire to be relieved of his post because of his alleged arthritic condition.[15]

The Imperial Commissioners' Report

The resignation of Ch'eng Te-ch'üan turned out to be an ephemeral victory for the local bannermen. Following the September 1, 1906, edict announcing its intention to reorganize the governmental system of the empire as a preparatory step toward the establishment of a constitutional monarchy, the court appointed fourteen high officials, among them Hsü Shih-ch'ang, Tsai-chen, and Yuan Shih-k'ai, to draw up plans for the reorganization of the central and provincial governments. A committee composed of Prince Ch'ing, Grand Secretary Sun Chia-nai, and Grand Councillor Ch'ü Hung-chi was entrusted with the task of examining the draft proposals prior to submitting them for imperial approval.[16] On November 6 the reorganization plan for the central government was promulgated.[17] In December 1906, on the suggestion of the military governor of Fengt'ien, Chao Er-sun, the court dispatched Hsü Shih-ch'ang and Tsai-chen, the ministers of Civil Affairs and of Commerce respectively, on a fact-finding mission to Manchuria.

The choice of Hsü Shih-ch'ang (1855–1939) and Tsai-chen as imperial commissioners to Manchuria indicated that the court was inclined to take seriously their recommendations. Tsai-chen was the son of Prince Ch'ing, the most powerful political figure of that period. Hsü was a protégé and close friend of Yuan Shih-k'ai, who was an ally of Prince Ch'ing in court politics and the creator of the Pei-yang Army, the best fighting force in the empire.[18] Unlike Tsai-chen, who was a mediocre figure remembered for his greed, Hsü was a man of ability. He obtained his *chin-shih* or metropolitan degree in 1886. In 1897 Yuan Shih-k'ai chose him, in spite of his lack of military background, as the chief-of-staff of the Pei-yang Army. In 1905 he was promoted probationary grand councillor and then concurrently minister of police and grand councillor. In the following year he was appointed minister of Civil Affairs—a post resulting from the merger of the ministries of Police and of Civil Appointment. Thus when Hsü went to Manchuria in 1906 he had an intimate knowledge of the political machinery of the imperial government and the backing of powerful colleagues.

The imperial commissioners toured Manchuria for three months. Their joint memorial, written by Hsü, jolted the court out of any lingering complacency. In regard to Kirin and Heilungkiang, their findings stressed the following points:[19]

The importance of immediate action. The commissioners were convinced that both Russia and Japan were aiming at territorial expansion. Unless China acted quickly to tighten its hold upon the Three Eastern Provinces, they stated, it would be difficult to prevent Russia and Japan from striking out for fresh conquests from their respective bases at Harbin and the Liao-tung Peninsula. The court, therefore, should not be satisfied with inconsequential remedies but should be prepared to initiate a well-thought-out program that would strengthen Manchuria militarily, economically, and politically for the struggle ahead.

Civil administration in Kirin. There were still too few local civil administrative units in Kirin, especially along the Sino-Russian frontier. On the other hand, there were too many corrupt and inefficient officials in the military government. The imperial commissioners received from the inhabitants well over a hundred petitions and complaints during the few days they were in Kirin city.

Agricultural settlements in Kirin. Many of the Chinese immigrants leased land from the bannermen who did not have to pay land tax. Since Kirin had suffered least from the Boxer Uprising and had sold large quantities of supplies to the Russians during the Russo-Japanese War, the populace, including the bannermen, was well-off. Opium growing, which in San-hsing and Yun-ch'un occupied thirty to forty percent of the land, was a serious problem.

Industry in Kirin. Neither the officials nor the people paid any attention to the development of industry. The importation of foreign commodities had been rising steadily.

The Kirin police force. The police was first organized in 1905 and a police department was established in 1906. Most of the policemen were illiterates and often deserted the force with their weapons and uniforms. The police officers were drawn from former soldiers or clerks. The fire brigade did not have any firefighting equipment.

Kirin finance. The annual revenue amounted to about 2,510,000 taels, of which 2,121,000 taels came from likin, excise taxes, customs, and commercial taxes; and about 388,000 taels came from land taxes. Of the annual appropriations, expenses for training a new army took about 1,200,000 taels and additional military expenses took about 600,000 taels. The rest was used for official salaries and administrative outlays. Tax collection was dispersed among various bureaus without central supervision and much of the money collected went into the pockets of the officials. There was a serious lack of silver and copper coins. Consequently, Russian ruble notes dominated the market. Local officials printed government notes to compete against the Russians. But the oversupply of government notes, which were backed by insufficient capital, caused great distress to the population.

Civil administration in Heilungkiang. Some progress in civil administration had been made. With the exception of Aigun, Hulun Buir, and Mergen where the old system was still in existence, areas like Tsitsihar, Hulan, T'ung-ken, and Buteha were changing to civil administration. There was a dearth of administrative talents. Military Governor Ch'eng Te-ch'üan had set up a school in his yamen to train candidates for various posts in the province. Police administration was still in an embryonic state.

Living conditions in Heilungkiang. The bannermen, who relied mainly on government stipends and avoided physical labor, were generally living in poverty. Agricultural immigrants, through hard work, were able to reap better harvests from the rich soil than they had ever done in Chihli and Shantung. Railroad workers had become unemployed since the completion of the railway and many of them had drifted into banditry.

Heilungkiang finance. The annual land tax totaled some 200,000 taels. Excise and miscellaneous taxes totaled some 750,000 taels. The biggest item in appropriations went to the military, amounting to about 400,000 taels. Some of the deficits were made up by subsidies from other provinces, which varied from 30,000 to 70,000 taels. Land sales throughout the years had totaled about 4,570,000 taels. After deducting administrative expenses and reimbursing the Mongol banners, about 1,500,000 taels still remained in the treasury. It was reported that this fund had been set aside to finance various government programs under consideration. There was also a dire shortage of hard currency in the market, so that the ruble had become the most common medium of exchange. A government bank with a capitalization of 500,000 taels, composed both of official and private shares had been set up with the specific purpose of issuing notes for circulation. However, the bank had already issued notes worth some 14 to 15 million strings of copper cash. Grave consequences were foreseen as a result of such mismanagement.

The imperial commissioners also found unsatisfactory conditions in the fields of education, military training, and economic development and were particularly disturbed by the aggressive attitudes of both the Russians and the Japanese on negotiations over such matters as railroad lands, lumbering rights, and Korean immigration.

Their report made a deep impression upon the court and several audiences were held between the commissioners and the emperor and Empress Dowager. The commissioners were instructed to suggest remedial actions which would assure the nation's control over Manchuria. Some days later they presented a secret memorial to the throne which eventually became the guide to government policy in Manchuria. The memorial proposed the following lines of action:[20]

Encouragement of colonization projects. The commissioners believed that colonization was essential for the development of Manchuria. They dismissed the objection that colonization interfered with the livelihood of the bannermen by castigating those who still wished to draw a line between bannermen and Chinese and reminded them that if Manchuria were lost to foreign nations, the bannermen would lose whatever they had.

They identified the Heilungkiang bannermen as most resistant to change because their officers were most afraid of losing their positions and the soldiers their benefits. The commissioners suggested that because the banner force no longer resembled an army, it would be much better to do away with the differentiation between bannermen and civilians. To ease the transition, the banner soldiers should still be paid their stipends and their officers be placed in suitable jobs.

Improvement of transportation. Because of the vastness of Manchuria, the commissioners pointed out, adequate means of transportation were necessary for its defense; otherwise, the foreign nations who controlled the major systems of transportation would have the manpower of the region at their disposal. For this reason, China should redeem the Japanese-built Hsin-min–Fengt'ien railway line and build as soon as possible the Ch'ang-ch'un–Kirin line, the Tsitsihar–Aigun line, the Kirin–Hun-ch'un line, the Harbin–San-hsing line, and the Hsin-min–Tsitsihar line. They emphasized that the fate of Manchuria was dependent upon whoever controlled its railroads.

Administrative integration. The commissioners believed that the problems of Fengt'ien, Heilungkiang, and Kirin could not be solved individually by the three separate military governments but must be approached regionally. This was especially true in matters concerning public finance, military reorganization, and diplomatic negotiations. They suggested, therefore, that in view of the gravity of the situation the court should disregard all precedents and appoint a single person as governor-general of the Three Eastern Provinces. The governor-general should rotate his official presence in each of the provinces and have complete control over their civil and military administrations except important diplomatic negotiations, which should be conducted only after consultation with the Ministry of Foreign Affairs. Under him there should be a governor in each of the three provinces who would be in charge of civil affairs and personnel administration. The governors, however, would have less power than their counterparts in China proper. The commissioners specifically recommended that the proposed governor-general should be given as much political latitude in Manchuria as Tseng Kuo-fan and Hu Lin-i were given in the Yangtze provinces during the T'ai-p'ing Rebellion; that is, he should have complete control over all fiscal, personnel, and administrative decisions.

The importance of being resolute. The development and defense of Manchuria would require large sums of money. Because the national treasury was quite empty, the commissioners urged the court to borrow the money from either domestic or foreign sources. But the court, they advised, must not procrastinate; otherwise, the foreign nations would discount China's determination to hold Manchuria and would redouble their aggressive acts, while the local inhabitants would become demoralized. They cautioned the court against vacillation in carrying out reforms by saying that the political structure of the state must change with the times. To reassure the conservative-minded, they pointed out that today's innovations would become the constitutional heritage of future generations.

It was a bold memorial, for it openly advocated the abdication of Manchu influence in the traditional political preserve of the Manchus and the concentration of regional political powers in the hands of a single governor-general. Both were sensitive issues at that time. By the turn of the century, antagonism between Chinese and Manchus was becoming a national political factor. The revolutionaries harped on the theme of the alien origin of the Manchu dynasty and the unequal distribution of political power between the two peoples, while the reformers, by insisting on constitutional government, were seen by the Manchu conservatives as attempting to overwhelm the Manchus through the electoral strength of the Chinese. Furthermore, since the T'ai-p'ing Rebellion, the growth of viceregal power among the provincial governors and governors-general, many of them Chinese, was a cause for apprehension to the Manchu elite. Consequently, beginning in 1906 when political and administrative reforms were being initiated in China proper, there was a growing struggle for power between Chinese and Manchu factions in the court as well as attempts by the central government to reduce the autonomous powers of the provincial governments, particularly in the fields of finance and defense.[21] For these reasons, the memorial of Hsü Shih-ch'ang and Tsai-chen might not have carried so much weight as it did if these men had not had the political support of Prince Ch'ing and Yuan Shih-k'ai.

Antecedents for Reorganization

Antecedents for the reorganization of the Manchurian administration had been created in Sheng-ching as early as 1876. In 1875, Ts'ung-shih, the acting military governor, memorialized the throne on the necessity of overhauling the political structure in Fengt'ien to overcome the divisive effects of the parallel lines of authority which existed between his office and the Sheng-ching five boards.[22] Basically, the troubles stemmed from the growing importance of civil affairs over military functions of the regional government, a problem that had also become an overriding concern in Kirin and Heilungkiang in the last decades of the nineteenth century. The military governor, nominally the head of the government, found himself shackled by the elaborate checks-and-balances safeguards installed in the past era.

In his memorial Ts'ung-shih maintained that the root of political ills in Sheng-ching was the disharmony between the civil and banner bureaucracies. The military governor was unable to impose his will on the officials of the five boards, particularly the head of the Board of Revenue, which had concurrent jurisdiction over prefectural affairs.[23] The prefects and magistrates who governed the local civilian population were hamstrung in their duties by the five boards and the zonal banner officers. This was true especially in the administration of justice. When disputes arose involving bannermen and civilians, the civilian party would bring the case to the magistrate's court, while the bannerman would take it to the Board of Punishments. The result was a stalemate, which provided excellent opportunities for bribery and extortion and infinite delay in the settlement of disputes.[24] The zonal banner officers had the responsibility of keeping peace, but the legal and administrative barriers separating the banner and civilian population also impeded their effectiveness. The bannermen were all related to each other by blood or friendship; consequently, they tended to let personal sentiments take precedence over impartiality in the conduct of public affairs. When crimes were committed by bannermen, they could count upon their *niru* officers and powerful clansmen to extricate them from any legal difficulty.[25]

Ts'ung-shih's recommendations for improving the quality of the Sheng-ching government were put into effect in 1876. The military governor was now given direct control of the boards of War and Punishments and clear supervisory power over the other three boards. He also regained the authority to oversee the administration of the metropolitan prefecture. The metropolitan prefect was given a rank equivalent to that of the provincial governor and administrative authority over the banner population. The zonal banner officers were deprived of any right to interfere in the administration of justice; their responsibilities were restricted to the management of banner land records and the maintenance of public order.[26] These changes represented the first step toward the elimination of the special political status of Manchuria. The second step was taken in 1905 when the five boards and the office of the metropolitan prefect were abolished, giving the military governor undivided authority over all provincial affairs.[27]

The Reorganization Plan of Hsü Shih-ch'ang

On April 20, 1907, the court announced the elimination of the posts of military governors of Fengt'ien, Kirin, and Heilungkiang and the institution of civil governors for the three provinces. Hsü Shih-ch'ang was appointed governor-general of the Three Eastern Provinces with the concurrent title of imperial commissioner. T'ang Shao-i was appointed acting Fengt'ien governor, Chu Chia-pao acting Kirin governor, and Tuan Chih-kuei acting Heilungkiang governor. (Tuan was dismissed before he took office, and on May 7 Ch'eng Te-ch'üan was appointed in his stead.)[28]

On the same day that it announced Hsü's appointment, the court also instructed Hsü to present his plan on the organization of provincial governments in Manchuria. On May 22 the court approved Hsü's plan, which had been agreed upon by the governors of Fengt'ien and Kirin. The governor of Heilungkiang was not in Peking and did not take part in the deliberations. The plan included the following major proposals.[29]

1. The governor-general should be clearly designated as the highest official in the three provinces with supervisory authority over the governors. Within the provincial government there should be established a *ch'eng-hsüan t'ing* or chancery to coordinate administrative matters, including the management of personnel, and a *tzu-i t'ing* or advisory council to make recommendations on legislative matters. Below the chancery and the advisory council there should be established the following bureaus: foreign affairs, banner affairs, civil affairs, education, finance, industries, and Mongol affairs. The chancery should be headed by a *tso ts'an-tsan* (left councillor) and the advisory council by a *yu ts'an-tsan* (right councillor). The seven bureaus should each be directed by a bureau chief. In order for the governor-general and the governors to exercise jurisdiction over the banner forces, the governor-general should have the concurrent military rank of *chiang-chün* (general) and the governor of *fu tu-t'ung* (lieutenant general).

2. All the administrative offices in each of the three provinces should be housed in one building so that the officials, through daily conferences, could expedite the transaction of public affairs and eliminate excess paper work.

3. The role of provincial governor should be definitely subordinated to that of the governor-general. All communications to the court should be presented together by the governor-general and the governor of the province concerned. When the governor-general was absent, the routine business of a province should be decided by the governor but important matters must be referred to the governor-general. In case of emergency, the governor should simultaneously notify the court and the governor-general of the measures that he had taken to meet the emergency. All official communications from the lower level governments in the province should be delivered to the chancery where they would be sent to the appropriate bureaus for consideration. The course of action decided upon by each of the bureaus would then be presented to the governor and governor-general for approval.

4. The judicial affairs of the provinces should come under the jurisdiction of the *t'i-fa-shih* (judicial commissioner) who should have his own yamen but come under the supervision of the governor and the governor-general.

5. More local governments should be established, especially in Heilungkiang. The district governments should be eliminated. The departmental, sub-prefectural, and prefectural governments should be controlled by a number of *ping-pei tao* (military circuit intendants), who should also have jurisdiction over garrison troops, thus eliminating the post of deputy military governor.

6. The salaries of the officials should be set higher than those in China proper to compensate for the higher cost of living and to minimize the temptation for official corruption.

7. The military affairs of the three provinces should be supervised by a *tu-lien ch'u* or provincial staff for troop training, which would be directed by the governor-general and assisted by the three governors. It should be made responsible for the training and administration of all military forces including the banner forces.

8. The governor-general should have the privilege of seeking an imperial audience whenever there were important matters warranting consultations with the court. The governors should have the privilege of visiting neighboring provinces for consultation on common problems.

9. Because the governor-general also held the posts of imperial commissioner and general of the garrison forces of the Three Eastern Provinces, he alone should have the authority to decide important matters concerning the banner forces relating to all three provinces.

10. The governor-general by himself or in agreement with the governors should be accorded the privilege of recommending personnel to all levels of the local government within the three provinces, and the power to disregard, if necessary, provisions in the existing code of civil appointments.

11. Because of the strategic location of the Three Eastern Provinces and the recent origin of the local civil governments, all existing precedents governing provincial administration should be relaxed to permit greater flexibility in solving local problems.

The most striking feature of Hsü's proposals was the impressive powers to be entrusted in the hands of the governor-general, who was to be given undisputed control in the conduct of regional civil, military, financial, and diplomatic affairs and over the personnel of the provincial governments. There was no longer to be any mechanism of checks-and-balances within the provincial structure. The governor by himself could not issue orders to the local governments or communicate directly with the court. Nor was the central government to retain direct supervision over financial, personnel, and military affairs of the three provinces. In many respects, Hsü's scheme merely formalized the greatly enhanced powers of governors-general during and after the T'ai-p'ing Rebellion.[30] But its acceptance by the court in a period when steps were being taken to reduce the powers of provincial authorities showed how seriously the court viewed the situation in Manchuria.

Perhaps the court was impressed by Hsü's sense of urgency as he asked for all the powers that he would need to push through his program of reform and development. He castigated the conservative critics by comparing them to the court officials of the late Ming period, who interfered with the work of able frontier officers by irresponsible and ruinous criticism.[31] To the court's credit, it gave him free rein during his tenure of office.

Hsü took up his office in June 1907 and resigned in the first lunar month of 1909 after the death of both the Empress Dowager and the emperor. He was succeeded by a Mongol bannerman, Hsi-liang, who was transferred to Jehol after the Wu-ch'ang uprising in 1911. The last governor-general of the Three Provinces was Chao Er-sun. Chu Chia-pao, the first Kirin governor, was transferred in 1908 and succeeded by Ch'en Chao-ch'ang. Ch'eng Te-ch'üan resigned from the governorship of Heilungkiang in 1908 and was succeeded by Chou Shu-mo. Both Ch'en and Chou stayed in office until 1911; but Chou was succeeded by Sung Hsiao-lien in the last days of the dynasty.[32]

The Provincial Government of Kirin

Upon arriving in Manchuria, Hsü toured the provinces and conferred with the governors on the reorganization plan. He arrived at Kirin on December 11 and in a memorial dated December 28 and approved by the court on January 21, 1908, Hsü and the Kirin governor, Chu Chia-pao, suggested certain modifications of Hsü's original proposals.[33] By April 1, 1908, a reorganized provincial government was beginning to function in Kirin.[34]

The new government was dominated by the executive branch despite tentative steps taken to separate the legislative and judicial functions from the executive. Assisting the governor-general and the governor (called the chief executives thereafter) in policy making was the Hsing-cheng hui-i ch'u or Administrative Council. Its membership included the chief executives as chairmen of the council, the directors of the government bureaus and the circuit intendants as councillors, and citizens experienced in law and government, as well as prefects and magistrates, as associate councillors. The council was convened periodically to discuss important administrative and legislative matters within the province. It was established in August 1909 by Hsi-liang and Ch'en Chao-ch'ang in accordance with the instructions issued by the Hsien-cheng pien-ch'a kuan or Committee for Drawing Up Regulations for Constitutional Government.[35] Although it was not provided for in Hsü's proposal, in essence, it institutionalized and extended Hsü's idea of gathering all important provincial offices in one building so that the officials could confer daily on administrative problems.[36] The life span of the council was too short and information on it too meager for anyone to appraise its effectiveness. Judging from its composition the council was probably too unwieldy to be a decision-making body, but it could have been utilized as a channel through which the chief executives explained their policies to the gentry class represented by the citizen members.

Because of its smaller size and intimate relationship with the chief executives, the Kung-shu wen-an ch'u or Secretariat probably exercised greater influence in the formulation and execution of public policies. The Secretariat took the place of the chancery and advisory council that Hsü had recommended and installed in Fengt'ien but decided was unnecessary for Kirin and Heilungkiang. It combined the functions of the above two organs as well as those of the traditional private secretariat of the provincial governor and governor-general.[37]

The Secretariat was divided into four sections: confidential matters, civil service grading, correspondence, and general affairs. The higher officials of the Secretariat included a number of secretaries of first, second, or third rank and the chief and deputy chiefs of the sections. The secretaries were responsible for the drafting of decrees and orders and the examination of regulations proposed by various government bureaus. The different sections of the Secretariat handled the flow of incoming and outgoing documents and correspondence, the keeping of records, the custody of the Provincial Seal of Office, and the business affairs of the Secretariat. As advisers to the chief executives, the secretaries might be asked to participate in official conferences.[38]

The public business of the provincial government was distributed among a number of bureaus. With the exception of the Bureau of Education, which was set up in 1905, all of them were established in 1907. Each bureau was headed by a director and assisted by section chiefs. The

Min-cheng ssu or Bureau of Civil Administration was divided into five sections:

1. The civil affairs section was in charge of such matters as the promotion of local self-government, custody of population registers, establishment of charitable institutions, surveillance of public morals, and preservation of ancient sites and monuments.

2. The police affairs section was in charge of the training and organization of police units.

3. The geographical survey section was responsible for the surveying and mapping of the public lands.

4. The public works section took over the functions of the Bureau of Public Works, which had existed under the military government, and was also made responsible for such innovations as the construction of modern roads and parks.

5. The general affairs section, the housekeeping unit of the Bureau, was also entrusted with matters concerning sanitation and public health, as well as the eradication of opium addiction.[39]

Provincial educational affairs were originally the responsibility of the *hsüeh-cheng* or educational commissioner of Fengt'ien. In January 1905 an Office of Education was set up in Kirin city and a number of schools with modernized curricula were opened for primary and normal students. Later in the year, as a part of the reform program, the court abolished the post of educational commissioner throughout the nation and substituted a system of provincial educational bureaus directly responsible to the governors and the governors-general.[40] The Bureau of Education, in accordance with the regulations of the Ministry of Education in Peking, was composed as follows:

1. The general affairs section handled all important correspondence and documents.

2. The general education section was responsible for primary, secondary, and normal education.

3. The accounting section took charge of the financial matters.

4. The textbook section was responsible for the compilation and examination of teaching materials. The establishment of the special education section, which would have been responsible for higher education and the sending of students abroad, and the vocational education section was postponed until a later date.[41]

The Bureau of Foreign Affairs was probably the most responsible and thankless division in the provincial government. As early as 1896 Yen-mao, the military governor of Kirin, had established a Kirin Foreign Affairs General Office at the city of Kirin which took charge of all matters relating to border disputes, and railroads, lumbering and mining concessions. In 1899 a General Office for Railway Diplomacy was set up at Harbin where the Russians had located their headquarters for the construction of the Chinese Eastern Railway. Branch offices were also set up at various places along the route. These offices were responsible for the collection of tariff and the adjudication of disputes between the railway company and the Chinese. In 1905 the military governors of Kirin and Heilungkiang jointly requested the appointment of a circuit intendant for foreign affairs and tariff collection to be stationed at Harbin. The request was granted and the post of *Pin-chiang-kuan tao,* or intendant of Pin-chiang Custom, was created with the concurrent title of associate director of the Office of Railway Diplomacy. In 1907 an Office of Foreign Affairs was also set up in Ch'ang-ch'un with the local prefect as director.[42]

When the provincial government was reorganized later in 1907, the Kirin Foreign Affairs General Office became the Bureau of Foreign Affairs with jurisdiction over the Harbin office, but the Ch'ang-ch'un office was put under the charge of the Southwest Circuit Intendant. The internal administration of the bureau was divided among three sections: international trade, boundary treaties, and general affairs. In 1909 all local foreign affairs offices, with the exception of the Harbin office, were abolished and the conduct of local negotiations was entrusted to the four circuit intendants.[43] Among them the *Pin-chiang-kuan tao*, whose full title was the Kirin Northwest Military Circuit intendant and concurrent director of the Pin-chiang Custom, had the most difficult position, for he was responsible not only to the governor-general and the Kirin governor but also to the Heilungkiang governor, the Ministry of Foreign Affairs, and the Custom Office.[44]

Prior to 1907, the financial administration of the province was divided among the bureau of revenue in the Military Governor's Office and various taxing authorities without any system of central accounting. The reorganization plan put all the agencies under the jurisdiction of the Bureau of Finance, which had the overall responsibility for the collection of taxes, the disbursement of appropriations, and the auditing of accounts. It had jurisdiction over all local tax offices, the Office of Government Scrips, and Office of Colonization.[45]

Fengt'ien and Kirin were the two provinces in which the imperial government experimented with the removal of the judicial process from the authority of local magistrates. In 1907 the Kirin Bureau of Justice was established to supervise the administration of civil and criminal justice for the civil population. The traditional bureau of punishments, which since 1882 had been made responsible only for cases involving bannermen, was abolished and its functions transferred to the Bureau of Justice. The latter bureau was divided into four sections: civil suits, criminal suits, prisons, and general affairs.[46]

The provincial court system was established according to regulations laid down by the Ministry of Justice. It comprised a Supreme Court and a number of appellate and lower courts. Because of the lack of funds and qualified personnel, up to 1898, only the Supreme Court, the Appellate Courts for Kirin, Pin-chou, and Ch'ang-ch'un, and two lower courts for Kirin had been established. Where the courts had not yet been set up, the local magistrates still exercised the traditional function of adjudications.[47] Together with the courts, a similar hierarchy of procurators' offices was expected to be established. But because of a similar lack of funds and personnel they were located only in Kirin, Pin-chou, and Ch'ang-ch'un.[48]

Although the separation of the judiciary from the executive was the goal of the new system, the provincial chief executives still retained a large measure of control over the administration of justice through their control of the Bureau of Justice, which was responsible for the appointment, promotion, and discipline of the judges and procurators.[49]

The *ch'üan-yeh tao* or intendant for economic development, a position established in 1907, had the responsibility of administering government industrial enterprises, standardizing weights and measures, promoting private industries and commerce, conducting experimental farms, running public utilities, and generally concerning itself with matters relating to economic development. It was composed of five sections: general affairs, agriculture, industry, commerce, and post and communication. By 1908 it had already established the following enterprises: an agricultural experimental station, a bureau of mining survey, an association for agricultural study, an electric light company, a forest products company, a government steamship company, a mail ship company, and a bureau of colonization and mining.[50]

The Office of Banner Affairs took over most of the functions originally exercised by the bureau of military affairs in the military government. It was composed of four sections: The rites section was responsible for the sending of tribute, the holding of sacrificial rites, and other ceremonial matters; the military section was responsible for the administration of the personnel of the banner force; the finance section took care of the salaries and monetary benefits of the banner force, the taxation of banner lands, and the registration of the banner population. The general affairs section was in charge of miscellaneous duties such as the internal administration of the office, the surveying of occupation opportunities for bannermen, and the education and training of bannermen for their eventual integration into the general population.[51] The office had under its jurisdiction not only the regular banner force but also the Heje tribes of the lower Amur basin.[52] Since the elimination of the political and social differences between the Manchus and Chinese was the stated objective of the imperial government, the Office of Banner Affairs was established with the view to easing the transitional pains of the banner population rather than the perpetuation of the existing differentiation between the banner and the civil population. For this reason the reeducation and retraining of the bannermen to prepare them for the future was a key provision in provincial reorganization plans.[53]

Attached to the Office of Banner Affairs was the Office of Mongol Affairs. In the fourth lunar month of 1907, a Bureau of Mongol Affairs for the Three Eastern Provinces was established in Fengt'ien at Hsü Shih-ch'ang's suggestion. It was the opinion of Hsü that the traditional system of governing the Mongol lands was no longer adequate to safeguard the national interest against the machinations of Russia and Japan, both of whom were interested in extending their influence into the Mongol territories for economic, political, and strategic reasons. Hsü advocated revision of the traditional system to permit a more direct administration of Mongol affairs by provincial authorities, the colonization of the Mongol lands and the building of railroads as defense measures, and the reeducation of the Mongol peoples to prepare them for adjustment to the changed environment.[54] The first director of the Bureau of Mongol Affairs was Chu Ch'i-ch'ien who traveled extensively in the Mongol territories to gather information on various aspects of the Mongol problem from the point of view of the provincial administrators.[55] In 1908, the Kirin Office of Mongol Affairs was set up to facilitate the implementation of Hsü's policy. In practice, most of the efforts were directed merely toward the opening of the Mongol lands for Chinese colonization.[56]

There were, on the provincial government level, also administrative organs for military affairs and for the promotion of constitutional government, as well as a semi-legislative body, the *tzu-i chü* or provincial assembly. These will be discussed under separate headings and in conjunction with similar establishments in Heilungkiang.

Local Governments in Kirin

Prior to 1907, the growth of local civil governments in Kirin had been due to the gradual, unplanned expansion of inhabited areas. After 1907, government promotion played an important role. In a memorial submitted to the throne on April 2, 1909, Hsü Shih-ch'ang proposed the immediate elevation from lower levels of six prefectures, one sub-prefecture, two departments, and three districts; the immediate establishment of two circuit intendancies, two sub-prefectures, one department, and four districts; and the eventual establishment of one sub-prefecture and four districts. These recommendations were in addition to the one circuit intendancy, one prefecture, one department, and two districts that he had set up in 1907.[57] In some areas the establishment of the various levels of local government was justified by the growth of population. In other areas, especially along the Sino-Russian and Sino-Korean frontiers, the establishment of the local governmental units was looked upon as primarily a means of promoting colonization and strengthening frontier defense.[58] Simultaneous with the establishment of civil governments in various parts of the province was the abolition of the posts of deputy military governor for Kirin, Hun-ch'un, San-hsing, Petuna, Ninguta, and Alchuka.

On the eve of the 1911 Revolution the local political division of Kirin province was as follows:

The Southwest Circuit Intendancy with its office at Ch'ang-ch'un had jurisdiction over two prefectures, one independent sub-prefecture, one sub-prefecture, and seven districts.

The Northwest Circuit Intendancy with its office at Harbin had jurisdiction over four prefectures, two independent departments, and two districts.

The Southeast Circuit Intendancy with its office at Hun-ch'un had jurisdiction over two prefectures, two departments, and four districts.

The Northeast Circuit Intendancy with its office at Ilan (San-hsing) had jurisdiction over three prefectures, one sub-prefecture, one department, and five districts.

The four intendants, in addition to their duties as civil and defense heads of their circuits also functioned as collectors of customs and local diplomatic representatives of the provincial government. In addition they were given the rank of colonel of the banner force to facilitate their handling of banner affairs within their jurisdictions.[59]

The progress of the modernization effort at the local government level varied according to localities. Because the prefect of Pin-chou, Li Shu-en, was highly praised by his superior for what he had done during his term of office, we may take the Pin-chou prefecture as an exceptional example of the modernization effort.[60]

Pin-chou, located on the bank of the Sungari River and some distance west of Harbin, had previously been under the jurisdiction of the deputy military governor of Alchuka. The first civil government, the Pin-chou sub-prefecture, was established there in 1882. In 1902 it was elevated to the status of independent sub-prefecture, and in 1910 to prefectural status. Li Shu-en was its first appointed prefect. The prefectural government was divided into executive and judicial branches. The prefect yamen was composed of the following offices: statistics, clerical, education, finance, and civil affairs. The Office of Finance, in addition to its principal duties of collecting taxes and disbursing payments, was also in charge of promoting agriculture, industry, and commerce. The Office of Civil Affairs was concerned primarily with public security, eradication of opium planting and smoking, and the promotion of self-government especially on the village level.[61]

An important reform in the new government was the payment of regular salaries to its employees. Hitherto many of the yamen personnel obtained their positions through bribery and were expected to recoup their expenses through their handling of court cases.[62] The separation of the executive and the judicial functions of the government eliminated this source of income and it was compensated by the payment of regular salaries. The procedure for instituting civil and criminal suits and the payment of court fees were regularized to minimize abuses by court underlings.[63]

Reform at the village level was effected by the elimination of the village militia, called *hui-lien,* which were often controlled by unscrupulous gentry and village tyrants. The responsibility for defense against bandits and maintenance of public order was given to a rural police force trained and controlled by the prefectural government.[64] Village administration was entrusted to an elected village chief, called *t'un-chang,* who was responsible for the carrying out of the educational, health, and agricultural policies of the prefectural government as well as the overseeing of the public order in the village.[65] The traditional village chief, called *hsiang-yueh*, who often obtained his appointment through bribery and had the power to levy contributions from the villagers to defray his personal and public expenses in the performance of his duties was replaced by a *hsiang-cheng* and an assistant, *hsiang-fu*, who were elected by the villagers and paid by the prefectural government. Since their duties were confined solely to the collection of taxes, they were under the supervision of the prefectural Office of Public Finance.[66] In other words, the coercive and taxing powers in the villages were taken away from the village landlords and centralized in the hands of the prefect, leaving the former only the control of what might be termed civic improvement projects.

Provincial Government in Heilungkiang

The structure of the Heilungkiang provincial government was similar to that of the Kirin government. However, because of the sparseness of the population and the lack of funds, the number of government bureaus was reduced to four: civil affairs, public finance, education, and justice. Diplomatic relations were handled by the Office of Railway Diplomacy and the General Office of Diplomatic Affairs in Tsitsihar. Economic development became the responsibility of the Bureau of Education. There was no Mongol Affairs Office and all problems relating to the minorities were referred to the Office of Banner Affairs. Unlike its counterpart in Kirin, the responsibility of the Office of Banner Affairs was limited to personnel administration of the banner force; its financial and educational problems were handled by the bureaus of Public Finance and Education respectively.[67]

Local Government in Heilungkiang

In a joint memorial submitted in June 1908, Hsü Shih-ch'ang and the acting governor of Heilungkiang, Chou Shu-mo, proposed the creation of three circuits: Aigun, Hulun Buir, and Hsing-tung. The last named, although established in 1906, did not yet have a permanent official site.[68]

All three circuits were located along the Sino-Russian frontier and the districts under their jurisdiction consisted mostly of unpopulated wilderness. The purpose of their establishment was to strengthen frontier defense and promote immigration.[69] According to the plan submitted by the memorialists, a number of prefectures, independent sub-prefectures, and districts were to be set up in each of the circuits in the course of time. The circuit intendant, subject to the instructions of the governor-general of the Three Eastern Provinces and governor of Heilungkiang, was responsible for all diplomatic, military, civil, and banner affairs within the territorial limits of his jurisdiction. The conduct of public business in the Office of the Intendant was shared by three bureaus, each headed by a senior assistant. The Judicial Bureau administered the judicial system within the jurisdiction of the intendancy and reviewed cases submitted by local authorities. The Finance Bureau, in addition to its fiscal duties, also was responsible for economic development. The Secretariat was responsible for the handling of official correspondence and documents as well as such important matters as military affairs, diplomatic relations, education, and police administration.[70] Thus, the power of the circuit intendant compared favorably with that of the deputy military governor whom he had displaced.

At the end of the Ch'ing dynasty, the entire Heilungkiang province boasted seven prefectures, three independent sub-prefectures, three sub-prefectures, one department, and seven districts. Practically all of them were founded between the years 1904 and 1910.[71] Unlike Kirin, all the local prefects and magistrates in Heilungkiang retained their traditional power over the administration of justice pending the eventual establishment of an independent court system, which, for the lack of qualified personnel and the sparseness of population, was never put into effect to the end of the dynasty.[72] Otherwise, there was no great difference between the two provinces in their systems of local government.

Reorganization of Tribal Enclaves

Reorganization of tribal enclaves in Heilungkiang began during the period of transition, again reflecting the political and economic forces that had brought about the end of the tributary system. The first move in this direction was made in 1872 when the Manchu general superintendent of the Buteha banners was given the rank of deputy military governor, putting his Buteha colleagues in a clearly subordinate position.[73] In 1894 the three superintendencies were abolished and all Buteha affairs were entrusted into the hands of a single deputy military governor; among the three deputy military governors appointed, the first two were Buteha natives and the last one a Tsitsihar Manchu.[74]

The final changes in the administration of the Buteha were made in 1906 when the Buteha territory was divided into East Buteha and West Buteha taking the Nonni River as the boundary. The post of deputy military governor was eliminated. Each of the new Buteha divisions was reorganized into eight banners under the supervision of a general superintendent. Each banner was commanded by a major, assisted by a lieutenant. Of the general superintendents, three had been Buteha natives, three Manchu bannermen, and one a Chinese bannerman.[75] These changes were effected together with the general reorganization of the provincial structure at that time. The reorganization was carried out along the lines suggested by Ch'eng Te-ch'üan, who had the arduous task of creating order out of the chaos that came in the wake of the Russian invasion. He had found that of the ninety-two *niru* that were created by the 1760 statute most of them had only a few score of soldiers and some had none at all. For this reason, he regrouped them into sixteen *niru* and eliminated the superfluous officers. Furthermore, he opened to all ethnic groups the Buteha posts, which had hitherto been reserved for Buteha and Manchu bannermen only.[76] The significance of this reorganization scheme was its pointing toward the direction of the gradual elimination of the vestiges of Buteha semi-autonomous status in Heilungkiang.

There were also changes regarding the administration of the Yafahan Orochon. After the left bank of the Amur was ceded to the Russians in 1858, a large number of the tribesmen were lost to the Manchurian government. In 1871, the military governor of Heilungkiang obtained the consent of the court to divide the Orochon and Birar tribesmen into the following five "routes," or regional groupings: Kumar, Birar, Ari, Tobukur, and T'o-ho.[77] In 1875 Military Governor Feng-shen decided to organize a reserve force of Orochon fighters as a measure of frontier defense. Five hundred Orochon sharpshooters were chosen for military training every year for forty days in the spring. They were compensated with cloth and money for their services. The number of men so trained was increased to 1,000 in 1880.[78]

In 1882, Military Governor Wen-hsü complained in a memorial that the Orochon were becoming increasingly antagonistic toward their *anda*, who took advantage of the military drill to exploit their charges. Wen-hsü suggested the organization of the 1,000 Orochon men under military training into banner companies like the Buteha. Each man would be paid a monthly stipend of one tael and be subject to the annual tribute of one sable. A Manchu general superintendent with the rank of deputy military governor would be sent to govern them, assisted by two Manchu deputy superintendents, eight Orochon deputy superintendents, sixteen majors, and sixteen lieutenants. The suggestion was acted upon, and in 1884 the town Hsing-an was built as the headquarters of the general superintendents.[79] The project failed because the Orochon were unused to regimentation and disliked leaving their mountain homes. The site for the town, located on marshy ground, was so badly chosen that many houses collapsed soon after they were built. Consequently, another reorganization was made in 1894. The general superintendents were eliminated. The eight majors of the Kumar route and the four majors of the Birar route were put under the jurisdiction of the Aigun deputy military governor; the two majors of the Ari route and the two majors of the Tobukur route were put under the jurisdiction of the Mergen deputy military governor; and the two majors of the T'o-ho route were put under the jurisdiction of the Hulun Buir deputy military governor. In addition, a colonel was appointed as supervising officer for each route, with the exception of Ari and Tobukur routes which together were assigned one colonel.[80] Each year the four colonels brought commodities worth a thousand taels to the mountains for distribution among the Orochon as a means of obtaining their good will and cooperation.[81] Apparently these measures failed to improve the relations between the Orochon and the government. In a 1905 memorial, Military Governor Ch'eng Te-ch'üan commented that the colonels and majors rarely came face to face with the men supposedly under their charge and that because imperial gifts had been abolished in recent years the Orochon had taken to brigandage as well as joining the ranks of the Russian army. Ch'eng advocated the appointment of a better type of officer, especially among the colonels. According to Ch'eng, they should be paid full salary and chosen without regard to ethnic origin but must be able to speak the Orochon language.[82] The system, however, remained unchanged to the end of the dynasty.

In 1880, Military Governor Ting-an requested the court to promote the Manchu general superintendent of the Hulun Buir tribes to the post of deputy military governor so as to give him greater prestige among his colleagues as well as to facilitate his dealings with foreigners.[83] In 1907 a Chinese official, Sung Hsiao-lien was appointed temporary deputy military governor to inaugurate changes which paved the way for the changeover from military to civil government. With the establishment of a civil government in 1909, the post of deputy military governor was eliminated. Hulun Buir became an administrative circuit within the provincial structure. The circuit intendant, in addition to his other duties, was also made responsible for the administration of the tribal banner troops, and for this reason he was also given the military rank of colonel.[84]

Military Reorganization

As early as 1867 some efforts had been made to improve the quality of the frontier troops by training special contingents of the banner soldiers for the suppression of bandits who infested the mountainous border between Kirin and the Russian territories.[85] However, the results were disappointing. Meanwhile, there were reports of incursions of Russian and Korean immigrants across the Chinese frontier as well as the formation of an outlaw kingdom composed of clandestine goldminers under the leadership of Han Pien-wai. It was imperative that something should be done about frontier defense. Consequently, in 1880 the Peking court dispatched Wu Ta-ch'eng to Kirin to organize an adequate defense system. Wu, together with the military governor of Kirin, Ming-an, suggested the organization of a special frontier force apart from the local banner troops. This was the origin of the Ching-pien chün, or Border Pacification Army. Significantly, the ranks of the Border Pacification Army totaling about 5,000 foot and mounted soldiers, were filled with former militiamen from Hunan and Anhwei, thus breaching the monopoly of military power by the banner forces. Its organization was patterned after those of the Hunan and Anhwei armies, who had suppressed the T'ai-p'ing Rebellion. Wu was appointed in 1881 as commissioner of Kirin Frontier Affairs.[86] During his term of office he established colonization offices in the Hun-ch'un district to encourage Chinese settlement, erected an arsenal in Kirin, and built fortifications at San-hsing and Hun-ch'un.[87] In 1884 Wu was ordered to Tientsin with the bulk of the Border Pacification Army to defend the port city against possible invasion by the French during the Sino-French conflict over Annam.[88]

After Wu's departure, the depleted ranks of the Border Pacification Army were filled by local bannermen and the military-governor assumed the concurrent office of commissioner of Kirin Frontier Affairs. The deputy military governor of Hun-ch'un was appointed deputy commissioner. The Border Pacification Army, however, continued to be independent of the local banner force.[89] In 1889 some hundred men and officers were selected from its Chinese cavalry units to form a naval squadron to patrol the Sungari River. The organization of the squadron was patterned after the naval auxiliary of the Anhwei Army.[90]

The exclusive control of the frontier armies by the military governors was again breached in 1885 when the court began to modernize the banner troops on a more serious scale than had been attempted previously. This change was in line with similar efforts to modernize the Lü-ying troops in the provinces within China proper.[91] Mu-t'u-shan was appointed commissioner for Troop Training for the Three Eastern Provinces, with headquarters located in Fengt'ien. The higher-echelon officers were all imperial guard officers sent from Peking. Although the military governors of the three Manchurian provinces were nominally associates of the commissioner in the training program, all decisions were made by the commissioner alone. Each of the three provinces was to train 10,000 men chosen from the ranks of the banner soldiers. The entire program was to be completed in three years. The Kirin and the Heilungkiang trainees were designated Chi-tzu-ying lien-chün, or the Kirin Training Battalion, and Ch'i-tzu-ying lien-chün, or the Tsitsihar Training Battalion. The trained troops were prohibited from being sent anywhere without permission from the court. Interestingly enough, the entire program was to be supervised from Peking by the Naval Office, which was established in the same year.[92] This move probably represented an effort on the part of the policy makers to remove the program from the control of the moribund banner hierarchy in the capital and entrust it to the more progressive-minded officials who sponsored the development of a modern navy.

The program was completed in 1889 but it failed to revitalize the banner force as the court had hoped. Mu-t'u-shan died about a year after the program was put into effect. His successor, Ting-an, was less energetic. Furthermore, the local military governors showed little interest in a program in which they had no direct control.[93] The officers in charge of training also had difficulties in disciplining the local recruits. When the Heilungkiang trainees learned that the court was planning to send some of them to construct a road across the Lesser Khingan Mountain to facilitate the exploitation of the Mo-ho goldmines, they threatened to desert *en masse*, thus forcing the government to drop the project.[94]

In 1890 I-ke-t'ang-a, the military governor of Heilungkiang, followed the example of Kirin, obtained court permission for the formation of the Chen-pien chün, or Border Garrison Army. This army, totalling seventeen battalions, was modeled after the Border Pacification Army of Kirin and was composed of both banner and Chinese soldiers recruited locally.[95]

Thus, prior to the Boxer Uprising, the armed forces on the Manchurian frontier consisted of the old-style banner troops, banner troops which had received some rudiments of modern training and equipped with firearms, and the Border Armies of Kirin and Heilungkiang modeled after the Hunan and Anhwei Armies, which were organized by Tseng Kuo-fan and Li Hung-chang. Some of these troops saw service during the Sino-Japanese War of 1894–1895 and were badly routed by the Japanese invaders. After that disaster, it was not surprising that they were in no position to resist the Russian invasion of Manchuria in 1900.

During the Russian occupation, the Border Armies and the Training Battalions practically ceased to exist. As a result there was a great surge of banditry. The military governor of Kirin, with the consent of the Russians, recruited from the population forty battalions of troops totaling 13,000 men for bandit suppression duties. Heilungkiang also organized some 3,700 troops for the same purpose. These troops, which included a large percentage of Chinese, were under the exclusive control of the military governors.[96] The court was then in no position to reconstitute its control over the military situation in Manchuria.

The delaying tactics employed by the Russians in withdrawing their occupation troops from Manchuria finally led to the Russo-Japanese War. After its conclusion, the slow task of reorganization of the military forces was resumed in conjunction with the political reorganization of the frontier provinces. In 1906 Ta-kuei, the military governor of Kirin organized the Ch'ang-pei chün, or Standing Army, composed of recruits selected from the banner force. A Tu-lien kung-so, or Provincial Staff for Military Training, was set up with the military governor as superintendent. Assisting the superintendent was a councillor and the directors of the Ping-pei ch'u, or Office of the Inspector-General, the Ts'an-mou ch'u, or Office of the Quartermaster-General, and the Chiao-lien ch'u, or Office of Military Schools. However, since only a single brigade was under training, the Ministry of the Army instructed the Kirin authorities in February 1907 to simplify the administrative structure by abolishing the Provincial Staff for Military Training and entrusting the entire program to the Office of the Inspector-General.[97] While efforts were being made toward this end, the edict for the abolition of the military government was announced in April. Governor-General Hsü Shih-ch'ang and Kirin Governor Chu Chia-pao suggested to the throne in January 1908 the establishment of a unified military administration for the three Manchurian provinces.[98] The result was the setting up in Fengt'ien of a Military Training Staff for the Three Eastern Provinces. The governor-general was appointed superintendent and the three governors, associate superintendents. Directly under the Military Training Staff were: the Office of the Inspector-General, which had jurisdiction over the personnel, fiscal, supply, and medical administration of the provincial armed forces; the Office of the Quartermaster-General, which had jurisdiction over planning, intelligence, and quartermaster administration; and the Office of Military Schools, which had jurisdiction over coastal defense, military schools, and troop training. Each of these offices was staffed by a general director and three assistant directors, one for each province.[99]

While new troops were being trained, the defense of the Manchurian provinces was bolstered by the Peiyang troops that Hsü Shih-ch'ang brought to his new post. These included the entire Third Division and two mixed brigades composed of units drawn from the Second, Fourth, Fifth, and Sixth Divisions. The Third Division commanded by Ts'ao K'un was stationed in Kirin with its main headquarters at Ch'ang-ch'un.[100] The old provincial armed units were also reorganized and redesignated as Hsün-fang-tui, or Patrol and Defense Troops. There were forty battalions of Patrol and Defense Troops in Fengt'ien, thirty-three in Kirin, and twenty-three in Heilungkiang.[101] In 1907 the Ministry of the Army decided that each of the three provinces should complete the training of a Lu-chün division within two years. (Lu-chün troops were trained according to new regulations laid down by the Ministry of the Army, also called Hsin-chün, or New Army.) But by 1909 Fengt'ien had completed the training of only six infantry battalions and one artillery battalion, Kirin only one infantry battalion, and Heilungkiang had not even begun its training program.[102] The expedient of converting the Hsün-fang-tui into Lu-chün was adopted to speed up the process.[103] Thus on the eve of the Revolution of 1911, the armed forces in the Manchurian frontier region consisted in Kirin of 16,258 banner troops, 3,412 Hsün-fang-tui and 24,112 Lu-chün and in Heilungkiang of 5,173 banner troops, 5,746 Hsün-fang-tui, and 2,940 Lu-chün.[104] The Peiyang troops were withdrawn to Chihli.

From the above account, it can be seen that, despite the profusion of programs, the process of military reorganization in the Manchurian frontier proceeded generally toward the direction of greater regional centralization, sinicization of the army personnel, including the officer corps, and the reduction of the banner forces.

Preparations for Constitutional Government

The Ch'ing court announced its intention of establishing a constitutional government on September 1, 1906. That very winter, the military governor of Kirin, Ta-kuei, gave permission to the gentry of Kirin to establish a Self-government Association. The association set up a research bureau and published a Self-government Bulletin.[105] The eagerness of the local gentry to promote the concept of self-government, according to Hsü Shih-ch'ang, was due to the realization of the precariousness of Kirin's position between two predatory powers and the conviction that any successful resistance to foreign encroachment was dependent upon the ability of the population to participate in the political processes. Apparently, the association, which included more than seven hundred members, did not confine itself merely to education but also tried, as Hsü stated, "to expand its powers and exceed its limits,"[106] probably a reference to attempts at influencing government decisions.

At the same time, Ta-kuei also established a Cheng-chih k'ao-ch'a chü, or Bureau for Political Study, which was intended to make a complete study of the general situation in Kirin so as to provide the government with pertinent information for decision making. In 1907 the Peking government instructed the provincial authorities to set up survey bureaus for the gathering of information necessary to the preparation of constitutional government. The Kirin authorities, thereupon, reorganized the Bureau for Political Study into the T'iao-ch'a chü, or Survey Bureau. Within the bureau, there were a school for the training of lecturers on constitutional government and an office of statistics.[107]

On September 30, 1907, the court decided that, prior to the convocation of the national parliament and provincial legislatures, there should be organized on the national level, a Tzu-cheng yüan or National Assembly, and on the provincial level, *tzu-i chü* or provincial assemblies. These were to serve as advisory councils to the national and provincial governments and as a training ground for future legislators.[108] Meanwhile, the mushrooming of private organizations for the promotion of constitutional government prompted the court to issue admonitions against their interfering with the legal authorities, A set of regulations was issued in December 24, 1907, which limited the scope of activities and freedom of discussion of these private associations.[109] It was under these regulations that the Self-government Association in Kirin was reorganized as the Bureau for Self-government of the Kirin Prefecture and attached to the Preparatory Office for Provincial Assembly. This move made it into a semi-official organization and restricted its activities to the realm of research and education. At the same time, under official encouragement, various districts in Kirin and Heilungkiang also set up their local self-government research bureaus.[110]

The organic laws for the National Assembly and provincial assemblies were promulgated on July 8 and 22, 1908. On August 27 the court further announced a schedule for the institution of constitutional government within nine years: preparations for the establishment of provincial assemblies were to be made in the first year (1908), election and convocation of provincial assemblies in the second year, convocation of the National Assembly in the third year, and proclamation of the Constitution and elections to the National Parliament in the ninth year.[111]

According to the electoral laws issued by the court, the provincial assemblies of Kirin and Heilungkiang were each to be composed of thirty members and were thus, together with Sinkiang, the smallest of all provincial assemblies. The members were to be elected indirectly: the voters in the primary election districts were to elect a number of electors who in turn were to assemble in the secondary election districts to choose from among themselves qualified candidates to the provincial assemblies. The provincial assembly itself would later elect from its membership qualified candidates to the National Assembly in Peking. The electorate was drawn on an exceedingly narrow basis. Only a male person, twenty-five years of age or more, and a native of the province who could satisfy one of the following qualifications was eligible to vote:[112] recognition in educational or public welfare work; a middle school or college education or their equivalent; a senior licentiate or a holder of higher degree; a former civil official of the seventh or higher rank or a former military official of the fifth or higher rank who had never been impeached or dismissed; a native of the province with a business capital or real estate worth 5,000 yuan or more, or a resident of the province for ten years or more with property worth 10,000 yuan or more.

In addition to these qualifications, a candidate to the provincial assembly was required to be at least thirty years of age, native of the province, or resident of the province for ten years or more. He could be disqualified for the following reasons: heretical ideas and unethical conduct; a sentence of imprisonment or severer punishments; previous engagement in a disreputable business or profession; proof in court of the loss of financial credit and its failure to be restored; opium addiction; mental illness; disreputable occupation; illiteracy.

There were also persons who were ineligible to vote and to be elected because of their professional status. These included provincial officials and members of their private secretariats, military officers, police officers, monks, priests, and students. Primary school teachers were eligible to vote but not to be elected, The bannermen were accorded a special quota of from one to three delegates in the assembly of the province where they resided but not in Manchuria where they were considered part of the civilian population.[113]

The electoral laws made it abundantly clear that only the wealthy and educated class, largely the gentry elements, would be permitted to participate in the highly limited form of popular government that the court envisaged for the country. These restrictions posed a delicate problem for the frontier region. For there the number of qualified persons was very small, especially in Heilungkiang. The ruling of the court further limited the size of the electorate by disqualifying Mongol lamas and persons who were literate in Manchu or Mongolian but not in Chinese.[114] For example, the Pin-chou prefecture in Kirin had a total population of 269,461.[115] Of the 98,705 adult males recorded in the census, only 818 were eligible to vote in the primary election and only 652 were eligible to become electors to vote in the secondary election which would then elect delegates to the provincial assembly.[116] For Kirin as a whole, the number of primary voters totaled only 15,370 in a population of 4,237,963.[117] In Heilungkiang, according to an admittedly inadequate census, the population in 1907 totaled 1,455,657 persons.[118] The number of eligible primary voters as recorded in 1909 totaled only 4,652.[119]

Circumscribed as it was, the provincial assembly was the first formalized channel in the history of imperial China through which the local elite could represent to the provincial government the interest of the population at large. They were convened throughout the nation on November 27, 1909, and Chang Chien, the speaker of the Kiangsu Assembly called for the immediate convocation of a national legislature with real power and the organization of a responsible cabinet. The provincial assemblies of Manchuria responded positively to his appeal. They sent representatives to Shanghai to confer with delegates from thirteen other provincial assemblies on steps to be taken toward that end. The result was the formation of an association, composed of members of various provincial assemblies, which undertook to petition the Peking government for the immediate election and convocation of a parliament. The association petitioned the court on three separate occasions in January, June, and October 1910. Finally the court promised to convoke the parliament in 1913. Some of the petitioners were satisfied; others were not. When the fourth petitioning move was being organized, the court singled out the Manchurian delegations and had them sent home under an official escort.[120] The suppression of the parliamentary movement alienated the moderates and accelerated the drift toward revolution.[121]

The Revolution of 1911

When the Russo-Japanese War was drawing to a close, Peking appointed Chao Erh-sun, one of its most energetic officials, to be the military governor of Fengt'ien. Chao, a Chinese bannerman, was determined to carry out the reform mandate in his province. In order to obtain the necessary funds for his projects, he had the court abolish the tax-free princely estates which were made available for purchase by their former Chinese tenants, conducted a land survey to flush out squatters occupying public lands who had hitherto escaped taxation, promoted the opening of Mongol lands to Chinese immigration, and increased the general rate of taxation.[122] These measures, while a financial success, aroused bitter opposition among many peasants and squatters. The village federations of Liaotung organized sporadic anti-tax riots. In 1907 some twenty thousand armed squatters barred government surveyors from their lands. When the disturbances were finally suppressed, some of the federation chiefs were punished, while others escaped to continue resistance in the mountainous districts, forming centers of revolutionary sentiment.[123]

Much of the new revenues obtained by Chao was spent on military reform: the training of the New Army and the reorganization of the Hsüan-fang-tui, the old provincial troops. The training task was given to Chiang Po-li, an outstanding graduate of the Japanese Military Academy and a close friend of Liang Ch'i-chao, the leader of the constitutional movement; the reorganization task was entrusted to Chang Hsi-luan, a product of the old army and a friend of Yuan Shih-k'ai. The officers of the Hsüan-fang-tui, knowing that their rice bowls would be broken as soon as the New Army was ready, were implacable foes of the young Japanese-educated cadres who occupied high positions in the New Army.[124] In 1911 there were three New Army groups stationed in Fengt'ien: the Sixth Division, which had been part of the Pei-yang force, trained by Yuan Shih-k'ai, was commanded by Wu Lu-ching; the Twentieth Division, made up of units drawn from various Pei-yang divisions, was commanded by Chang Shao-tseng; and the Second Mixed Brigade, trained in Fengt'ien, was commanded by Lan T'ien-wei. All three officers were members of the Liao-tung branch of the T'ung-meng hui, organized in 1907 under the leadership of Sung Chiao-jen.[125] Another revolutionary officer was Chang Yung, a native of Fengt'ien. In 1905 Chang Yung, together with Wu Yüeh, had attempted to assassinate the five imperial commissioners, who were at the Peking station on their way to study constitutional governments abroad. Wu was blown to death by their homemade bomb. Chang was arrested. While in prison, he persuaded the warden to escape with him to Japan. Chang then studied at the Japanese Military Academy and joined the T'ung-meng hui. In 1911 after his return to Fengt'ien, he was appointed military counsellor by Chao Erh-sun, now governor-general of the Three Eastern Provinces.[126]

The educational reform, also initiated by Chao in 1905, was responsible for drawing to Fengt'ien many young intellectuals, who had acquired a modern education in China and abroad, to staff the new school system. The T'ung-meng hui found many eager recruits from their ranks.[127] The Provincial Assembly, the stronghold of the local gentry, after its demand for the immediate convocation of a national parliament was rebuffed by the court conservatives, was also becoming more sympathetic to revolutionary views. Finally the bandit bands, with their anti-government bias, were willing to listen to the blandishments of the revolutionaries.

On the eve of the revolution, three major factions emerged in the Fengt'ien political scene. There was the clandestine T'ung-meng hui, headed by Chang Yung and Hsü Ching-hsin, with a membership of about a hundred young intellectuals drawn from the ranks of teachers, students, army officers, and village federation chiefs. Its armed backing included a number of village federations in Liao-tung, which possessed about four thousand Russian rifles, several bandit bands in western and northern Fengt'ien, totaling about eight hundred men, and most important of all, units of the New Army with about thirty thousand well-equipped soldiers. A reform faction, led by Wu Ching-lien, the president of the Provincial Assembly, had a following among the educational circles. Finally, there was a conservative gentry bloc, headed by Yuan Chin-k'ai, vice-president of the Provincial Assembly, and backed by the old provincial army officers under the leadership of Chang Tso-lin and Feng Te-lin.[128] In Kirin and Heilungkiang, the revolutionary strength was slight, the local gentry were inclined to work with the officials, while the young teachers and students of the new schools favored reformism.

Chao Erh-sun had returned to Manchuria in April 1911 as governor-general. In October Chang Shao-tseng, Wu Lu-ching, and Lan T'ien-wei left Fengt'ien with their troops to participate in the projected autumn maneuvers to be held near Peking. Because of the Wu-ch'ang uprising, the maneuvers were canceled. The troops under the command of Chang and Lan were held at Luan-chou, east of Peking; those under Wu were at Shih-chia-chuang, south of Peking. They were in an excellent position to threaten the imperial capital. However, because these troops were of Pei-yang origin, the majority of the middle- and lower-echelon officers were still loyal to Yuan Shih-k'ai, who was biding his time in enforced retirement after the death of the Empress Dowager in 1909. On October 27, 1911, the regent, who had wanted to put Yuan to death for his betrayal of the emperor during the abortive Hundred Days Reform of 1898, was compelled by the exigency of the military situation to appoint Yuan commander-in-chief of the imperial forces. On October 29, Chang Shao-tseng and Lan T'ien-wei began to show their hands by calling on the court to institute constitutional government immediately. Two days later, they blocked a shipment of Russian arms which was being sent from Fengt'ien to Peking by Chao Erh-sun. On November 2, Wu Lu-ching similarly withheld a shipment of arms and ammunition on its way to the Hupei front where the imperial troops were locked in combat with the revolutionaries.[129] These mutinous acts staged by Chang and Wu were a greater menace to the safety of the imperial government than the distant fighting in central China. Yuan Shih-k'ai moved quickly to nullify the threat. On November 6, both men were relieved of their commands. The next day, Wu was assassinated by two of his subordinates.[130] Lan had returned to Fengt'ien where some of his troops were guarding Sheng-ching (Mukden), the provincial capital.

The revolutionaries in Fengt'ien now decided to detach Manchuria from imperial control by declaring its independence. Wu Ching-lien, as president of the Provincial Assembly, was to convene a meeting of all provincial leaders with the declared objective of establishing a pao-an hui, or peace preservation association to maintain order in the province. During the meeting, attempts would be made to elect Wu as president of the association and Lan as vice-president. It was hoped that Chao Erh-sun, his authority thus undermined, would have to leave the province. The next step would be to make Wu the civil governor and Lan the military commander.[131]

This plan was upset by Chao's countermove. Knowing the unreliability of Lan's force, Chao secretly ordered the Hsüan-fang-tui, under the command of Wu Chün-sheng, to take over the defense of the provincial capital. The order became known to Chang Tso-lin's liaison officer in Sheng-ching, who quickly transmitted the message to him. Chang immediately sent his troops to Sheng-ching, passing on their way through the territory of Wu, who had not yet received Chao's order. Upon their arrival at the capital, Chao accepted Chang's offer of help and put him in command of all the provincial troops in the area, totaling about fifteen battalions. These troops were strong enough to checkmate the New Army units and to intimidate the Provincial Assembly.[132]

On November 11, Wu Ching-lien called for the holding of a public meeting as planned. Next day, about two hundred local notables attended the meeting, including Chao Erh-sun, Yuan Chin-k'ai, and Chang Tso-lin. During the meeting Chang Tso-lin, who had ringed the building with his men, brandished his pistol and declared his support for Chao. Those in attendance were cowed by this threat of force. As a result Chao was elected president and Wu vice-president of the Fengt'ien Peace

Preservation Association.[133] Chao then declared that the province would stay neutral in the civil conflict. On November 14 Lan was relieved of his command. Following Fengt'ien's example, the Kirin Peace Preservation Association under the presidency of Governor Ch'en Ch'ao-ch'ang was organized in November 16 and the Heilungkiang Peace Preservation Association under the presidency of Governor Chou Shu-mo emerged in November 17. While waiting for the dust of the revolution to settle, they discouraged any attempt to overthrow the local established authorities.

In desperation, the revolutionaries started a series of uprisings by village associations, bandit bands, and Lan's troops during the month of November, all of which were easily suppressed. Wu Ching-lien and Lan fled to China proper. Chang Yung was assassinated by Yuan Chin-k'ai's men.[134] The revolution was stillborn in Manchuria.

After the establishment of the republic with Yuan Shih-k'ai as president, Chao Erh-sun resigned as governor of Fengt'ien in November 1912 and was succeeded by Chang Hsi-luan. Because Chang Hsi-luan had been their military superior, Chang Tso-lin and Feng Te-lin, now powerful divisional commanders, were content to serve under him with appropriate humbleness. In August 1915, Chang Hsi-luan was transferred to Hupei. Tuan Chih-kuei, as his successor, did not have the prestige or ability to exact obedience from his Manchurian subordinates. Chang Tso-lin led the local opposition to Tuan, but was always tactful enough to declare his loyalty to Yuan Shih-k'ai. When Yuan's monarchical dream ran into mounting provincial opposition in 1916, Chang made it known that he might declare Fengt'ien independent of Peking. Tuan took the hint and resigned. Yuan, not willing to antagonize Chang and his fellow Manchurian officers, appointed him commander-in-chief of the Fengt'ien military forces and concurrent provincial governor. Chang had become in reality the undisputed leader of Manchuria. By 1918 all the high political and military posts in the three Manchurian provinces were held by his trusted lieutenants.[135]

Conclusion

The reorganization of the Manchurian frontier administration was the logical outcome of the nineteenth-century social and economic transformations which had rendered obsolete the existing structure of the military government. If China had remained isolated from outside influences, the direction of administrative change would probably have followed that of the Sheng-ching government: the gradual shifting of power and prestige from the banner officers to civilian officials and the de facto changeover from military government to a provincial government of the traditional type.

However, under the pressure of domestic politics and foreign menace, such Western concepts as separation of powers, popular legislature, and government as an instrument of social and economic progress were introduced into the reorganization plans, placing a veneer of modernity over a bureaucracy whose members were still largely the products of the traditional society. As far as the structure of government was concerned, the regional unity of Manchuria, founded upon political and economic realities, was preserved in the republican era by the dominant role assumed by the Fengt'ien leadership over the provincial authorities in Kirin and Heilungkiang. Both Chang Hsi-luan and Chang Tso-lin exercised, to even greater degree, the viceregal powers that had been entrusted to the late Ch'ing governors-general. There was only one important structural change: the simplification of local administrative hierarchy. The prefectures, sub-prefectures, and independent districts were eliminated; only the districts and circuits survived under the centralized authority of the provinces.[136] Politically, the overriding difference between the republican era and the preceding age was, of course, the emergence of warlords. The imperial administrators had always been responsive to the will of the emperor, while the warlords were responsible only to themselves.

The late Ch'ing reform efforts had left two permanent imprints. The district governments set up by Hsü Shih-ch'ang and his successors, many of them hastily located in sparsely populated areas, remained viable concerns as the tide of immigration ran unabated throughout the period of warlord politics. The ideal of an independent judiciary, although it left much to be desired in its actual operation, nevertheless had become a reality as a court system, however imperfect, gradually came into being, staffed by men more or less trained in modern legal procedure and concepts.[137]

The chief casualty was the embryonic popular legislature. A contemporary writer described the situation in Kirin, which may be considered typical throughout Manchuria, as follows:

During the election of the Kirin Provincial Assembly and, in the first year of the republic, the election of the First Provincial Legislature and representatives to the National Parliament, because of their novelty, people were hesitant to come forward as candidates and the supervisors of the elections had to urge them to run in thousands of ways. The voters cast their ballots with discrimination and the elected behaved with circumspection and self-respect. For this reason, although the events were unprecedented, the spirit of those involved in them was commendable. Since then, people gradually came to consider the elections as steps to power and doors to prominence. When an election is being held, the strong and unscrupulous persons would try in every way to gain control by recommending staff workers and forging voter registrations. The voter registrars, writing furiously in their offices, would produce within several days, a list of names of several hundred thousand voters. Consequently, the real qualified voters, without having to make a decision or cast a ballot, would find that the ballot boxes had been filled and the election was over. But this is merely corruption in the primary elections.

The corruption that occurs during the final elections is shameful beyond words. Every successful primary candidate usually takes along about a dozen aides to the city where the final election is to be held. They are there to entertain the electors and garner their votes. Their crudities in this endeavor are shown in hundreds of unseemly scenes: entertaining with prostitutes and opium, begging on bended knees, bribing with the promise of official position or with a high price, going as far as a thousand to eight or nine thousand *yuan* for a single vote. Consequently, an elected representative could spend up to several tens of thousands of *yuan* and a president of the legislature up to two hundred thousand *yuan*. Some of them have squandered their family fortunes without being elected. Some of them have piled up an immense debt which could not be repaid even after serving several terms as representatives. As a result, those who are elected think only of climbing the official ladder and enriching themselves without ever thinking of the welfare of the people and the nation. . . . As time goes on, they are looked upon with contempt by the local officials who use them for their own purposes and the suffering of the people becomes ever greater. The few

> upright legislators are weak in strength and their words do not carry weight. They are being ridiculed as fools and scolded for their obstinacy.[138]

The truth seems to be that Manchuria was governed neither better nor worse than the average warlord-dominated region. It had one advantage that other Chinese provinces did not have—a favorable population-land ratio and an exportable agricultural surplus. The wealth of Manchuria, if properly utilized and reinvested under a government that had the welfare of its people as its first concern, could have given its leaders the moral prestige to rally the entire nation behind them for the reunification of China. This was not done. Chang Tso-lin and his lieutenants squandered the regional assets on expanding their armies in a futile quest for national supremacy through military conquest. Government as a force for progress proved to be a concept easy to grasp but infinitely more difficult to translate into action. The frontier had come of age politically only to serve as a pawn in a modernized version of the traditional struggle for dynastic succession.

8

The Transformation of the Ch'ing Manchurian Frontier Policy

Basically, the Manchurian frontier policy of the early Ch'ing emperors was an attempt to preserve political control of that northeastern corner of the empire exclusively in the hands of the Manchus and their military instrument, the banner forces, and to minimize its cultural contacts with China proper. Consequently, the administration of the region was entrusted to a hierarchy of military garrison commanders, the great majority of whom were Manchus, presiding over a political structure that was essentially a pyramidal military organization having jurisdiction over civil affairs. In order to perpetuate the predominant military and political positions of the Manchus, Chinese immigration was prohibited and the adoption of Chinese cultural traits were officially discouraged in the frontier region.

The founders of the Manchu dynasty were keenly aware of the assimilative power of Chinese culture vis-à-vis their own and the resulting political implications. For this reason, although they found it advantageous to employ Chinese advisers and generals and adopt Chinese institutions and ideology while engaging in an all-out struggle against the Ming empire, they were uneasy about the long-range effects of their policy. Thus, Abahai, who in 1631 admonished his Manchu, Chinese, and Mongol officials to encourage their sons and brothers to study the Confucian classics and in 1636 inaugurated the presentation of sacrifices to the Temple of Confucius in Mukden, thought it necessary to remind his Manchu courtiers not to forget the Manchu heritage in their eagerness to adopt Chinese culture.[1] This ambivalent attitude of the Manchu rulers was again expressed by the Yung-cheng emperor in a message to the Grand Secretariat on September 10, 1724, rejecting a proposal made by Chao Tien-tsui, a junior metropolitan censor who was managing the dockyard in Kirin city. Chao had petitioned the court for permission to build a Temple of Confucius in Kirin and to establish schools for the children of the local Manchu and Chinese population. The emperor remarked that for those Manchus who lived in China proper, because of their proximity to the Chinese population, it was understandable that they were being gradually estranged from their ancestral customs, the preservation of which was now dependent upon the soldiers garrisoning the Manchurian frontier posts. He made it clear that the frontier Manchus should not divert their attention from practicing their ancestral arts to the studying of Chinese classics.[2] The Yung-cheng emperor's sentiments were later reaffirmed by the Ch'ien-lung emperor in a decree issued on November 14, 1759, which stressed the emperor's desire for the Manchus to retain their ancestral virtues.[3]

The preoccupations of the Ch'ing emperors with the preservation of their ancestral values stemmed from the fact that theirs was an alien dynasty of conquest, the imposition of the rule of a racial minority upon a vast population which believed implicitly in its own cultural superiority. Knowing that the Manchu minority would be submerged in the ocean of Chinese humanity if no precautions were taken to retain its identity, the Ch'ing emperors tried, through the banner system, to set the Manchus apart as a distinct social and military caste from their Chinese subjects. But the bannermen in China could not help being influenced by the pervading Chinese cultural environment, especially when the court itself was committed to govern the empire according to Confucian ideology and traditional Chinese practices. The emperors might have reasoned that only in the Manchurian frontier region, where the Manchu and tribal population outnumbered greatly the Chinese population in the beginning of the dynasty, could the tradition and spirit of Manchu culture remain unsullied by contacts with the Chinese. Thus, by barring Chinese immigration into the frontier and prohibiting the frontier bannermen from acquiring a Chinese education, the frontier would function as a fountainhead of ancestral virtues and a reservoir of military power for the ruling Manchu elite in Peking.

From another point of view, the cultural isolation of the Manchurian frontier was also politically advantageous to the ruling house. This was so because of a recurring problem in the history of Chinese imperial governments: the challenge to the dynastic house by frontier authorities. The Ch'ing emperors probably remembered that the founders of their dynasty were able to conquer the much bigger and wealthier Ming empire with the assistance of defecting Chinese officers and men of the

Ming frontier in the southern Manchurian region of Liao-tung. The possibility of the frontier Manchus allying with the Chinese of neighboring provinces to challenge the imperial authority could not be ruled out entirely. Consequently, the fewer the contacts between the frontier peoples and China proper the better it would be for the ruling house of Aisin Giror.

Finally, whatever the ethnic origin of the occupant of the Chinese throne, the assurance of political stability in the frontier region and tranquility among the tribal elements was an important consideration in the administration of the empire. During the Ch'ing dynasty such stability was achieved largely by the preservation of the political and cultural equilibrium of the various ethnic groups living on the frontier which entailed: (1) the barring of Chinese immigration so as to prevent the upsetting of racial and cultural balance; (2) the maintenance of the traditional political and social organization of the tribal peoples and the minimization of their contacts with other ethnic groups; (3) the placing of limitations upon the territorial and occupational mobility of the bannermen.

These measures complemented the overall policy of keeping the political control of the frontier in the hands of the Manchus and isolating the frontier culturally from China proper. But the overall policy of the Ch'ing emperors could not be completely carried out because of their role as rulers of an empire where the centers of political and economic gravity were located in China proper. From the viewpoint of the safety of the empire as a whole, the importance of the Manchurian frontier as the homeland of the Manchus and the fountainhead of ancestral virtues became secondary to its strategic role as a buffer zone between China proper and any hostile power coming from the north, be it the Ölöt Mongols or the Russians. The loss of Manchuria would open the gateway for an enemy to march upon Peking. It was to strengthen frontier defenses against the Russians that Chinese exiles and convicts were conscripted into the banner organization and distributed to various parts of the frontier defense line during the latter part of the seventeenth century. Similarly, in the latter part of the nineteenth century, when the frontier was again threatened by foreign aggression, Chinese peasants, soldiers, and administrators were brought into the region in a frantic move to stave off its alienation.

The policy of cultural isolation was also undermined by the economic attractions of the frontier region. The profits to be had from trading in furs and ginseng were so great that they attracted many legitimate traders as well as illegitimate hunters, trappers, and diggers. Its virgin lands were an irresistible magnet to the peasants of overcrowded north China, plagued by recurring natural calamities. The obligation of the Peking court to provide for the relief of famine-stricken subjects made it morally impossible to block their exodus to the frontier.

Lastly, the form of political control also worked against the cultural isolation of the frontier. In order to assure court control over the frontier administration, the leadership of the military governments was drawn from the sinicized Manchu elite in China proper who functioned, knowingly or not, as an effective channel for the transmission of Chinese cultural values to their bannerman subjects.

The most effective agents of cultural transmission, however, were the Chinese immigrants. They brought from China proper to the frontier their accustomed ways of life, their occupational and social skills, and their ethical and religious concepts. They transformed the frontier landscape by creating farms out of the wilderness and erecting villages, towns, and cities in the mountains, forests, and plains. Outlawed by the legal authorities, they organized their own governments. Their armed bands challenged directly the military might of the local government and exposed their weakness and incompetency. Their labor produced an agricultural surplus which was processed, transported, and sold by their trade networks not only to China proper but also to foreign lands. They built schools and participated in state examinations which trained them for local political leadership.

The process of cultural change within the frontier region was accelerated by the belated reversal of Ch'ing policy toward Chinese immigration and toward the caste differentiation between Chinese and bannermen in the latter part of the nineteenth century. This reversal of policy was prompted by fundamental changes in the balance of political forces within China proper as the result of the Ta'i-p'ing Rebellion and the growth of reformist and revolutionary movements, and by the radical shifts in the balance of power in the Far Eastern international order as the result of the encroachment of Western imperialism and the rise of Japanese militarism. The traditional laissez-faire policy which sought only to preserve the political and cultural equilibrium of the frontier ethnic groups had to be discarded in favor of a policy which encouraged the rapid economic and demographic growth of the frontier region. The implementation of the new policy necessitated the replacement of the old frontier political structure with a somewhat modernized administration and the shifting of the frontier political and military power from the bannermen to the Chinese.

The transition from military to civil administration was accomplished with surprising ease. The bannermen, that segment of the population which had most to lose in the change of political leadership, offered very little effective resistance to the new order. They were numerically overwhelmed by Chinese immigrants, economically impoverished because of their dependence upon government subsidies and their inability to hold on to their lands and acquire new skills, and culturally demoralized as their ancestral virtues proved incapable of coping with the problems of the new age; their assimilation of Chinese culture lacked the intellectual depth necessary for the production of a new and enlightened leadership among themselves.

The reorganized governments of the Manchurian frontier were a combination of the traditional and the modern, reflecting the political thinking of a new generation of officialdom coming into prominence in China after the disastrous defeat in the Sino-Japanese War of 1895. The imperial court, chastised by the Boxer fiasco of 1900 and faced by a growing revolutionary movement, was willing to inaugurate political reforms which, it announced, would lead ultimately to a form of constitutional monarchy. Manchuria was chosen as the experimental ground in which the piecemeal reform program was to be tested in actual practice.

Hsü Shih-ch'ang, the first governor-general, pleading the dangers of Russian and Japanese aggression and the need for undiluted authority to deal with problems that arose in the aftermath of the Russo-Japanese War and to overcome the traditional bureaucratic inertia, obtained strong viceregal powers for his office. Despite the tentative moves toward constitutional reforms, such as the beginning of an independent judiciary and popular legislatures, the reorganized frontier administration was essentially autocratic in structure and spirit, albeit "progressive" in its willingness to discard outworn forms and to engage in activities not hitherto considered to be within the scope of governmental concern. The frontier had been sinicized but neither the political leadership nor the population was really ready for a complete break with the political traditions of the past as the subsequent era of frontier warlordism testified.

Notes, Bibliography,
Glossary and Index

ABBREVIATIONS USED IN THE NOTES

CLTC *Chi-lin t'ung-chih* (Gazetteer of Chi-lin)

HCK *Heilungkiang chih kao* (Draft gazetteer of Heilungkiang)

PCTC *Pa-ch'i t'ung-chih ch'u-chi* (Collected documents on the eight banners, first collection)

SCTC *Sheng-ching t'ung-chih* (Gazetteer of Sheng-ching)

TSCL *Tung-san-sheng cheng-lüeh* (The administration of the Three Eastern Provinces)

Notes

1. Foundation of the Ch'ing Manchurian Frontier Policy

1. Alexander Malozemoff, *Russian Far Eastern Policy, 1881–1904* (Berkeley, 1958), p. 1.

2. For a review of the events leading to the signing of the treaty, see Liu Hsuan-ming, "Russo-Chinese Relations up to the Treaty of Nerchinsk," *The Chinese Social and Political Science Review,* 23.4:397–415 (1940); also, Joseph Sebes, *The Jesuits and the Sino-Russian Treaty of Nerchinsk, 1689: The Diary of Thomas Pereira, S.J.* (Rome, 1961), pp. 56–75.

3. Liu Hsuan-ming, pp. 421–422. For a Chinese translation of the Manchu text of the treaty, which differed slightly from the Chinese text, see Ts'ao T'ing-chieh, *Tung-pei pien-fang chi-yao* (Commentaries on selected works related to the defense of the northeastern frontier) in *Liao-hai ts'ung-shu* (Collected works on the Liao-hai area; Shanghai, 1936), 2:14a–b. For a discussion of the different texts of the treaty, see Sebes, pp. 150–164.

4. For a list of the outposts, see Hsi-ch'ing, *Heilungkiang wai chi* (A study of the Heilungkiang area; Shanghai, 1894), p. 24.

5. Manchuria was surveyed in 1707–1710 by Frs. Regis, Jartoux, and Fridel. See Tu Wei-yun et al., *Chung-kuo li-shih ti-li* (A historical geography of China; Taipei, 1954), III, 5.

6. Wang Chun-heng, *A Simple Geography of China* (Peking, 1958), pp. 63–72.

7. E. G. Ravenstein, *The Russians on the Amur* (London, 1861), p. 342. The total area of Kirin and Heilungkiang excluding the Mongol territories is about 251,000 sq. mi. Hulun Buir has an area of about 75,000 sq. mi.

8. *Ibid.,* pp. 80–81.

9. H. E. M. James, *The Long White Mountain* (London, 1888), p. 243.

10. *Ibid.,* pp. 15–16.

11. Yang Pin, *Liu-pien chi-lüeh* (Notes on the willow frontier; 1894), p. 1.

12. Liu Hsüan-min, "Ch'ing-tai Tung-san-sheng i-min yü k'ai-k'en" (Immigration and colonization in the Three Eastern Provinces during the Ch'ing); in *Shih-hsüeh nien-pao* (Journal of history), 2.5:70 (1938).

13. Wang Chung-han, *Ch'ing-shih tsa-k'ao* (Essays on Ch'ing history; Peking, 1957), pp. 6–9. Hatada Takashi, "Mindai joshin jin no tekki ni tsuite" (Development of the use and manufacture of ironware by the Juchen in the Ming period) in *Tōhō Gakuhō* (Journal of Oriental studies), no. 11, pt. 1, pp. 262–266 (1940).

14. Wang Chung-han, pp. 14–19.

15. Meng Shen, "Pa-ch'i chih-tu k'ao-shih" (The origin and growth of the eight-banner system); in *Bulletin of the Institute of History and Philology,* vol. 6, pt. 3, p. 343 (1936).

16. *Ibid.*, p. 396.

17. *Shih-erh-ch'ao tung-hua-lu* (Tung-hua records of the twelve reigns), ed. Wang Hsien-ch'ien et al. (Taipei, 1963), Ts'ung-te reign, II, 35.

18. For the details of these cases, see Hsieh Kuo-chen, *Ch'ing-ch'u liu-jen k'ai-fa tung-pei shih* (A history of the early Ch'ing exiles in the development of the northeast; Shanghai, 1948), pp. 16–33, 40–60.

19. Fang Kung-ch'ien, *Chüeh-yü chi-lüeh* (Notes on a remote land; 1894), p. 1.

20. Yang Pin, p. 4.

21. Fang Kung-ch'ien, pp. 1–2; Yang Pin, pp. 9, 11b, 12b, 13; Wu Chen-ch'en, *Ninguta chi-lüeh* (Notes on Ninguta; 1894), pp. 2b, 4.

22. Fang Kung-ch'ien, p. 1b; Wu Chen-ch'en, p. 4b; Yang Pin, p. 4.

23. Fang Kung-ch'ien, p. 2b.

24. *Ibid.*, p. 2; Yang Pin, pp. 11b–12.

25. Fang Kung-ch'ien, p. 2b; Yang Pin, p. 7b; Wu Chen-ch'en, p. 4b.

26. Fang Kung-ch'ien, p. 2b; Yang Pin, p. 11; Wu Chen-ch'en, p. 3b.

27. *Ibid.*, p. 4b; Yang Pin, pp. 11a–b.

28. Fang Kung-ch'ien, p. 2.

29. Yang Pin, p. 12.

30. Fang Kung-ch'ien, p. 2.

31. Wang Chung-han, p. 84.

32. Hsiao I-shan, *Ch'ing-tai t'ung-shih* (A history of the Ch'ing dynasty; Taipei, 1963), I, 383–384.

33. S. M. Shirokogoroff, *Social Organizations of the Manchus* (Shanghai, 1934), pp. 100–101.

34. Fang Kung-ch'ien, pp. 2a–b; Wu Chen-ch'en, pp. 4b–5; Yang Pin, p. 12b.

35. Fang Kung-ch'ien, p. 2b.

36. Meng Shen, *Ch'ing-ch'ao ch'ien-chi* (The origins of the Ch'ing dynasty; Shanghai, 1930), p. 208.

37. Arthur W. Hummel, ed., *Eminent Chinese of the Ch'ing Period* (Washington, D.C., 1943–1944), I, 302.

38. *Sheng-ching t'ung-chi* (Gazetteer of Sheng-ching), comp. Wei shu et al. (Taipei, 1965), II, 31a–b.

39. Hsi-ch'ing, p. 27.

40. Shirokogoroff, *Social Organizations*, pp. 16–17.

41. *Ibid.*, p. 53.

42. *Ibid.*, pp. 54–55.

43. *Ibid.*, pp. 93, 96, 98.

44. *Ibid.*, p. 106.

45. Wu Chen-ch'en, p. 3; Yang Pin, pp. 7a–b. For a discussion of the term Heje and its variants, see Ling Shun-sheng, *Sung-hua-chiang hsia-yu ti Heh-che-tsu* (The Gold tribes of the lower course of the Sungari River), Chung-yang yen-chiu yüan li-shih yü-yen yen-chiu so (National Research Institute of History and Philology) monographs, series A, no. 14, pp. 45–51 (Nanking, 1934).

46. Wang chung-han, pp. 104–109. See also Ts'ao T'ing-chieh, *Tung-pei pien-fang chi-yao*, 2:1b–5.

47. Hsi-ch'ing, p. 12b. See also, Meng Ting-kung, *Buteha chih-lüeh* (Notes on

Buteha; Shanghai, 1936), p. 5. Meng, a Dagur, served as the superintendent of West Buteha under the republic.

48. Hsi-ch'ing, p. 10b.

49. *Hulun Buir chih-lüeh* (Short gazetteer of Hulun Buir), comp. Chang Chia-fan et al. (Shanghai, 1922), p. 194. Owen Lattimore stated that the Old Barga were of Buriat origin; see Lattimore, *The Mongols of Manchuria* (New York, 1934), p. 159.

50. *Hulun Buir chih-lüeh,* p. 194.

51. Lattimore, *Mongols,* pp. 159–160.

52. *Hulun Buir chih-lüeh,* p. 195.

53. Ling Shun-sheng, pp. 225–226. See also Ts'ao T'ing-chieh, *Hsi-po-li tung-p'ien chi-yao* (Notes on a journey to eastern Siberia; Shanghai, 1936), p. 33b.

54. Ling Shun-sheng, p. 226.

55. *Ibid.*

56. *Ibid.,* pp. 226–227.

57. *I-lan hsien-chih* (Gazetteer of I-lan *hsien*), comp. Yang Pu-ch'ih et al. (1920), p. 63.

58. See Ts'ao T'ing-chieh's excellent summary in *Tung-pei pien-fang chi-yao,* 1:8–10b.

59. It began at the town of Kirin and followed the Sungari and Nonni northward to Petuna, Tsitsihar, and Mergen. From Mergen it crossed the Lesser Hsingan mountains to Aigun. See Hsi-ch'ing, pp. 7b–8b.

60. *Ibid.,* pp. 7a–b.

61. Hsiao I-shan, "Ch'ing-tai tung-pei chih t'un-k'en yü i-min" (Military colonization and immigration in the northeast during the Ch'ing) in *Hsüeh-shu chi-k'an* (Academic quarterly), 6.3:36–43 (1951). For various decrees concerning illegal settlements on Mongol lands from the reigns of Ch'ien-lung to T'ung-chih, see *Ch'ing-tai pien-cheng t'ung-k'ao* (Classified laws and decrees on frontier administration during the Ch'ing), comp. Ch'en Ping-kuang (Nanking, 1934), pp. 224–229.

62. Sa-ying-e, *Chi-lin wai-chi* (A private account of Kirin; 1894), pp. 15a–b. *HCK,* 24:1a–b.

63. Sa-ying-e, p. 5.

64. Hsi-ch'ing, p. 24.

65. Shirokogoroff, *Social Organizations,* pp. 3–4.

2. *The Banner System*

1. Nakayama Hachirō, "Min-matsu Jockoku to hachiki teki tōsei ni kansuru sobyō" (A sketch of the Jurched tribes at the end of the Ming dynasty and the control of the eight banners) in *Manshū shi kenkyū* (Studies in Manchu history; Tokyo, 1935), p. 125. Also Mo Tung-yin, *Man-tsu shih lun ts'ung* (Collected essays on the history of the Manchus; Peking, 1958), pp. 63–64.

2. Nakayama, pp. 125–126; Mo Tung-yin, p. 67.

3. *PCTC,* 32:3b–4b.

4. *PCTC,* 32:6–8. For the origin of the Mongol *niru* and banners, see Wang Chung-han, pp. 119, 121–125. *CLTC* maintains that the Mongol *niru* were first organized in 1623 and the first Chinese *niru* in 1630 without stating its sources; see 50:3.

5. Mo Tung-yin, p. 69.

6. *CLTC,* 51:1–3.

7. Mo Tung-yin, p. 145; Ch'en Wen-shih, "Man-chou pa-ch'i niu-iu ti kou-ch'eng" (The formation of the Manchu eight-banner *niru*); in *Ta-lu tsa-chih* (Mainland magazine), 31.9:14; Jonathan D. Spence, *Ts'ao Yin and the K'ang-hsi Emperor, Bond-servant and Master* (New Haven, 1966), p. 7.

8. Mo Tung-yin, pp. 145–146; Spence, pp. 7–8.

9. Mo Tung-yin, p. 146.

10. Ch'i Chin, *Tung-pei chang-ku* (Historical notes on the northeast; Taipei, 1959), pp. 13–14, 18–19.

11. Ch'en Wen-shih, 31.10:28–29.

12. *PCTC,* 36:15b–18b; *CLTC,* 50:3b.

13. *Ibid., HCK,* 36:15b–18b.

14. Sa-ying-e, p. 5b.

15. Chin Te-shun, *Ch'i-chün chih* (The banner army; n.p., n.d.), p. 3; *Ning-an hsien chih* (Gazetteer of Ning-an *hsien*), comp. MeiWen-ch'ao et al. (1924), 4:70b–71; *Man-Mō sosho* (Encyclopedia of Manchuria and Mongolia), ed. Naitō Konan (Dairen, 1922), II, 1007–08.

16. *HCK,* 26:37b–40b.

17. *HCK,* 26:34b.

18. *HCK,* 26:35.

19. *HCK,* 26:2.

20. *PCTC,* 36:20.

21. *Shih-erh ch'ao tung-hua-lu,* T'ien-ch'ung reign, II, 8b–9.

22. *PCTC,* 36:20–21b.

23. Hsiao I-shan, *Ch'ing-tai t'ung-shih,* I, 597.

24. *CLTC,* 47:14a–b; Hsu Tsung-liang, *Heilungkiang shu-lüeh* (A brief account of Heilungkiang; Shanghai, 1894), p. 1.

25. *CLTC,* 47:2b.

26. Hsiao I-shan, *Ch'ing-tai t'ung-shih,* I, 597.

27. Nakayama, p. 142.

28. *Ning-an hsien chih,* 4:71.

29. Wei Yüan, *Sheng wu chi* (A history of imperial campaigns; 1842), 11:1b–3. According to Fang Chao-ying, the number of *niru* increased steadily from 1601 to 1735. After 1735, it remained almost unchanged until 1911. In 1735 there were 678 Manchu *niru,* 207 Mongol *niru* and 270 Chinese *niru* in Peking. The number of men per *niru* after 1644 varied from 100 to 200. See Fang, "A Technique for Estimating the Numerical Strength of the Early Manchu Military Forces," *Harvard-Yenching Journal of Asiatic Studies,* 13:193, 204 (1950). Fang's estimate probably errs in not making a clear distinction between *ch'i-ting,* able-bodied male, and *ch'i-ping,* soldier.

30. See table in Sutō Yoshiyuki, "Shin-cho ni okeru Manshū chūbo no toku-shusei kansuru ni ichi kōsatsu" (A study of the characteristics of the bannermen garrisons in Manchuria); in *Tōhō Gakuhō,* no. 11, pt. 1, pp. 182 (1940).

31. Lo Erh-kang, *Lü-ying ping chih* (The Green Standard Army; Chungking, 1945), pp. 5–9, 17–21, 195–198.

32. Figures from *Ch'ing-ch'ao wen-hsien t'ung-k'ao* (Encyclopedia of the historical records of the Ch'ing dynasty; Shanghai, 1936). See table in Sutō, p. 179.

33. Sa-ying-e, p. 5.

34. *Ibid.*; *CLTC*, 51:3–4b.

35. *I-lan hsien chih*, pp. 63a–b.

36. *HCK*, 26:35b–36. Hsu Tsung-liang, p. 14.

37. Sa-ying-e, p. 5b. The Ḳhalkhas of Inner Mongolia were members of a confederation composed of the Jarud, Barin, Bayud, Khunggirad and Uijiged tribes. See H. Serruys, *Genealogical Tables of the Descendants of Dayan-Qan* (The Hague, 1958), pp. 151–152, 154.

38. *Ibid.*

39. Yang Pin, p. 3b.

40. *HCK*, 11:3a–b.

41. Sa-ying-e, p. 5b.

42. *Ta-Ch'ing shih-ch'ao sheng-hsün* (Imperial edicts of ten Ch'ing emperors; Taipei, 1965), 290:5b.

43. Sa-ying-e, p. 6.

44. *Hu-lan fu chih* (Gazetteer of Hu-lan prefecture), comp. Huang Wei-han *et al.* (1915), 12:16–18.

45. Sa-ying-e, p. 6.

46. *CLTC*, 50:11; Sa-ying-e, p. 1.

47. *CLTC*, 50:10a–b.

48. For a discussion of the land expropriation measures, see Wang Ch'ing-yün, *Shih-ch'ü yü-chi* (Essays on public affairs; 1888), pp. 40b–41b; Yang Hsüeh-shen, "Ch'ing-tai ch'i-ti hsing-chih chi ch'i pien-hua" (The nature and transformation of the banner lands during the Ch'ing); in *Li-shih yen-chiu*, no. 4:175–178 (1963).

49. *Mambun Rōtō* (Essays written in old Manchu script), tr. Kanda Nobuo *et al.* (Tokyo, 1955), I, 55–56, 356. See also, Wang Chung-han, pp. 61–63.

50. Sa-ying-e, p. 18b. The size of *shang* varied according to localities from six to ten *mou*. (One acre equals about 6.6 *mou*.)

51. Sa-ying-e, p. 18b; *CLTC*, 30:7.

52. Sa-ying-e, p. 18b.

53. *CLTC*, 30:8–12.

54. *CLTC*, 30:7–8; Hsü Tsung-liang, p. 8b.

55. Wu Chen-ch'en, p. 1b.

56. Sa-ying-e, p. 18. The picul in this case is a granary picul, which is smaller than the market picul.

57. *CLTC*, 30:1–4.

58. *Hu-lan fu chih*, 3:48.

59. *Hu-lan fu chih*, 3:5a–b; Hsi-ch'ing, p. 16; Hsü Tsung-liang, pp. 10b–11. Hsü gave the date of the establishment of the farms as 1735.

60. Hsi-ch'ing, p. 16; Hsü Tsung-liang, pp. 10b–11.

61. Hsi-ch'ing, pp. 14–15.

62. Sa-ying-e, pp. 26b–35.

63. *Ibid.*, pp. 35a–b; Hsü Tsung-liang, p. 11.

3. Political Control of the Tribal Peoples

1. Fu, Lo-shu, *A Documentary Chronicle of Sino-Western Relations, 1644–1820* (Tucson, 1966), I, 94–95; Sebes, p. 73; *Shih-erh-ch'ao tung-hua-lu,* K'ang-hsi reign, 10:10b–11.

2. *CLTC*, 7:8b–9.

3. See *Ta-Ch'ing hui-tien shih-li* (Cases and precedents of the collected statutes of the Ch'ing dynasty; 1908), *chüan* 518.

4. Chao-lien, *Hsiao-t'ing tsa-lu* (Random notes from the Whistling Pavilion; 1880), 4:66. Also Wei Yüan, 1:16.

5. Ts'ao T'ing-chieh, *Hsi-po-li tung-p'ien chi-yao*, p. 22.

6. Mamiya Rinzō, *Mamiya Rinzō no Kokuryūkō tanken—Tōdatsu kikō* (The exploration of the Amur river by Mamiya Rinzō), ed. Mantetsu Koho Ka (Information Bureau of the South Manchurian Railway; Mukden, 1940), pp. 106–107.

7. Ch'eng Ping-kuang, p. 293.

8. *Ta-Ch'ing hui-tien shih-li,* 523:4a–b.

9. Wu Chen-ch'en, pp. 7a–b.

10. Yang Pin, pp. 7a–b.

11. Sa-ying-e, p. 22b. The number of tribute sables remained unchanged down to 1909. See Hsü Shih-ch'ang, chapter on Chi-lin, p. 23b; in *TSCL*, vol. 8.

12. Mamiya's journey to Sakhalin and the Amur territory was an attempt by the Japanese government to ascertain the extent of Russian advance in the Far East. Mamiya crossed the Tatar Strait from Sakhalin on July 2, 1809, arrived at Deren on July 11 and returned to Japan on September 18. See Mamiya, pp. 108–109.

13. *Ibid.*, p. 29.

14. *Ibid.*, p. 30.

15. *Ibid.*, pp. 30–31.

16. *Ibid.*, p. 32.

17. *Ibid.*, p. 32.

18. *Ibid.*, p. 33.

19. *Ibid.*, pp. 34–36.

20. *Ibid.*, pp. 36–37.

21. *Ibid.*, pp. 38–39.

22. Ravenstein, pp. 82–83.

23. Ts'ao T ing-chieh, *Hsi-po-li tung-p'ien chi-yao,* pp. 35a–b.

24. Meng Ting-kung, p. 3.

25. Hsi-ch'ing, p. 21.

26. Ying-ho, *P'u-k'uei ch'eng fu* (Poems on the city of P'u-kei; c. 1829), p. 15b.

27. Hsü Tsung-liang, p. 10b.

28. Hsi-ch'ing, p. 20b.

29. *Ibid.*, p. 21b.

30. *Ibid.*, pp. 11, 21. The census did not take into account the Birars and Orochons who were not organized into banners. They probably numbered over a thousand households.

31. *Ibid.*, pp. 20b–21.

32. *Ibid.*, p. 10b.

33. *Ta-Ch'ing hui-tien shih-li,* 1127:7.

34. Fang Shih-chi, *Lung-sha chi-lüeh* (Frontier notes; Shanghai, 1894), p. 5.

35. Figures from *SCTC.* See table in Sutō, p. 182.

36. *Ch'ing-shih kao* (A draft history of the Ch'ing dynasty), ed. Chao Erh-sun (Shanghai, 1936), p. 483.

37. Hsi-ch'ing, p. 12b.

38. For biography of Hai-lan-ch'a, see *Ch'ing-shih kao,* pp. 1200–1202. Meng Ting-kung identified Hai-lan-ch'a as a Solon from a village on the bank of the Ha-o-lun river in the West Buteha, see Meng Ting-kung, pp. 12–16.

39. *Ta-Ch'ing hui-tien shih-li,* 1127:7b. Hsi-ch'ing gave the number as 1,984 men, see Hsi-ch'ing, p. 13. Hsü Tsung-liang's figure for 1887 was 2,600 men, see Hsü Tsung-liang, p. 14b.

40. Hsi-ch'ing, p. 15. The soldiers received 12 taels a year, an amount which was kept fixed almost to the end of the dynasty. See also Hsü Tsung-liang, p. 14.

41. Hsi-ch'ing, pp. 10b–11.

42. *HCK,* 26:26a–b.

43. *Ibid.,* p. 26b.

44. Hsi-ch'ing, p. 12b.

45. On the conferment of lama titles by the imperial government, see Ch'eng Ping-kuang, chap. 3.

46. *Hulun Buir chih-lüeh,* pp. 205–206.

47. Liu Hsuan-ming, pp. 393–397.

48. Ravenstein, p. 25.

49. Liu Hsuan-ming, pp. 397–398. For biographical information on Gantimur, see J. F. Baddeley, *Russia, Mongolia, China* (New York, 1965), II, 428–429.

50. Ravenstein, pp. 45–53.

51. Similar limitation was also imposed upon all Mongol tribes. This measure had the effect of preventing the Mongols from forming a powerful coalition to challenge the imperial authority. For a discussion of this aspect of Manchu frontier policy, see Lattimore, *Mongols,* p. 151.

52. Ho Ping-ti, *Studies on the Population of China, 1368–1953* (Cambridge, Mass., 1959), p. 270.

4. *Bureaucratic Administration*

1. *PCTC,* 27:11.

2. *Ch'ing-ch'ao wen-hsien t'ung-k'ao,* 271:7275.

3. *Ibid.*

4. *Ibid.*

5. *HCK,* 1:3b.

6. *HCK,* 43:1b.

7. *SCTC,* 19:1b–6.

8. *Ch'ing-ch'ao t'ung-tien* (Encyclopedia of Ch'ing institutional history; Shanghai, 1936), 25:2173–74.

9. *Ibid.,* 25:2173. *Shih-erh-ch'ao tung-hua-lu,* Yung-cheng reign, 5:16a–b, 54.

10. Ch'ung-hou, *Sheng-ching tien-chih pei-k'ao* (The administrative system of Sheng-ching; 1878), 8:3b–4. Ch'ung-hou (1826–1893) was the acting military governor of

Sheng-ching (1876–1878). See also Chin-tai tung-pei jen-min yün-tung shih (A history of the modern revolutionary movement of the people of the Northeast), comp. Chung-kuo k'o-hsüeh-yüan Chi-lin fen-yüan li-shih yen-chiu so (The History Institute of the Kirin Branch of the Chinese Academy of Sciences) and Chin-lin shih-fan ta hsüeh li-shih-hsi (History department of Kirin Normal College; Chang-ch'un, 1960), p. 5.

11. *SCTC*, 1:6.
12. *Ch'ing-ch'ao t'ung-tien*, 33:2205.
13. Ch'ung-hou, 8:1–4.
14. *Ch'ing-shih kao*, p. 420.
15. *Ta-Ch'ing hui-tien shih-li*, 1121:5b.
16. Ravenstein, p. 25.
17. *Ibid.*, pp. 28–32. *HCK*, 30:37b–40b.
18. *Ibid.*, *CLTC*, 1:9b–10.
19. Hummel, II, 630–631. *HCK*, 43:1a–b.
20. *CLTC*, 1:12b–13b.
21. *HCK*, 43:1b.
22. See *CLTC*, 1:14a–b for an account of the defensive preparations against Galdan.
23. *Ch'ing-shih kao*, p. 420.
24. *CLTC*, 60:1.
25. *PCTC*, 37:1.
26. *CLTC*, 61:1–5b. Kuo T'ing-i, *Chin-tai Chung-kuo shih-shih jih-chih* (A daily chronological account of modern Chinese history, late Ch'ing period; Taipei, 1963). app. II, 45.
27. Hsi-ch'ing, p. 28b. *HCK*, 44:1–22.
28. Sa-ying-e, p. 6.
29. *Ibid.*, pp. 7b–8; also, *CLTC*, 57:1–21b.
30. Hsi-ch'ing, p. 7; also, *HCK*, 42:40–47.
31. *CLTC*, 56:1–5; *HCK*, 42:1–4.
32. *CLTC*, 56:1.
33. *CLTC*, 57:22–23b.
34. *CLTC*, 57:34b.
35. *HCK*, 42:46b.
36. Sa-ying-e, pp. 8b–9; Hsi-ch'ing, pp. 8a–b.
37. *Hulun Buir chih-lüeh*, pp. 46–51.
38. *Ibid.*, p. 71.
39. Sa-ying-e, pp. 12b–13; *CLTC*, 39:1–4; *HCK*, 13:19a–b.
40. Sa-ying-e, p. 13; *CLTC*, 39:4–6b.
41. Sa-ying-e, p. 24b; *CLTC*, 51:27–32b; Hsi-ch'ing, p. 18b; *HCK*, 26:42–47b.
42. *CLTC*, 51:31b–32b; *HCK*, 26:47a–b.
43. *HCK*, 24:2, 20b; *CLTC*, 49:2b–11b.
44. *CLTC*, 36:1–17b. Hsi-ch'ing, p. 9.
45. *CLTC*, 60:7b–8b; Hsi-ch'ing, pp. 18b–19.
46. *CLTC*, 60:7b–8b; Sa-ying-e, pp. 12b–13; Hsü Tsung-liang, p. 8.
47. Sa-ying-e, pp. 14a–b; Hsi-ch'ing, p. 20.

48 *CLTC*, 60:7b–9b. *Lang-chung* may be translated as department director and *yuan-wai-lang* as assistant department director.

49. *HCK*, 43:2a–b.

50. Hsi-ch'ing, p. 20; Hsü Tsung-liang, p. 8.

51. *HCK*, 43:3b; *CLTC*, 60:9b–10.

52. Sa-ying-e, pp. 13a–b.

53. *Ibid.*, pp. 13b–14.

54. *Ibid.*, p. 14b.

55. *HCK*, 43:3.

56. *Ibid.*; *CLTC*, 60:9b–10.

57. Hsü Tsung-liang, p. 8.

58. *Ibid.*

59. *CLTC*, 60:3b–4.

60. *HCK*, 43:14–22b.

61. Liu Wen-feng, *Tung-ch'ui chi-hsing* (Journey to the eastern frontier; n.d.), p. 6b; also, *HCK*, 43:18, 24b–25.

62. *Hu-lan fu chih*, 2:3b–4.

63. *Chih-chou* was rated junior fifth rank and *chih-hsien* seventh rank in the civil service hierarchy. For more information on the powers and duties of magistrates see Ch'u T'ung-tsu, *Local Government in China under the Ch'ing* (Cambridge, Mass., 1962), chap. 2.

64. *CLTC*, 60:38b. 47b, 56b–57.

65. *CLTC*, 60:57.

66. *CLTC*, 60:38b.

67. Sa-ying-e, p. 15.

68. *Ibid.*, pp. 84–85.

69. *CLTC*, 60:45.

70. *CLTC*, 60:48.

71. Wu T'ing-hsieh, *Tung-san-sheng yen-ko piao* (Tables of geographical changes in the Three Eastern Provinces; 1909), table 6, p. 9.

72. See Meng Shen, "Pa-ch'i chih-tu k'ao-shih," p. 399.

73. See table in *CLTC*, 61:1–5b. *HCK*, 44:1–22; *Ch'ing-shih kao*, pp. 865–898.

74. Hsü Tsung-liang, p. 8.

75. *CLTC*, 38:24b–25; Hsi ch'ing, p. 41.

76. Sa-ying-e, pp. 12a–b, 17a–b. There were two revolving funds: one for the benefit of soldiers who needed loans for living expenses, the other for military colonists who needed loans for the purchase of draft oxen.

77. Hsi-ch'ing, pp. 14b–15b.

78. P'eng Yü-hsin, "Ch'ing-mo chung-yang yü ko sheng ts'ai-cheng kuan-hsi" (The fiscal relationship between the central government and the provinces during the late Ch'ing); in *She-hui k'o-hsüeh tsa-chih*, 9.1:86–91 (1937).

79. Hsü Shih-ch'ang, chap. on Heilungkiang, p. 1; in *TSCL*, vol. 7.

80. *Ibid.*, p. 9.

81. *CLTC*, 60:55b–56b; *HCK*, 43:5a–b. *Ch'ing-ch'ao t'ung-tien*, 26:2178.

82. Sa-ying-e, p. 22.

83. *Ibid.*, pp. 13–14b.

5. Sinicization of the Manchurian Frontier

1. Ho Ping-ti, p. 283.
2. Hsü Shih-ch'ang, chap. on Chi-lin, pp. 21–24; in *TSCL*, vol. 6.
3. *HCK*, 12:5b–7.
4. Hsü Shih-ch'ang, chap. on Heilungkiang, pp. 11–12; in *TSCL*, vol. 6.
5. *SCTC*, 23:1b.
6. Liu Hsüan-min, p. 68.
7. *SCTC*, 23:1b.
8. Kao Shih-ch'i, *Hu-ts'ung tung-hsün jih-lu* (Diary of an eastern journey in the emperor's entourage; Shanghai, 1894), 2:6.
9. Liu Hsüan-min, p. 68.
10. Yang Pin, p. 11. The term "ten-thousand" as used here means a large but unspecified number.
11. Liu Hsüan-min, p. 74.
12. Wu Chen-ch'en, pp. 1, 3. See also Yang Pin, p. 11.
13. Sa-ying-e, pp. 10b–11. The list of Chinese officials given in this account showed only such lower ranking officials as *hsüeh-cheng*, director of schools, and *hsün-chien*, sub-district magistrate.
14. *CLTC*, 52:14.
15. *CLTC*, 53:1.
16. See the names of higher ranking officials recorded in Shen Ch'ao-t'i, *Chi-lin chi-shih shih* (Narrative poems on Chi-lin; Nanking, 1911), *chüans* 3 and 4, and the table of officials in *HCK*, 45:32–34b.
17. Yang Pin, p. 9.
18. Liu Hsüan-min, p. 68.
19. *CLTC*, 1:8, 13b.
20. The foregoing is a composite account derived from the descriptions of frontier life as experienced and seen by the authors of *Ninguta chi-lüeh, Liu-pien chi-lüeh, Heilungkiang wai-chi,* and *Lung-sha chi-lüeh.*
21. Yang Pin, pp. 13b–14.
22. Fang Kung-ch'ien, p. 2b.
23. This information is found on p. 58 of the Ts'ung-shu chi-ch'eng ed. of Yang Pin's work (Shanghai, 1936).
24. Yang Pin, pp. 9b–11.
25. Sa-ying-e, p. 5.
26. Chao-lien, 2:17b–18.
27. Hsi-ch'ing, p. 29.
28. *CLTC*, 46:1b, 3a–b.
29. Hsi-ch'ing, pp. 23a–b.
30. *CLTC*, 1:19a–b.
31. Hsi-ch'ing, p. 23b.
32. *CLTC*, 2:6b–8.
33. *CLTC*, 2:12b–13b.
34. Ch'eng Te-ch'üan, *Ch'eng chung-ch'eng tsou-kao* (Memorials of Governor Ch'eng; 1910), 17:36a–b.

35. See "Hsü ch'in-ch'a ch'a-fu ts'an-an che" (Memorial by Imperial Commissioner Hsü [Shih-ch'ang] on the result of an investigation into the impeachment of [Ch'eng Te-ch'uan]); in *ibid.*, app., p. 3.

36. *Ibid.*, pp. 3a–b; also Hsü Shih-ch'ang, chap. on Heilungkiang; in *TSCL*, VIII, 14.

37. Hsi-ch'ing, p. 28b.

38. *Ibid.*, pp. 28a–b.

39. *Ibid.*, p. 25.

40. For a discussion of Ming-Manchu trade see Inaba Iwakichi, *Zōtei Manshū hattatsu shi* (Enlarged edition of the history of the development of Manchuria; Tokyo, 1935), chap. 5.

41. *Ibid.*, pp. 286–289.

42. Imamura Tomo, *Ninjin shi* (Encyclopedia of Jinseng; Seoul, 1934–1940), II, 162.

43. *Ibid.*, II, 163, 166.

44. See pp. 57–58 of the Ts'ung-shu chi-ch'eng ed. of Yang Pin's work.

45. Imamura, III, 24.

46. Yang Pin, pp. 8b, 9b.

47. *Ibid.*, p. 8.

48. *Ibid.*

49. Sa-ying-e, p. 22b.

50. *Ibid.*, pp. 22b–23. See also Ch'ung-hou, 5:25–39b.

51. *CLTC*, 35:12a–b.

52. See Li T'ing-yü, "T'iao-ch'a Ch'ang-pai-shan pao-kao chih i-chien-shu" (A report on the investigations in Ch'ang-pai-shan and related proposals); in *Tung-san-sheng pien-wu chi-yao* (Selected documents on frontier affairs of the Three Eastern Provinces; Peking, 1917), 3:22. The report was made in 1908.

53. V. K. Arseniev, *Dersu, the Trapper*, trans. Malcolm Burr (New York, 1941), pp. 85–87.

54. *Ibid.*, pp. 182–183.

55. Ts'ao T'ing-chieh, *Hsi-po-li tung-p'ien chi-yao*, pp. 36b–37.

56. Arseniev, pp. 131, 176.

57. *Shih-erh-ch'ao tung-hua-lu*, T'ien-ming reign, 1:9b.

58. *CLTC*, 41:1b–2.

59. *Chi-lin hsin-chih* (New gazetteer of Chi-lin), comp. Liu Shuang (Hsin-ching, 1934), 2:210.

60. I am basing my biography of Han on the following sources: *Hua-tien hsien chih* (Gazetteer of Hua-tien), comp. Ch'en T'ieh-mei et al. (1931), 9:14b–15b; *Chi-lin hsin chih*, 2:210–211; Inaba, pp. 338–339; *CLTC*, 4:21a–b; 5:7a–b.

61. *Hua-tien hsien chih*, 9:15b–18; 5:4a–b.

62. *Hu-lan fu chih*, 8:21–23; *Chin-tai tung-pei jen-min ko-ming yün-tung shih*, pp. 53–54.

63. Fang Kung-ch'ien, p. 2.

64. Yang Pin, p. 3b.

65. Hsü Shih-ch'ang, chap. on *chün-cheng* (military administration), p. 1; in *TSCL*, vol. 4.

66. *Li-shu hsien chih* (Gazetteer of Li-shu *hsien*), comp. Meng Ch'ing-chang et al. (1934), 7:83a–b.

67. *Ibid.*, 1:2b. *Chin-tai tung-pei jen-min ko-ming yün-tung shih*, pp. 23–36.

68. Hummel, II, 854.

69. Chang Tso-lin served with the Japanese and Chang Tsung-ch'ang with the Russians. See *Li-shu hsien chih*, 7:85b–86; Ch'i Chin, pp. 7–8; *Chin-tai tung-pei jen-min ko-ming yün-tung shih*, pp. 192–193.

70. Archibald R. Colquhoun believed that it began in the 1860's. See his *Overland to China* (New York, 1900), p. 238.

71. *CLTC*, 43:11–13; *Hu-lan fu chih*, 3:25b–26, 10–18; Yü En-te, *Chung-kuo chin-yen fa-ling pien-ch'ien shih* (The history of opium prohibition in China; Shanghai, 1934), p. 102.

72. *Ibid.*, pp. 124, 141–142.

73. Owen Lattimore, *Manchuria, Cradle of Conflict* (New York, 1935), pp. 195–196. See Ch'in Tai-yüan, *Tung-ch'ui chi-wen* (Notes on the eastern frontier; 1912), pp. 11b–12b, for a report on collusion between opium growers, bandits, and soldiers in eastern Kirin.

74. Lattimore, *Manchuria*, p. 229.

75. Hsü Tsung-liang, p. 19.

76. Mo Tung-yin, pp. 50–52, 101–103.

77. Yang Pin, p. 64. Fang Shih-chi, p. 5b.

78. Yang Pin, p. 11; Hsi-ch'ing, p. 18.

79. Ravenstein, p. 82.

80. *Ibid.*, pp. 104–105.

81. Ts'ao T'ing-chieh, *Hsi-po-li tung-p'ien chi-yao*, p. 37.

82. Kawakubo Teiro, "Shindai Mansh ni okeru shoka no zokusei ni tsuite" (On the prosperity of *shao-kuo* in Manchuria during the Ch'ing period); in *Wada hakushi koki kinen Tōyōshi ronsō* (Oriental studies presented to Sei [Kiyoshi] Wada on his seventieth birthday; Tokyo, 1960), pp. 304–305.

83. James, pp. 320–321.

84. *Ibid.*, p. 171.

85. Hsü Tsung-liang, p. 13.

86. Chu Ch'i-ch'ien, *Tung-san-sheng Meng-wu kung-tu hui-pien* (Collected public correspondence on Mongol affairs in the Three Eastern Provinces; 1909), 2:19.

87. Inaba, pp. 332–333.

88. Hsü Tsung-liang, p. 4. For information on the founder of the Ts'ui clan, see *HCK*, 54:14a–b.

89. Liu Wen-feng, *Tung-ch'ui chi-hsing*, pp. 45a–b.

90. Ch'en Ch'i-t'ien, *Shansi p'iao-chuang k'ao lüeh* (A brief history of Shansi banks; Shanghai, 1936), pp. 27–28, 132, 134.

91. Yang Tuan-lu, *Ch'ing-tai huo-pi chin-yung shih kao* (A draft history of currency and finance during the Ch'ing; Peking, 1962), p. 133.

92. *Manshu tsushi* (Gazetteer of Manchuria), comp. Tōa Dobunkai (Tokyo, 1906), pp. 425–426.

93. Ch'i Chin, pp. 39–40.

94. *Ibid.*, p. 41; *CLTC*, 40:11b–12a; *HCK*, 21:4b

95. Li Shu-t'ang, *Tung-chiao chi-hsing* (Journey to the eastern frontier; 1899), pp. 14a–b. Li was sent by the government to Mo-ho to investigate the business affairs

of the mining company. The company was in difficulty largely because of the excessive contributions it had to make to the local government's military budget.

96. Hsi-ch'ing, p. 11.

97. Liu Hsüan-min, p. 31.

98. Hsiao I-shan, "T'un-ken yu i-min," 6.3:36–43 (1951).

99. *CLTC*, 29:3b.

100. *HCK*, 12:4.

101. *HCK*, 17:2b.

102. Hsi-ch'ing, p. 11.

103. *HCK*, 8:11b–14b.

104. *HCK*, 8:20b, 33b–34.

105. Kuo T'ing-i, "Tung-pei ti k'ai t'o" (The opening of the northeast); in *Pien-chiang wen-hua lun-chi* (Collected essays on frontier culture; Taipei, 1953), I, 55.

106. *Ibid.*, p. 56.

107. James, p. 371.

108. Inaba, p. 332.

109. *Chi-lin hsin-chih*, 2:83; *Chu-ho hsien chih* (Gazetteer of Chu-ho hsien), comp. Sung Ching-wen et al. (1929), 15:2.

110. Inaba, p. 332.

111. *Chi-lin hsin chih*, 2:84; Tung Ch'iu-shui, *Tung-pei feng-t'u hsiao chih* (Customs of the northeast; Hong Kong, 1948), p. 16. Meng Shen, "Meng-ku Kuo-lo-ssu hou-ch'i lü-hsing tsa-chi" (Miscellaneous notes on a journey through the Gorlos Rear Banner); in *Man-yü chi-i* (Interesting journeys; Shanghai, 1918), I, 4.

112. Ch'i Chin, pp. 20–21; Tung Ch'iu-shui, pp. 16–17. *Chuang-ho hsien chih* (Gazetteer of Chuang-ho *hsien*), comp. Li Ch'i-shih et al. (1934), 13:12.

113. James, pp. 251–254.

114. Ts'ao T'ing-chieh, *Hsi-po-li t'ung-pien chi-yao*, p. 37b.

115. Arseniev, pp. 179–180.

116. Li T'ing-yü, pp. 19–21.

117. *Ibid.*

118. Arseniev, pp. 185, 213–214, 222–225.

119. Hsü Shih-ch'ang, chap. on Ch'ang-Lin, pp. 28b–30; in *TSCL*, vol. 1. The term *hsiang-yüeh* as used in China proper referred generally to a system of village lectures. See Hsiao Kung-ch'uan, *Rural China: Imperial Control in the Nineteenth Century* (Seattle, 1960), p. 185.

120. Yang Pin, pp. 12b–13. James, p. 435.

121. Sutō, p. 178.

122. Sa-ying-e, p. 17b.

123. *Ibid.*, p. 13.

124. Hsi-ch'ing, pp. 25b–26; Hsü Tsung-liang, pp. 17a–b.

125. Wu Chen-ch'en, p. 4.

126. Yang Pin, p. 9b; Hsi-ch'ing, pp. 22b, 25.

127. Wu Chen-ch'en, pp. 5b–6; Yang Pin, p. 11.

128. James, pp. 372–373.

129. See *Hu-lan fu chih*, 8:20–32. Hsü Shih-ch'ang, chap. on chün-cheng, pp. 142–143b; in *TSCL*, vol. 4.

6. The Frontier Government in Transition

1. Ho Ping-ti believes that by 1750–1775 the optimum condition for population increase had been reached in China. Thereafter, further growth produced corresponding depression in the living standard of the people. See Ho Ping-ti, p. 270.

2. *CLTC*, 51:23b–24.

3. *HCK*, 59:24; also, Hsü Tsung-liang, p. 12b.

4. See Teng Ssu-yü and John K. Fairbank, *China's Response to the West* (Cambridge, Mass., 1954), for examples of their writings on this subject.

5. Lo Erh-kang, pp. 55–57.

6. Kuo T'ing-i, "Tung-pei ti k'ai-t'o," pp. 54–56.

7. Arseniev, pp. 71–72.

8. Estimate by Lopatin. Cited in S. M. Shirokogoroff "Northern Tungus Migrations in the Far East," *The Journal of the North China Branch of the Royal Asiatic Society*, 57:172–173 (1926).

9. See biographies of Buteha personalities in Meng Ting-kung, pp. 3b–38.

10. Hsü Ts-ung-liang, pp. 14a–b; also *HCK*, 26:58b–59b.

11. Meng Ting-kung, pp. 8b–9b; also, Liu Weng-feng, p. 34.

12. Hsü Shih-ch'ang, chap. on Hulun Buir, pp. 31–32; in *TSCL*, vol. 1.

13. Hsü Hsi, pp. 155–156.

14. Tsou Shang-yu and Chu Chen-hsin, *Hulun Buir k'ai-yao* (General information on Hulun Buir; n.p., n.d.), p. 56.

15. Chu Ch'i-ch'ien, 1:1a–b. Chu was the director of the Mongol Affairs Bureau in Manchuria 1907–1909. See also Lattimore, *Manchuria,* pp. 230–231.

16. See Hsiao I-shan, *Ch'ing-tai t'ung-shih*, I, 557–559.

17. Hsü Shih-ch'ang, *T'ui-keng-t'ang cheng-shu* (Public papers from the Studio for Retirement; 1914), 6:19b–20, 8:7, 27. See also *CLTC*, 52:14b–16.

18. Hsü Shih-ch'ang, *T'ui-keng-t'ang cheng-shu,* 7:5a–b.

19. Hsü Tsung-liang, p. 11b. See also Ch'eng Te-ch'üan, *Ch'eng chung-ch'eng tsou-kao,* app., 1:16–17b.

20. Hsü Shih-ch'ang, *T'ui-keng-t'ang cheng-shu,* 11:8a–b.

21. *Hu-lan fu chih,* 3:6, 7b.

22. Hsü Tsung-liang, p. 19.

23. *Ibid.,* p. 14b.

24. Ch'eng Te-ch'üan, "Tz'u-fu-lou ch'i-shih" (Correspondence from the Tz'u fu-lou); in *Ch'eng chung-ch'eng tso-kao,* 1:16–17.

25. Hsü Tsung-liang, pp. 15b–17.

26. Ts'ao T'ing-chieh, *Tung-san-sheng yü-ti t'u-shuo* (Notes on the geography of the Three Eastern Provinces; Shanghai, 1936), app., pp. 10b–11. The imperial gifts were known locally as *urin*, a Manchu term for fabrics and other forms of wealth.

27. Hsü Shih-ch'ang, chap. on Chi-lin, p. 21; in *TSCL*, vol. 8.

28. *Ibid.,* p. 23b.

29. Hsü Tsung-liang, p. 10b; also, Hsü Shih-ch'ang, chap. on Heilungkiang, pp. 26a–b; in *TSCL*, vol. 8.

30. *Ibid.,* p. 24.

31. *HCK*, 8:11b–14b.

32. *Hu-lan fu chih*, 2:5b.
33. *Ibid.*, 2:4a–b.
34. *Ibid.*, 2:5b.
35. *HCK*, 8:20b–25b.
36. For an account of the organization and functions of the village schools, granaries, and *pao-chia* units in China proper, see Hsiao Kung-ch'uan, chaps. 3, 5, 6.
37. *HCK*, 8:26b–27.
38. *Wang-k'uei hsien chih* (Gazetteer of Wang-k'uei *hsien*), comp. Chang Yü-shu et al. (1919), 1:41b.
39. *Hu-lan fu chih*, 2:39a–b.
40. *Ibid.*, 2:39b–41b.
41. There are many conflicting details on Chang's early career. The following sketch is a composite picture drawn from these sources: Wang T'ieh-han, "Chang Yü-t'ing hsien-sheng ti ch'u-nien" (Chang Yü-t'ing's early years); in *Chuan-chi wen-hsüeh*, 5.6:28 (1964); Ts'ao Te-hsüan, "Wo so chih-tao ti Chang Tso-lin" (The Chang Tso-lin whom I knew); in *ibid.*, 5.6:24; "Chang Tso-lin," in *Biographical Dictionary of Republican China*, ed. Howard L. Boorman (New York, 1967), I, 115–122.
42. Wang T'ieh-han, "Chang Yü-t'ing ti ch'u-nien," 5.6:28.
43. Ch'i Chin, pp. 29–31.
44. *Ibid.*, p. 32.
45. Ts'ao Te-hsüan, 5.6:24; "Chang Tso-lin," p. 116.
46. Wang T'ieh-han, "Chang Yü-t'ing ti ch'u-nien," 5.6:28.
47. Wu T'ing-hsüeh, *Tung-san-sheng yen-k'o piao*, tables, 4, 5, and 6.
48. *CLTC*, 52:1; also *HCK*, 27:1.
49. Hummel, II, 880. *Yang-wu yün-tung* (The Westernization movement), ed. Chung-kuo shih-hsüeh-hui (Chinese historical association; Shanghai, 1926), IV, 393–406.
50. *CLTC*, 43:2–3b, 6b–7, 11–13.
51. *HCK*, 18:3b–4.
52. *HCK*, 18:12b–20b.
53. *CLTC*, 43:1b.
54. *HCK*, 23:2b–4b.
55. *CLTC*, 41:3b–8b.
56. *CLTC*, 41:12b–20; also, *Yang-wu yün-tung*, 7:145–149.
57. See *TSCL*, vol. 3 for accounts of diplomatic negotiations between frontier authorities and the Russians.
58. Hsü Shu-hsi, *China and her Political Entity* (New York, 1926), p. 285.
59. Hsü Shih-ch'ang, app. to Yen-chi, chap. 7, pp. 13–15; in *TSCL*, vol. 1.
60. Hsü Shu-hsi, pp. 286–287.
61. Hsü Shih-ch'ang, chap. on Ch'ou Meng (Mongol policy), pp. 41–44b; in *TSCL* vol. 2.
62. Hsü Shih-ch'ang's chap. on Meng-ch'i (Mongol banners), pp. 39a–b; in *ibid.*
63. Shen Chao-t'i, 1:4b–5.
64. Hsü Shih-ch'ang, chap. on Ch'ou Meng, pp. 39a–b; in *TSCL*, vol. 2.
65. Hsü Shih-ch'ang, Introduction, pp. 1b–2b; in *ibid.*
66. The proceeds of the land sale were usually divided equally between the govern-

ment and the Mongol banners. The land tax was commonly fixed at 660 copper coins per *shang*, from which amount the government received 240 coins and banner 420 coins. See Hsü Shih-ch'ang chap. on Ch'ou Meng, pp. 38–39b; in *ibid.*

67. Hsü Shih-ch'ang, chap. on Meng-ch'i, pp. 2b–4; in *ibid.*

7. Reorganization of the Frontier Government

1. Kudō Takeshige *Konoe Atsumaro kō* (Prince Konoe Atsumaro; Tokyo, 1938), pp. 251–252

2. *Ibid.*, pp. 189–190.

3. Chang Chih-tung *Chang Wen-hsiang-kung ch'üan-chi* (The complete works of Chang chih-tung; Peiping, 1928), 55:2–15b.

4. The following biographical sketch of Ch'eng's career is put together from various memorials written by Ch'eng's superiors. See Ch'eng Te-ch'üan *Ch'eng chung-ch'eng tsou-kao* (Memorials of Governor Ch'eng) 1910, 3, pp. 1–14. For Ch'eng's own account of his activities during the Russian invasion, see *Keng-tzu chiao-she yü-lu* (An aspect of the 1900 negotiations), a volume of Ch'eng's letters written in 1900 and included in his *Ch'eng chung-ch'eng tsou-kao.*

5. The record of this highly interesting audience is kept in *Tz'u-fu-lou pi-chi* (Journal from the Tower of Happiness Bestowed), pp. 1–7b also included in *Ch'eng chung-ch'eng tsou-kao.*

6. *Ibid.*, pp. 8b–9b.

7. *Ibid.*, pp. 8b–9.

8. *Ibid.*, pp. 9b–10.

9. *Ibid.*, pp. 12–17.

10. *Tz'u-fu-lou ch'i-shih*, 1:15b–18b. This is a collection in four *chüan* of Ch'eng Te-ch'üan's official correspondence from 1994 to 1907. It is also included in his *Ch'eng chung-ch'eng tsou-kao.*

11. See Li Chien-nung, *Chung-kuo chien-pai-nien cheng-chih shih* (The political history of China in the last hundred years; Shanghai, 1947), pp. 227–230. Li believes that the Empress Dowager had no real intention of carrying out a thorough reform program.

12. For a summary of the points discussed in the treaty conference, see Huang Ta-shou, *Chung-kuo chien-tai shih* (A history of modern China; Taipei, 1955), I, 255–263.

13. In reality among the new ministers appointed to the reorganized Peking government in 1906, seven were Manchus, four Chinese, one Mongol bannerman, and one Chinese bannerman, a distribution which put the Chinese at a greater disadvantage than ever before. See Li Chien-nung, p. 255.

14. Ch'eng Te-ch'üan, *Ch'eng chung-ch'eng tsou-kao,* 7:39–50.

15. *Ibid., chüan* 7, app. 2, pp. 1–6b.

16. The fourteen officials included six grand councillors, seven ministers, five *cheng-wu ta-ch'en* (ex-officio members of the Nei-ko hui-i cheng-wu ch'u or Committee of Ministers), the governor-general of Chihli, and a senior president of the censorate. Many of the above members held concurrent posts. For text of the edict, see *Ta-Ch'ing Kuang-hsü hsin fa-ling* (New laws and decrees of the Kuang-hsü reign of the Ch'ing dynasty; Shanghai, 1909), *ts'e* 1 (Edicts), pp. 16a–b.

17. *Ibid.*, pp. 17a–b.

18. For the relationship between Prince Ch'ing and Yuan and their positions in the court, see Li Chien-nung, pp. 230–231. Mrs. Fang Lien-che wrote a preliminary biographical sketch of Hsü Shih-ch'ang for the Research Project on Men and Politics in Modern China, Columbia University.

19. The memorial, included in a collection of Hsü's memorials, official correspondence, and telegrams is undated. See Hsü Shih-ch'ang, *T'ui-keng-t'ang cheng-shu*, 5:1–10b, 6:1–30.

20. *Ibid.*, 7:11–16.

21. See Li Chien-nung, pp. 243–246 for a full discussion of Manchu-Chinese antagonism existing in this period.

22. Ch'ung-hou, 8:1–5.

23. *Ibid.*, 8:1.

24. *Ibid.*, 8:3.

25. *Ibid.*, 8:4.

26. *Ibid.*, 8:17b; *Fengt'ien t'ung-chih* (Gazetteer of Fengt'ien), comp. Pai Yung-ching et al. (1934), 124:1b.

27. *Ibid.*, 49:29a–b.

28. Wu Tseng-ch'i, *Ch'ing-shih kang-yao* (A chronology Ch'ing history; Shanghai, 1913), pp. 581–582. Tuan was dismissed because he was impeached for presenting a singsong girl to Tsai-chen after the latter's return from Manchuria. T'ang, Chu, and Tuan were all members of the Yuan Shih-k'ai clique.

29. Hsü Shih-ch'ang, *T'ui-Keng-t'ang cheng-shu*, 8:21–30.

30. See Shen Nai-cheng, "Ch'ing-mo chih tu-fu chi-ch'üan, chung-yang chi-ch'üan, yü 't'ung-shu pan-kung'" (On the powers of the viceroys and governors of provinces in the last years of the Ch'ing); in *She-hui k'o-hsüeh*, 2.1:316–324 (1937).

31. Hsü Shih-ch'ang, 7:14. See also chap. on Fengt'ien, pp. 2–8b; in TSCL, vol. 2.

32. See tables in *Ch'ing-shih kao*, pp. 820–864.

33. Hsü Shih-ch'ang, chap. on Chi-lin, pp. 3–4; in *TSCL*, vol. 5.

34. Shen Chao-t'i, 2:3.

35. *Ibid.*, 2:5b–6.

36. See Hsi-liang's memorial on the establishment of a similar council in Fengt'ien in *Hsi-liang i-kao; tsou-kao* (Collected works of Hsi-liang; memorials), ed. Chung-kuo k'o-hsüeh-yuan li-shih yen-chiu-so ti-san-so (Institute of History, Third Institute, Chinese Academy of Sciences; Peking, 1959), II, 1129–30.

37. Hsü Shih-ch'ang, chap. on Chi-lin, p. 5, and chap. on Heilungkiang, p. 5; in *TSCL*, vol. 5.

38. *Ibid.*

39. Hsü Shih-ch'ang, chap. on Chi-lin, p. 7, and chap. on Heilungkiang, p. 6; in *ibid.* Also, Shen Chao-t'i, 2:9–12.

40. *Ibid.*, 2:22a–b.

41. *Ibid.*, 2:22b–23b; also, Hsü Shih-ch'ang, chap. on Chi-lin, p. 8, and chap. on Heilungkiang, p. 7; in *TSCL*, vol. 5.

42. Kuo Hsi-leng, *Chi-lin hui-cheng* (Topical notes on Chi-lin; 1914), pp. 70–71. See also Shih Chao-chi, *Shih Chih-chih hsien-sheng tsao nien hui-i lu* (Reminiscences of the early years of Mr. Shih Chih-chih; 1954), pp. 33–38, for his experience as Pin-chiang kuan tao.

43. Kuo Hsi-leng, p. 71. Shen Chao-t'i, 2:12–14.

44. Shih Chao-chi, pp. 35–36.

45. *TSCL*, V, 9, 12. Shen Chao-t'i, 2:25–26. The Office of Government Scrips was an agency empowered to issue scrips for general circulation without the usual banking safeguards. The over-issuance of these unbacked scrips caused serious financial losses to their holders prior to 1907. For a discussion of the origin of *kuan-t'ieh* (government scrips) see *Chi-lin chih kuan-t'ieh wen-t'i* (Government scrips in Chi-lin; n.d.), pp. 1–2.

46. Hsü Shih-ch'ang, chap. on Chi-lin, p. 1; in *TSCL*, vol. 10.

47. *Ibid.,* pp. 7a–b, 13–14.

48. *Ibid.,* pp. 16a–b.

49. *Ibid.,* p. 3.

50. *TSCL*, V, 10, 12a–b. Shen Chao-t'i, 3:1–2.

51. Hsü Shih-ch'ang, chap. on Chi-lin, p. 11; in *TSCL*, vol. 5. Shen Chao-t'i, 3:15–16b.

52. *Ibid.,* 3:18a–b.

53. Hsü Shih-ch'ang, chap. on Chi-lin, pp. 9–16; in *TSCL*, vol. 8.

54. Hsü Shih-ch'ang, Introductions, pp. 2b–4; in *TSCL*, vol. 2.

55. Hsü Shih-ch'ang, chap. on Ch'ou Meng, pp. 22–28; in *ibid.*

56. Shen Chao-t'i, 3:17a–b, 20a–b.

57. Hsü Shih-ch'ang, chap. on Chi-lin, pp. 29–33; in *TSCL*, vol. 5.

58. *Ibid.*, pp. 29a–b.

59. Kuo Hsi-leng, pp. 32–48.

60. Li was a returned student from Japan. He served successively in Kirin as a district magistrate, prefect of Pin-chou, prefect of Kirin, and intendant of the southwest circuit. See *Hsi-liang i-kao, tsou-kao*, 2:1236.

61. Li Shu-en, *Pin-chou fu cheng shu* (Public papers of the Pin-chou prefectural administration; Shanghai, 1909), Sect. 3, pp. 18–19.

62. *Ibid.*, p. 19. For a full discussion of this problem, see Ch'u T'ung-tsu, chaps. 3–6.

63. Li Shu-en, Sect. 3, pp. 20–26.

64. *Ibid.,* p. 59.

65. *Ibid.,* Sect. 2, pp. 15–16.

66. *Ibid.,* pp. 38–41.

67. Hsü Shih-ch'ang, chap. on Heilungkiang, pp. 2–3; in *TSCL*, vol. 5. *HCK*, 45:13–15, 28b–31b.

68. Hsü Shih-ch'ang, chap. on Heilungkiang, p. 17; in *TSCL*, vol. 5.

69. *Ibid.,* pp. 15–16.

70. *HCK*, 45:19b.

71. *HCK*, 45:24–26b.

72. *HCK,* 45:19.

73. *HCK,* 43:20b–21.

74. Meng Ting-kung, pp. 3a–b.

75. *Ibid.,* pp. 3b–4.

76. Hsü Shih-ch'ang, chap. on Heilungkiang, pp. 9a–b; in *TSCL*, vol. 8.

77. *HCK*, 43:28b–29. This account makes a mistake in identifying the military governor as T'e-p'u-ch'in, who served in that capacity from 1862 to 1865. The incumbent was actually Te-ying.

78. *HCK*, 26:31b.

79. *HCK*, 26:30. See also *Ai-hun hsien chih* (Gazetteer of Ai-hun hsien), comp. Hsu Hsi-lien et al. (1920), 13:2–3b.

80. *Ibid.*, 13:3b; also, *HCK*, 26:30–31b.

81. Ch'eng Te-ch'üan, *Ch'eng chiang-chün shou chiang tsou-kao* (Memorials of Military Governor Ch'eng in Heilungkiang; n.d.), 7:42b.

82. *Ibid.*, 7:43b–44.

83. *Hulun Buir chih lüeh*, p. 55.

84. *Ibid.*

85. *CLTC*, 52:1a–b.

86. *CLTC*, 53:1a–b.

87. Hummel, II, 881.

88. *CLTC*, 53:1.

89. *CLTC*, 53:3a–b.

90. *CLTC*, 53:18–19b.

91. See Ralph Powell, *The Rise of Chinese Military Power, 1895–1912* (Princeton, 1955), pp. 36–42.

92. *CLTC*, 54:1a–b, 11a–b. *HCK*, 27:5–7b.

93. *CLTC*, 54:11a–b.

94. Hsü Tsung-liang, pp. 17, 19b–20.

95. *Ibid.*, pp. 7b–8.

96. Hsü Shih-ch'ang, chap. on *chün-cheng*, pp. 118–129; in *TSCL*, vol. 4.

97. Shen Chao-t'i, 3:22b. The organization of the Provincial Staff followed the regulation drawn up by the Ministry of Army, see H. S. Brunnert and V. V. Hagelstrom, *Present Day Political Organization of China*, tr. A. Beltchenko and E. E. Moran (Shanghai, 1912), pp. 304–306.

98. Hsü Shih-ch'ang, chap. on *chün-cheng*, pp. 4–5b; in *TSCL*, vol. 4.

99. *Ibid.*, pp. 5b–10b.

100. *Ibid.*, pp. 11a–b. For the history of the Peiyang Army see Powell, pp. 200–219. Also Jerome Chen, *Yuan Shih-k'ai, 1859–1916* (Stanford, 1961), pp. 77–84.

101. Hsü Shih-ch'ang, chap. on *chün-cheng*, p. 1b; in *TSCL*, vol. 4.

102. Hsi-liang, 2:932.

103. *Ibid.*, 2:1107.

104. Shen Chien, "Hsin-hai ko-ming ch'ien-hsi wo-kuo chih lu-chün chi ch'i chün-fei" (China's land army and its finances on the eve of the revolution); in *She-hui k'o-hsüeh tsa-chih*, 2.2:389 (1937).

105. Hsü Shih-ch'ang, chap. on Chi-lin, pp. 14a–b; in *TSCL*, vol. 6.

106. *Ibid.*

107. *Ibid.*, p. 8.

108. *Ch'ing-shih kao*, p. 404.

109. See "Chieh-she chi-hui lu" (Regulations on associations and public gatherings); in *Hsin fa-ling chi-yao* (Selected new laws and decrees; Shanghai, 1910), pp. 1–9.

110. Hsü Shih-ch'ang, chap. on Chi-lin, pp. 14b–16; in *TSCL*, vol. 6.

111. For the texts of the imperial proclamations and the organic laws, see *Ta-Ch'ing Kuang-hsü hsin-fa-ling*, 1:26–27b; 2:1–32.

112. *Ibid.*, 2:4b–6.

113. *Ibid.*, 2:5–7.

114. *HCK*, 50:11b. In a telegram dated April 16, 1909, the court informed the Heilungkiang authorities to permit some 200 Manchus and Mongols who were literate in their own language but not in Chinese to vote in the first election but emphasized that it was not to be regarded as a precedent, see *Hsin fa-ling chi-yao*, p. 151.

115. See statistical reports in Li Shu-en, p. 36.

116. *Ibid.*, p. 39.

117. The number of eligible voters from *Hsin fa-ling chi-yao*, p. 141. The population figures from Hsü Shih-ch'ang, chap. on Chi-lin, pp. 22b, 24; in *TSCL*, vol. 6.

118. Hsü Shih-ch'ang, chap. on Heilungkiang, p. 10; in *ibid.* The actual number was probably greater than the official returns indicated because of the difficulties in counting the tribal peoples and immigrants.

119. *HCK*, 50:23b.

120. For an account of the petitioning movement, see *Hsin-hai ko-ming* (The 1911 Revolution), ed. *Chung-kuo shih hsüeh hui* (Shanghai, 1957), IV, 1–9.

121. Such assembly leaders as Chang Chien of Kiangsu, T'ang Shou-ch'ien of Chekiang, Sun Hung-i of Chihli, T'ang Hua-lung of Hupei, T'an Yen-k'ai of Hunan, and P'u Tien-chien of Szechwan all joined the revolutionary camp in 1911. For details see accounts of revolutionary activities in chapters devoted to these provinces in *ibid.*

122. Ch'i Chin, p. 51; also, Ning Wu, "Tung-pei Hsin-hai ko-ming chien shu" (An account of the 1911 Revolution in the northeast); in vol. 5 of *Hsin-hai ko-ming hui-i-lu* (Reminiscences of the 1911 Revolution), ed. Chung-kuo jen-min cheng-chih hsieh-shang hui-i and the Ch'üan-kuo wei-yüan-hui wen shih tzu-liao yen-chiu wei-yüan-hui (Peking, 1961–1963), p. 538.

123. *Ibid.*, pp. 538–539.

124. T'ien Pu-i, *Pei-yang chün-fa shih hua* (The story of the Peiyang warlords; Taipei, 1965), I, 105, 108.

125. Ning Wu, pp. 536–537.

126. *Ibid.*, p. 537.

127. *Ibid.*, p. 536.

128. *Ibid.*, p. 541.

129. T'ien Pu-i, I, 162.

130. *Ibid.*, I, 163–164.

131. Ning Wu, pp. 373–374.

132. Wang T'ieh-han, "Chang Yu-t'ing hsien-sheng chang-wo Tung-san-sheng chün-cheng-ch'üan ti ching-kuo" (How Mr. Chang Yü-t'ing obtained military and political power in the Three Eastern Provinces); in *Chüan-chi wen-hsüeh*, 5.3:31 (1964).

133. Ning Wu, pp. 536–537.

134. *Chin-tai tung-pei jen-min ko-ming yün-tung shih*, pp. 217–220, 232.

135. Wang T'ieh-han, "Tung san-sheng chün-cheng-ch'üan," 5.3:32–34.

136. *Chi lin hsin-chih*, 2:452.

137. *Tung-pei yao-lan* (Handbook of the northeast), comp. Chin Yü-fu et al. (Chungking, 1944), p. 235.

138. *Chi-lin hsin chih*, 2:465–466.

8. Transformation of the Ch'ing Manchurian Frontier Policy

1. *Man-chou lao-tang mi-lu* (Secret records of the old Manchu archives), ed. Chin-liang (1929), 2:34b–35, 44a–b; also, *Mambun Rōtō*, VII, 1223, 1438–41.

2. *CLTC*, 1:17–18b.

3. *CLTC*, 1:28–29.

Bibliography

Ai-hun hsien chih 瑷琿縣志(Gazetteer of Ai-hun hsien), comp. Hsü Hsi-lien 徐希廉 et al. 20 *chüan;* 1920.

Arseniev, V. K. *Dersu the Trapper,* tr. Malcolm Burr. New York, 1941.

Baddeley, J. F. *Russia, Mongolia, China.* Reprint; 2 vols.; New York, 1965.

Brunnert, H. S. and V. V. Hagelstrom. *Present Day Political Organization of China,* tr. A. Beltchenko and E. E. Moran. Shanghai, 1912.

Chang Chih-tung 張之洞. *Chang Wen-hsiang-kung ch'üan-chi* 張文襄公全集 (The complete works of Chang Chih-tung). 229 *chüan;* Peiping, 1928.

Chao-lien 昭槤. *Hsiao-t'ing tsa-lu* 嘯亭雜錄 (Random notes from the Whistling Pavilion). 6 *chüan;* 1880.

Ch'en Ch'i-t'ien 陳其田. *Shansi p'iao-chuang k'ao lüeh* 山西票莊考畧 (A brief history of Shansi banks). Shanghai, 1936.

Ch'en, Jerome. *Yuan Shih-k'ai, 1859–1916.* Stanford, 1961.

Ch'en Wen-shih 陳文石. "Man-chou pa-ch'i niu-lu ti kou-ch'eng" 滿洲八旗牛彔的構成 (The formation of the Manchu eight-banner *niru*); in *Ta-lu tsa-chih* 大陸雜誌 (Mainland magazine), vol. 31, nos. 9 and 10 (1965).

Ch'eng Te-ch'üan 程德全. *Ch'eng chiang-chün shou-chiang tsou-kao* 程將軍守江奏稿 (Memorials of Military Governor Ch'eng in Heilungkiang). 17 *chüan;* n. d. The memorials are dated from 1903 to 1906.

——— *Ch'eng chung-ch'eng tsou-kao* 程中丞奏稿 (Memorials of Governor Ch'eng). 19 *chüan;* 1910.

Chi-lin chih kuan-t'ieh wen-t'i 吉林之官帖問題 (The problem of government scrips in Chi-lin). n.p.; n.d.

Chi-lin hsin chih 吉林新志 (New gazetteer of Chi-lin), comp. Liu Shuang 劉爽. Hsin-ching, 1934.

Chi-lin t'ung-chih, see *CLTC.*

Ch'i Chin 祁瑾. *Tung-pei chang-ku* 東北掌故 (Historical notes on the northeast). Taipei, 1959.

Chin Te-shun 金德純. *Ch'i-chün chih* 旗軍志 (The banner army); in *Chao-tai ts'ung-shu* 昭代叢書 (Reprinted works of a glorious era). n.d.

Chin-tai tung-pei jen-min ko-ming yün-tung shih 近代東北人民革命運動史 (A history of the recent revolutionary movement of the people of the northeast), comp. Chung-kuo k'o-hsüeh-yüan Chi-lin fen-yüan li-shih yen-chiu-so 中國科學院吉林分院歷史研究所 (The History Institute of the Kirin Branch of the Chinese Academy of Sciences) and Chi-lin shih-fan ta-hsüeh li-shih-hsi 吉林師範大學歷史系 (The history department of Kirin Normal College). Chang-ch'un, 1960.

Ch'in Tai-yüan 秦岱源. *Tung-ch'ui chi-wen* 東陲紀聞 (Notes on the eastern frontier),

Preface. 1912.

Ch'ing-ch'ao hsü wen-hsien t'ung-k'ao 清朝續文獻通考 (Encyclopedia of the historical records of the Ch'ing dynasty, continued), 1921. Reprint; Shanghai, 1936.

Ch'ing-ch'ao t'ung-tien 清朝通典 (Encyclopedia of Ch'ing institutional history), 1785. Reprint; Shanghai, 1936.

Ch'ing-ch'ao wen-hsien t'ung-k'ao 清朝文獻通考 (Encyclopedia of the historical records of the Ch'ing dynasty), 1785. Reprint; Shanghai, 1936.

Ch'ing-shih kao 清史稿 (A draft history of the Ch'ing dynasty), ed. Chao Erh-sun 趙爾巽, 1927. Reprint; Shanghai, 1936.

Ch'ing-tai pien-cheng t'ung-k'ao 清代邊政通考 (Classified laws and decrees on frontier administration during the Ch'ing), comp. Ch'en Ping-kuang 陳炳光. Nanking, 1934.

Chu Ch'i-ch'ien 朱啟鈐. *Tung-san-sheng Meng-wu kung-tu hui-pien* 東三省蒙務公牘彙編 (Collected public correspondence on Mongol affairs in the Three Eastern Provinces). 5 *chüan;* 1909.

Chu-ho hsien-chih 珠河縣志 (Gazetteer of Chu-ho hsien), comp. Sung Ching-wen 宋景文 et al. 20 *chüan;* 1929.

Ch'u T'ung-tsu. *Local Government in China under the Ch'ing*. Cambridge, Mass., 1962.

Chuang-ho hsien-chih 莊河縣志 (Gazetteer of Chuang-ho hsien), comp. Li Ch'i-shih 李其實 et al. 18 *chüan;* 1934.

Ch'ung-hou 崇厚. *Sheng-ching tien-chih pei-k'ao* 盛京典制備考 (The administrative system of Sheng-ching). 8 *chüan;* 1878.

CLTC: Chi-lin t'ung-chih 吉林通志 (Gazetteer of Chi-lin), comp. Li Kuei-lin 李桂林 et al. 122 *chüan;* 1891. Reprint; 10 vols.; Taipei, 1965.

Colquhoun, Archibald R. *Overland to China*. New York, 1900.

Fang Chao-ying. "A Technique for Estimating the Numerical Strength of the Early Manchu Military Forces," *Harvard-Yenching Journal of Asiatic Studies,* vol. 13 (1950).

Fang Kung-ch'ien 方拱乾. *Chüeh-yü chi-lüeh* 絶域紀畧 (Notes on a remote land), Hsiao-fang-hu-chai yü-ti ts'ung-ch'ao 小方壺齋輿地叢鈔 (The little square vase studio geographical series); 1894.

Fang Shih-chi 方式濟. *Lung-sha chi-lüeh* 龍沙紀畧 (Frontier notes), Hsiao-fang-hu-chai yü-ti ts'ung-ch'ao (The little square vase studio geographical series); 1894.

Feng-t'ien t'ung-chih 奉天通志 (Gazetteer of Feng-t'ien), comp. Pai Yung-cheng 白永貞 et al. 260 *chüan;* 1934.

Fu Lo-shu. *A Documentary Chronicle of Sino-Western Relations, 1644–1820*. 2 vols.; Tucson, 1966.

Hatada Takashi 旗田巍. "Mindai joshinjin no tekki ni tsuite" 明代女眞人の鐵器について (Development of the use and manufacture of ironware by the Juchen in the Ming period); in *Tōhō Gakuhō* 東方學報 (Journal of Oriental studies), no. 11, pt. 1 (1940).

HCK: Heilungkiang chih kao 黒龍江志稿 (Draft gazetteer of Heilungkiang), comp. Chang Po-ying 張伯英 et al. 62 *chüan;* appendix, 4 *chüan;* Peiping, 1933. Reprint; 8 vols.; Taipei, 1965.

Heilungkiang chih kao, see *HCK*.

Ho Ping-ti. *Studies on the Population of China, 1368–1953*. Cambridge, Mass.; 1959.

Hsi-ch'ing 西清. *Heilungkiang wai-chi* 黒龍江外記 (A study of the Heilungkiang area),

Hsiao-fang-hu-chai yü-ti ts'ung-ch'ao (The little square vase studio geographical series); 1894.

Hsi-liang 錫良. *Hsi-liang i-kao, tsou-kao* 錫良遺稿，奏稿 (Collected works of Hsi-liang, memorials), ed. Chung-kuo k'o-hsüeh-yüan li-shih yen-chiu-so ti-san-so 中國科學院歷史研究所，第三所 (Institute of History, Third Institute, Chinese Academy of Sciences). 2 vols.; Peking, 1959.

Hsiao I-shan 蕭一山. "Ch'ing-tai tung-pei chih t'un-k'eng yü i-min" 清代東北之屯墾與移民 (Military colonization and immigration in the northeast during the Ch'ing); in *Hsüeh-shi chi-k'an* 學術季刊 (Academic quarterly), vol. 6, no. 3 (1951).

——— *Ch'ing-tai t'ung-shih* 清代通史 (A history of the Ch'ing dynasty). 5 vols.; Taipei, 1961–1963.

Hsiao Kung-chuan. *Rural China: Imperial Control in the Nineteenth Century*. Seattle, 1960.

Hsieh Kuo-chen 謝國楨. *Ch'ing-ch'u liu-jen k'ai-fa tung-pei shih* 清初流人開發東北史 (A history of the development of the northeast by early Ch'ing exiles). Shanghai, 1948.

Hsin fa-ling chi-yao 新法令輯要 (A selection of new laws and decrees). Shanghai, 1910.

Hsin-hai ko-ming 辛亥革命 (The 1911 Revolution), ed. Chung-kuo shih-hsüeh hui 中國史學會 (The Chinese historical society). 8 vols.; Shanghai, 1957.

Hsü Shih-ch'ang 徐世昌. *T'ui-keng't'ang cheng-shu* 退耕堂政書 (Public papers from the studio for retirement). 55 *chüan;* 1914.

——— *Tung-san-sheng cheng-lüeh,* see *TSCL.*

Hsü Shu hsi. *China and her Political Entity*. New York, 1926.

Hsü Tsung-liang 徐宗亮. *Heilungkiang shu-lüeh* 黑龍江述畧 (A brief study of Heilungkiang), Hsiao-fang-hu-chai yü-ti ts'ung-ch'ao (The little square vase studio geographical series); 1894.

Hu-lan fu-chih 呼蘭府志 (Gazetteer of Hulan prefecture), comp. Huang Wei-han 黃維翰 et al. 12 *chüan;* 1915.

Hua-tien hsien-chih 樺甸縣法 (Gazetteer of Hua-tien), comp. Ch'en T'ieh-mei 陳鐵梅 et al. 10 *chüan;* 1931.

Huang Ta-shou 黃大受. *Chung-kuo chin-tai shih* 中國近代史 (A history of modern China). 3 vols.; Taipei, 1955.

Hulun Buir chih-lüeh 呼倫貝爾志畧 (Short gazetteer of Hulun Buir), comp. Chang Chia-fan 張家璠 et al. Shanghai, 1922.

Hummel, Arthur W., ed. *Eminent Chinese of the Ch'ing Period*. 2 vols.; Washington, D. C., 1943–1944.

I-lan hsien-chih 依蘭縣志 (Gazetteer of I-lan hsien), comp. Yang Pu-ch'ih 楊步墀 et al. 1920.

Imamura Tomo 今村鞆. *Ninjin shi* 人參史 (Encyclopedia of Jinseng). 7 vols.; Seoul, 1934–1940.

Inaba Iwakichi 稻葉岩吉. *Zōtei Manshū hattatsu shi* 增訂滿洲發達史 (Enlarged edition of the history of the development of Manchuria). Tokyo, 1935.

James, H. E. M. *The Long White Mountain*. London, 1888.

Kao Shih-ch'i 高士奇. *Hu-ts'ung tung-hsün jih-lu* 扈從東巡日錄 (Diary of an eastern journey in the emperor's entourage), Hsiao-fang-hu-chai yü-ti ts'ung-ch'ao (The little square vase studio geographical series); 1894.

Kawakubo Teirō 川久保悌郎. "Shindai Manshū ni okeru shōka no zokusei ni tsuite" 清代滿洲における燒鍋の簇生について (On the prosperity of *shao-kuo* in Manchuria during the Ch'ing); in *Wada hakushi koki kinen Tōyōshi ronsō* 和田博士古稀紀念東洋史論叢 (Oriental studies presented to Sei [Kiyoshi] Wada on his seventieth birthday). Tokyo, 1960.

Kudō Takeshige 工藤武重. *Konoe Atsumaro kō* 近衛篤麿公 (Prince Konoe Atsumaro). Tokyo, 1938.

Kuo Hsi-leng 郭熙楞. *Chi-lin hui-cheng* 吉林彙徵 (Topical notes on Chi-lin). 1914.

Kuo T'ing-i 郭廷以. "Tung-pei ti k'ai-t'o" 東北的開拓 (The opening of the northeast); in *Pien-chiang wen-hua lun-chi* 邊疆文化論集 (Collected essays on frontier culture). 3 vols.; Taipei, 1953.

——— *Chin-tai Chung-kuo shih-shih jih-chih, Ch'ing chi* 近代中國史事日誌，清季 (A daily chronological account of modern Chinese history, late Ch'ing period). 2 vols.; Taipei, 1963.

Lattimore, Owen. *The Mongols of Manchuria*. New York, 1934.

——— *Manchuria, Cradle of Conflict*. New York, 1935.

Li Chi. "Manchuria in History," *The Chinese Social and Political Science Review*, vol. 16, no. 2 (1932).

——— *The Formation of the Chinese People*. Cambridge, Mass., 1928.

Li Chien-nung 李劍農. *Chung-kuo chin pai-nien cheng-chih shih* 中國近百年政治史 (A political history of China in the last hundred years). Shanghai, 1947.

Li Shu-en 李澍恩. *Pin-chou fu cheng-shu* 賓州府政書 (Public papers of the Pin-chou prefectural administration). Shanghai, 1909.

Li-shu hsien-chih 梨樹縣志 (Gazetteer of Li-shu hsien), comp. Meng Ch'ing-chang 孟慶璋 et al. 8 *chüan*; 1934.

Li Shu-t'ang 李樹棠. *Tung-chiao chi-hsing* 東徼紀行 (Journey to the eastern frontier), Preface. 1899.

Li T'ing-yü 李廷玉. "T'iao ch'a Ch'ang-pai shan pao-kao chih i-chien-shü" 調査長白山報告意見書 (A report on the investigations in Ch'ang-pai shan and related proposals); in *Tung-san-sheng pien-wu chi-yao* 東三省邊務輯要 (Selected documents on frontier affairs of the Three Eastern Provinces), 3:22. Peking, 1917.

Ling Shun-sheng 凌純聲. *Sung-hua-chiang hsia-yu ti Heh-che-tsu* 松花江下游的赫哲族 (The Gold tribes of the lower course of the Sungari River); in Chung-yang yen-chiu-yüan li-shih yü-yen yen-chiu so 中央研究院歷史語言研究所 (National Institute of History and Philology) monographs, series A, no. 14. Nanking, 1934.

Liu Hsuan-ming. "Russo-Chinese Relations up to the Treaty of Nerchinsk," *The Chinese Social and Political Science Review*, vol. 23, no. 4 (1940).

Liu Hsüan-min 劉選民. "Ch'ing-tai Tung-san-sheng i-min yü k'ai-k'en" 清代東三省移民與開墾 (Immigration and colonization in the Three Eastern Provinces during the Ch'ing); in *Shih-hsüeh nien-pao* 史學年報 (Journal of history), vol. 2, no. 5 (1938).

Liu Wen-feng 劉文鳳. *Tung-ch'ui chi-hsing* 東陲紀行 (Journey to the eastern frontier). n.p., n.d.

Lo Erh-kang 羅爾綱. *Lü-ying ping-chih* 綠營兵志 (The Green Standard army). Chungking, 1945.

Malozemoff, Andrew. *Russian Far Eastern Policy, 1881–1904*. Berkeley, 1958.

Mambun Rōtō 満文老檔 (Chronicles written in old Manchu script), tr. Kanda Nobuo 神田信夫 et al. 7 vols.; Tokyo, 1955–1963.

Mamiya Rinzō 間宮林藏. *Mamiya Rinzō no Kokuryūkō tanken— Tōdatsu kikō* 間宮林藏の黒龍江探檢—東韃紀行 (The exploration of the Amur River by Mamiya Rinzō), ed. Mantetsu Koho Ka 滿鐵弘報課編 (Information bureau of the South Manchurian Railway). Mukden, 1940.

Man-chou lao-tang mi-lu 滿州老檔秘錄 (Secret records from the old Manchu archive), ed. Chin-liang 金梁. 2 *ts'e;* 1929.

Man-Mo sosho 滿蒙叢書 (Encyclopedia of Manchuria and Mongolia), ed. Naito Konan 內藤湖南. 7 vols.; Dairen, 1922.

Manshū tsūshi 滿州通志 (Gazetteer of Manchuria), comp. Tōa Dōbunkai 東亞同文會 (East Asian cultural association). Tokyo, 1906.

Meng Shen 孟森. *Ch'ing-ch'ao ch'ien-chi* 清朝前記 (The origin of the Ch'ing dynasty). Shanghai, 1930.

——— "Pa-ch'i chih-tu k'ao-shih" 八旗制度考實 (The origin and growth of the eight-banner system); in *Bulletin of the Institute of History and Philology,* vol. 6, pt. 3 (1936).

——— "Meng-ku Kuo-lo-ssu hou-ch'i lü-hsing tsa-chi" 蒙古郭羅斯後旗旅行雜記 (Miscellaneous notes on a journey through the Gorlos Rear Banner); in *Man-yu chi-i* 漫游誌異 (Interesting journeys), vol. 1. Shanghai, 1918.

Meng Ting-kung 孟定恭. *Buteha chih-lüeh* 布特哈志畧 (Notes on Buteha), a private compilation in the local gazetteer format, preface. 1932. Reprinted in *Liao hai ts'ung-shu* 遼海叢書 (Reprinted works on the Liao region); 1936.

Mo Tung-yin 莫東寅. *Man-tsu shih lun-ts'ung* 滿族史論叢 (Collected essays on the history of the Manchus). Peking, 1958.

Nakayama Hachirō 中山八郎. "Min-matsu Jochoku to hachiki teki tōsei ni kansuru sobyō" 明末女直と八旗的統制に關する素描 (A sketch of the Jurched tribes at the end of the Ming dynasty and the control of the eight banners); in *Manshū shi kenkyū* 滿洲史研究 (Studies in Manchu history). Tokyo, 1935.

Ning-an hsien-chih 寧安縣志 (Gazetteer of Ning-an hsien), comp. Mei Wen-chao 梅文昭 et al. 4 *chüan;* 1924.

Ning Wu 寧武. "Tung-pei Hsin-hai ko-ming chien-shu" 東北辛亥革命簡述 (An account of the 1911 Revolution in the northeast); vol. 5 of *Hsin-hai ko-ming hui-i-lu* 辛亥革命回憶錄 (Reminiscences of the 1911 Revolution), ed. Chung-kuo jen-min cheng-chih hsieh-shang hui-i ch'üan-kuo wei-yüan-hui wen-shih tzu-liao yen-chiu wei-yüan-hui (The research committee on literary and historical materials of the National Committee of the Chinese People's Political Consultative Conference). Peking, 1961–1963.

Pa-ch'i t'ung-chih ch'u-chi, see *PCTC.*

PCTC: Pa-ch'i t'ung-chih ch'u-chi 八旗通志初集 (Collected documents on the eight banners, first collection), ed. O-er-t'ai 鄂爾泰 et al. 250 *chüan;* 1739.

P'eng Yü-hsin 彭雨新. "Ch'ing-mo chung-yang yü ko sheng ts'ai cheng kuan-hsi" 清末中央與各省財政關係 (The fiscal relationship between the central government and the provinces during the late Ch'ing); in *She-hui k'o-hsüeh tsa-chih* 社會科學雜誌 (Journal of the social sciences), vol. 9, no. 1 (1937).

Powell, Ralph L. *The Rise of Chinese Military Power, 1895–1912.* Princeton, 1955.

Ravenstein, E. G. *The Russians on the Amur*. London, 1861.

Sa-ying-e 薩英額. *Chi-lin wai-chi* 吉林外記 (A private account of Chi-lin), 1825. Hsiao fang-hu-chai yü-ti ts'ung-ch'ao (The little square vase studio geographical series); 1894.

SCTC: Sheng-ching t'ung-chih 盛京通志 (Gazetteer of Sheng-ching), comp. Wei Shu 魏樞 et al. Reprint; 3 vols.; Taipei, 1965.

Sebes, Joseph. *The Jesuits and the Sino-Russian Treaty of Nerchinsk, 1689: The Diary of Thomas Pereira, S. J.* Rome, 1961.

Shen Chao-t'i 沈兆禔. *Chi-lin chi-shih shih* 吉林紀事詩 (Narrative poems on Chi-lin). 4 *chüan;* Nanking, 1911.

Shen Chien 沈鑑. "Hsin-hai ko-ming ch'ien-hsi wo-kuo chih lu-chün chi ch'i chün-fei" 辛亥革命前夕我國之陸軍及其軍費 (China's land army and its finances on the eve of the 1911 Revolution); in *She-hui k'o-hsüeh* (Social sciences), vol. 2, no. 2 (1937).

Shen Nai-cheng 沈乃正. "Ch'ing-mo tu-fu chi-ch'üan, chung-yang chi-ch'üan, yü 't'ung-shu pan-kung' " 清末督撫集權，中央集權，與'同署辦公' (On the powers of the viceroys and governors of provinces in the latter years of the Ch'ing); in *She-hui k'o-hsüeh,* vol. 2, no. 1 (1937).

Sheng-ching t'ung-chih, see *SCTC.*

Shih Chao-chi 施肇基. *Shih Chih-chih hsien-sheng tsao-nien hui-i-lu* 施植之先生早年回憶錄 (Memoirs of the early years of Mr. Shih Chih-chih). Privately printed; 1954.

Shih-erh-ch'ao tung-hua-lu 十二朝東華錄 (Tung-hua records of the twelve reigns), ed. Wang Hsien-ch'ien 王先謙 et al. Reprint; 30 vols.; Taipei, 1963.

Shirokogoroff, S. M. "Northern Tungus Migration in the Far East," *The Journal of the North-China Branch of the Royal Asiatic Society,* vol. 57 (1926).

——— *Social Organizations of the Manchus*. Shanghai, 1934.

Spence, Jonathan D. *Ts'ao Yin and the K'ang-hsi Emperor, Bondservant and Master*. New Haven, 1966.

Sutō Yoshiyuki 周藤吉之. "Shin-chō ni okeru Manshū chūhō no toku-shusei ni kansuru ichi kōsatsu" 清朝に於ける滿州駐防の特殊性に關する一考察 (A study of the characteristics of the bannermen garrisons in Manchuria); in *Tōhō Gakuhō,* no. 11, pt. 1 (1940).

Ta-Ch'ing hui-tien shih-li 大清會典事例 (Cases and precedents of the collected statutes of the Ch'ing dynasty). 1220 *chüan;* 1908.

Ta-Ch'ing Kuang-hsü hsin fa-ling 大清光緒新法令 (New laws and decrees of the Kuang-hsü reign of the Ch'ing dynasty). 20 *ts'e;* Shanghai, 1909.

Ta-Ch'ing shih-chao sheng-hsün 大清十朝聖訓 (Imperial edicts of ten Ch'ing emperors). Taipei, 1965.

Teng Ssu-yü and John K. Fairbank. *China's Response to the West*. Cambridge, Mass., 1954.

T'ien Pu-i 田布衣. *Pei-yang chün-fa shih hua* 北洋軍閥史話 (The story of the Peiyang warlords). 4 vols.; Taipei, 1965.

Ts'ao Te-hsüan 曹德宣. "Wo so chih-tao ti Chang Tso-lin" 我所知道的張作霖 (The Chang Tso-lin whom I knew); in *Chüan-chi wen-hsüeh* 傳記文學 (Biographical literature), vol. 5, no. 6 (1964).

Ts'ao T'ing-chieh 曹廷杰. *Hsi-po-li tung-p'ien chi-yao* 西伯林東偏紀要 (Notes on a journey to eastern Siberia), 1885. Reprinted in *Liao-hai ts'ung-shu,* 1936.

——— *Tung-pei pien-fang chi-yao* 東北邊防輯要 (Commentaries on selected works related to the defense of the northeastern frontier). 2 *chüan;* 1885. Reprinted in *Liao-hai ts'ung-shu,* 1936.

——— *Tung-san-sheng yü-ti t'u-shuo* 東三省輿地圖說 (Notes on the geography of the Three Eastern Provinces), appendix, 1895. Reprinted in *Liao-hai ts'ung-shu,* 1936.

TSCL: Tung-san-sheng cheng-lüeh 東三省政畧 (The administration of the Three Eastern Provinces). Reprint; 10 vols.; Taipei, 1956.

Tsou Shang-yu 鄒尚友 and Chu Chen-hsin 朱枕薪. *Hulun Buir kai-yao* 呼倫貝爾概要 (General information on Hulun Buir). n.d.

Tu Wei-yün 杜維運 et al. *Chung-kuo li-shih ti-li* 中國歷史地理 (A historical geography of China). 3 vols.; Taipei, 1954.

Tung Ch'iu-shui 董秋水. *Tung-pei feng-t'u hsiao-chih* 東北風土小誌 (Customs of the northeast). Hong Kong, 1948.

Tung-pei yao-lan 東北要覽 (Handbook of the northeast), comp. Chin Yü-fu 金毓黻 et al. Chungking, 1944.

Tung-san-sheng cheng-lüeh, see *TSCL.*

Wang Ch'ing-yün 王慶雲. *Shih-ch'ü yü-chi* 石渠餘記 (Essays on public affairs). 6 *chüan;* 1888.

Wang Chun-heng. *A Simple Geography of China.* Peking, 1958.

Wang Chung-han 王鍾翰. *Ch'ing-shih tsa-k'ao* 清史雜考 (Essays on Ch'ing history). Peking, 1957.

Wang-k'uei hsien-chih 望奎縣志 (Gazetteer of Wang-k'uei hsien), comp. Chang Yü-shu 張玉書 et al. 4 *chüan;* 1919.

Wang T'ieh-han 王鐵漢. "Chang Yü-t'ing hsien-sheng chang-wo Tung-san-sheng chün-cheng-ch'üan ti ching-kuo" 張雨亭先生掌握東三省軍政權的經過 (How Mr. Chang Yü-t'ing obtained military and political power in the Three Eastern Provinces); in *Chüan-chi wen-hsüeh,* vol. 5, no. 3 (1964).

——— "Chang Yü-t'ing hsien-sheng ti ch'u-nien" 張雨亭先生的初年 (Chang Yü-t'ing's early years); in *Chüan-chi wen-hsüeh,* vol. 5, no. 6 (1964).

Wei Yüan 魏源. *Sheng wu chi* 聖武記 (A history of imperial campaigns). 14 *chüan;* 1842.

Wu Chen-ch'en 吳振臣. *Ninguta chi-lüeh* 寧古塔紀畧 (Notes on Ninguta), Hsiao-fang-hu-chai yü-ti ts'ung-ch'ao; 1894.

Wu T'ing-hsieh 吳廷燮. *Tung-san-sheng yen-ko piao* 東三省沿革表 (Tables of geographical changes in the Three Eastern Provinces). 6 *ts'e;* 1909.

Yang Hsüeh-shen 楊學琛. "Ch'ing-tai ch'i-ti ti hsing-chih chi ch'i pien-hua" 清代旗地的性質及其變化 (The nature and transformation of the banner lands during the Ch'ing); in *Li-shi yen-chiu,* no. 3 (1963).

Yang Pin 楊賓. *Liu-pien chi-lüeh* 柳邊紀畧 (Notes on the willow frontier), Hsiao-fang-hu-chai yü-ti ts'ung-ch'ao (The little square vase studio geographical series); 1894.

Yang-wu yün-tung 洋務運動 (The Westernization movement), ed. Chung-kuo shih-hsüeh hui. 8 vols.; Shanghai, 1962.

Yang Tuan-liu 楊端六. *Ch'ing-tai huo-pi chin-yung shih k'ao* 清代貨幣金融史稿 (A draft history of Chinese currency and finances during the Ch'ing). Peking, 1962.

Ying-ho 英和. *P'u-k'uei ch'eng-fu* 卜魁城賦 (Poems on the city of P'u-k'uei), n.p., n.d.

Yü En-te 于恩德. *Chung-kuo chin-yen fa-ling pien-ch'ien shih* 中國禁煙法令變遷史 (The history of opium prohibition in China). Shanghai, 1934.

Glossary

Adi 阿吉
Alantai 阿蘭泰
Alchuka 阿勒楚喀
amban janggin 昂邦章京
anda 安達
Ari 阿里
Ayushi 阿玉喜

Barga 巴爾呼
bayara 巴牙喇
Bayensusu 巴彥蘇蘇
beile 貝勒
beise 貝子
Birar 畢拉爾
booi 包衣
Buriat 布萊雅

Chang Ch'ien 張謇
Chang Ching-hui 張景惠
Ch'ang-ch'un 長春
Chang Hsi-luan 張錫鑾
Chang Shao-tseng 張紹曾
Chang Tso-hsiang 張作相
Chang Tso-lin 張作霖
Chang Tsung-ch'ang 張宗昌
Chang Yung 張榕
Ch'ang-ling 長嶺
Ch'ang-ning 長寧
Ch'ang-pai-shan 長白山
Ch'ang-pei-chün 常備軍
Chao Erh-sun 趙爾巽
Chao Tien-tsui 趙殿最
chen 鎮
chen-shou Sheng-ching tsung-kuan 鎮守盛京總管
Chen-pien chün 鎮邊軍
Ch'en chao-ch'ang 陳昭常
Ch'en Ching-yin 陳敬尹
ch'en-hsüan t'ing 承宣廳
Cheng-chih k'ao-ch'a chü 政治考察局
cheng tang-chia 正當家
ch'eng shou-wei 城守尉
Ch'eng Te-ch'üan 程德全
Chi-tzu-ying lien-chün 吉字營練軍
Ch'i-chi 奇集，齊集
ch'i-chieh 旗界
ch'i-jen 旗人
Ch'i-san 奇三
ch'i-ting 旗丁
ch'i-t'un 旗屯
ch'i-t'ien 旗田
Ch'i-tzu-ying lien-chün 齊字營練軍
Ch'i-ya Hala 欺牙喀喇
Chia-p'i-kou 夾皮溝
chiang-chün 將軍
Chiang Pai-li 蔣百里
chiao-lien ch'u 教練處
chiang-i 匠役
chieh-kuan 界官
Chien-chou 建州
chien-kuan Feng-t'ien fu-yin shih-wu ta-ch'en 兼管奉天府尹事務大臣
ch'ien-feng 前鋒
chih-chou 知州
chih-hsien 知縣
Chin 金
ching-ch'i 京旗
Ching-hsi-li 淨溪里，精奇利
Ching-pien chün 靖邊軍
Ch'ing, Prince 慶親王
Ch'ing-shih kang-yao 清史綱要
Chou Shu-mo 周樹模
Chu Ch'i-ch'ien 朱啟鈐
Chu Chia-pao 朱家寶

chu-fang 駐防
Chü-li 句驪
Ch'ü Hung-chi 瞿鴻禨
chuan-ch'üeh 專缺
ch'uan-kuan 穿官
ch'üan-yeh tao 勸業道
chuang-t'ou 莊頭
cūlgan 出勒罕，楚勒罕

da 達
Dagur 達呼爾
Deren 德勒恩，德楞
Dondon 敦敦
Dörbet 土伯特

ejen 額眞
En-tse 恩澤

fang-ying 防營
fang-yü 防禦
Fe Manchu 佛滿洲
fen-kuan 分營
Feng Lin-ko 馮麟閣
Feng-shen 豐紳
Fiatka 非牙喀
Fu-chün 富俊
fu tu-t'ung 副都統

Gantimur 根特木爾
gashen 嘎山
gashenda 嘎山達
gusai 固山
Güwalca 瓜勒察，卦勒察

Hai-ch'eng 海城
Hai-lan-ch'a 海蘭察
hala 哈賚，哈拉
halada 哈賚達
han 汗
Han-chün 漢軍
Han Hsiao-chung 韓効忠
Han Hsien-tsung 韓現淙
Han Pien-wai 韓邊外
Han Teng-chü 韓登擧
Heje 黒哲，黒斤，赫哲
Heng-kun 恆滾

Heta Ala 赫圖阿拉
Hoi Ryŏng 惠寧
hosei beile 和碩貝勒
hoton 霍通
hsi-hsin 細辛
Hsi-shan 西山
hsi-tan 西丹
hsiang-cheng 鄉正
hsiang-fu 鄉副
hsiang-yüeh 鄉約
hsiao-ch'i-chiao 驍騎校
Hsiao-hsien 孝獻
hsieh-ling 協領
Hsien-cheng pien-ch'a kuan 憲政編查舘
Hsien-nung-t'an 先農壇
hsien-san 閑散
Hsin-chün 新軍
Hsin-min 新民
Hsing-cheng hui-i ch'u 行政會議處
hsing-ssu 刑司
Hsing-tung 興東
hsiu-ts'ai 秀才
Hsü Ching-hsin 徐鏡心
Hsü Hsi 徐曦
Hsü Shih-ch'ang 徐世昌
hsün-chiu 勳舊
Hsün-fang-tui 巡防隊
hu-kuan 互管
hu-ssu 戶司
hui-fang 會房
hui-lien 會練
hui-shou 會首
Hui-tien shih-li 會典事例
Hun-ch'un 琿春
hung-hu-tzu 紅鬍子
Hurka 虎免哈

Ice Manchu 伊徹滿洲，異齊滿洲
I-k'e-t'ang-a 依克唐阿
Ilan Hala 依蘭哈拉
Imin 依敏
i min shih pien 移民實邊
irgen 伊爾根
I-shan 奕山
i-ts'ang 義倉

GLOSSARY

Jalait 扎賚特
jalan 甲喇，扎蘭
janggin 章京
Jerim (Cherim) 哲里木
Juchen 女眞

K'ai-ch'eng 開城
K'ai-hu-jen 開戶人
kao-liang 高梁
karun 卡倫
Keike 葛克勒，葛依克哷
Khingan (Hsingan) 興安
Kiakar 恰喀爾
Kile 欺勒爾，奇勒爾
K'u-er-han 庫爾瀚
K'u-ya-la 庫牙喇
K'u-yeh 庫頁
kuan-chuang 官莊
kuan-fang-kuan 關防官
kuan-tang chu-shih 營檔主事
Kuan-ti 關帝
kuan-t'ieh 官帖
kuan-t'un 官屯
Kumar 庫瑪爾
kung-ch'üeh 公缺
kung-chung 公中
Kung Kuang-ts'ai 孔廣才
Kung-shu wen-an ch'u 公署文案處
kung-ssu 工司
kung-t'ien 公田
kung-ts'ang 公倉

Lalin 拉林
Lan T'ien-wei 藍天蔚
lang-chung 郎中
Li-fan yüan 理藩院
li-hsing chu-shih 理刑主事
li-hsing yüan-wai-lang 理刑員外郎
li-shih t'ung-p'an 理事通判
Li Hung-chang 李鴻章
Li, Prince 禮親王
Liao-tung 遼東
Liao-yang 遼陽
lien-chuang-hui 聯莊會
lien-hui 練會
Lin-chiang 臨江

ling-ts'ui 領催
Liu K'un-i 劉坤一
liu-min 流民
Lo-ch'a 羅刹
Lu-chün 陸軍
Lü-ying 綠營
Lung-t'an 龍潭

ma-chia 馬甲
ma-tse 馬賊
Man-chou 滿洲
Manegir 瑪涅克爾
Mao-ming-an 茂名安
meiren 梅勒
Mergen 墨爾根
min-cheng ssu 民政司
min-hu 民戶
min-jen 民人
min-t'un 民屯
min-wu t'ing 民務廳
Ming-an 銘安
Meng-ku 蒙古
Mo-ho 漠河
mokun 莫昆
mokunda 莫昆達
moringa 摩淩阿
Mu-ch'eng 木城
Mu-ch'i-ho 木奇河，穆欽河
Mu-t'u-shan 穆圖善
Muren 穆連

Nara 那拉
nei-ta-ch'en 內大臣
Nei-wu fu 內務府
Nipchu 尼布潮
niru 牛彔
Ni-ya-hu-t'u 尼雅胡圖
Niu-man 牛滿
Nonni 嫩江
Nung-an 農安

obo 鄂博
Ölöt 額魯特，厄魯特
Orochon 鄂倫春

p'ai-t'ou 牌頭

pang tang-chia 幇當家
pao-an hui 保安會
pao-cheng 保正
pao-chia 保甲
pao-i 包衣
p'ao-t'ou 砲頭
pei-mu 貝母
Petuna 伯都納
Pi-le-erh 畢喇爾
piao-chü 鏢局
p'iao-hao 票號
pien-t'ai 邊臺
Pin-chiang-kuan tao 濱江關道
ping-pei ch'u 兵備處
ping-pei tao 兵備道
ping-ssu 兵司
ping t'eh ch'ü ch'ien 憑帖取錢
P'u-k'uei 卜魁
Pulu 普祿

Sa-pao 薩保
Sabsu 薩布素
San-hsing 三姓
Sarhuda 沙爾虎達
shang 晌
shang-shu 尚書
She-chi-t'an 社稷壇
shen 神
shen-chi-ying 神機營
Shen-yang 瀋陽
Sheng-tsu 聖祖
shih-kuan 世營
shih-lang 侍郎
shiregetü 西勒圖
Shou-shan 壽山
Shuang-ch'eng pao 雙城堡
Sibe 席百，錫伯
So-e-t'u 索額圖
Solon 索倫
So-so-k'u 索索庫
su-tzu 蘇子
sui-ch'üeh ti 隨缺地
Sui-hua 綏化
sula 蘇拉
Sun Chia-nai 孫家鼐
Sung Hsiao-lien 宋小濂
Sungari 松阿里，松花江

Ta-kuei 達桂
ta-tzu 韃子
t'ai-ch'i 抬旗
T'ai-ning 泰寧
tang-chia-ti 當家的
t'ang-chu-shih 堂主事
T'ang-ho 湯河
T'ang Shao-i 唐紹儀
T'ang Yü-lin 湯玉麟
t'ang-ssu 堂司
Tardai 塔爾岱
Te-hui 德輝
Te-sheng 德勝
T'e-p'u-ch'in 特普欽
t'i-fa-shih 提法使
T'iao-ch'a chü 調查局
t'iao-shen 跳神
t'ieh-tzu 帖子
T'ien-ch'i 天攸
Ting-an 定安
t'ing 廳
Tobukur 多布庫爾
To-lung-a 多隆阿
T'o-ho 托河
t'ou-mu 頭目
Tsai-chen 載振
ts'ai-tung 財東
ts'an-ling 參領
ts'an-mou ch'u 參謀處
Ts'ao K'un 曹琨
Tseng-ch'i 曽祺
Tsitsihar 齊齊哈爾
tso-ling 佐領
tso-ssu 左司
tso ts'an-tsan 左參贊
Ts'ui 崔
tsung-kuan 總管
Ts'ung-shih 崇實
Ts'ung-shu chi-ch'eng 叢書集成
tu-lien ch'u 督練處
Tu-lien kung-so 督練公所
tu-t'ung 都統
Tumen 圖們
t'u-ssu 土司

Tuan Chih-kuei 段芝貴
t'un-chang 屯長
t'un-kuan 屯官
t'un-t'ien 屯田
t'un-ting 屯丁
Tung-san-sheng chi-lüeh 東三省紀畧
T'ung-k'en 通肯
t'ung-ling 統領
T'ung-meng hui 同盟會
Tzu-cheng yüan 資政院
tzu-i chü 諮議局
tzu-i t'ing 諮議廳
Tzu-kuang-ko 紫光閣

Ula 烏拉
urin 烏綾

Wan-li 萬曆
Warka 瓦爾喀
Wen-ch'üan 文全
Wen-hsiang 文祥
Wen-hsü 文緒
wo-p'eng 窩棚
Wu-cha-la 烏扎拉
Wu Ching-lien 吳景濂
wu-chi 烏稽，窩集
Wu Chün-sheng 吳俊陞
Wu-ho-t'u 烏活圖
Wu Tseng-ch'i 吳曾祺
Wu Ta-ch'eng 吳大澂
Wu Yüeh 吳樾

yafahan 雅發罕
Yaksa 雅克薩
yang-yü ping 養育兵
Yen-ch'u 嚴楚
Yen-mou 延茂
yin-fang 印房
yin-k'u 銀庫
yin-k'u chu-shih 銀庫主事
yin-wu ch'u 印務處
Ying-ko 英格
yu-i shih-kuan 優異世管
yu-ssu 右司
yu ts'an-tsan 右參贊
Yüan Chin-k'ai 袁金鎧
Yüan Shih-k'ai 袁世凱
yüan-wai-lang 員外郎
Yung-chi chou 永吉州

Index

INDEX

INDEX

Harvard East Asian Series

1. *China's Early Industrialization: Sheng Hsuan-huai (1844–1916) and Mandarin Enterprise.* By Albert Feuerwerker.
2. *Intellectual Trends in the Ch'ing Period.* By Liang Ch'i-ch'ao. Translated by Immanuel C. Y. Hsü.
3. *Reform in Sung China: Wang An-shih (1021–1086) and His New Policies.* By James T. C. Liu.
4. *Studies on the Population of China, 1368–1953.* By Ping-ti Ho.
5. *China's Entrance into the Family of Nations: The Diplomatic Phase, 1858–1880.* By Immanuel C. Y. Hsü.
6. *The May Fourth Movement: Intellectual Revolution in Modern China.* By Chow Tse-tsung.
7. *Ch'ing Administrative Terms: A Translation of the Terminology of the Six Boards with Explanatory Notes.* Translated and edited by E-tu Zen Sun.
8. *Anglo-American Steamship Rivalry in China, 1862–1876.* By Kwang-Ching Liu.
9. *Local Government in China under the Ch'ing.* By T'ung-tsu Ch'ü.
10. *Communist China, 1955–1959: Policy Documents with Analysis.* With a foreword by Robert R. Bowie and John K. Fairbank. (Prepared at Harvard University under the joint auspices of the Center for International Affairs and the East Asian Research Center.)
11. *China and Christianity: The Missionary Movement and the Growth of Chinese Antiforeignism, 1860–1870.* By Paul A. Cohen.
12. *China and the Helping Hand, 1937–1945.* By Arthur N. Young.
13. *Research Guide to the May Fourth Movement: Intellectual Revolution in Modern China, 1915–1924.* By Chow Tse-tsung.
14. *The United States and the Far Eastern Crises of 1933–1938: From the Manchurian Incident through the Initial Stage of the Undeclared Sino-Japanese War.* By Dorothy Borg.

15. *China and the West, 1858–1861: The Origins of the Tsungli Yamen.* By Masataka Banno.
16. *In Search of Wealth and Power: Yen Fu and the West.* By Benjamin Schwartz.
17. *The Origins of Entrepreneurship in Meiji Japan.* By Johannes Hirschmeier, S.V.D.
18. *Commissioner Lin and the Opium War.* By Hsin-pao Chang.
19. *Money and Monetary Policy in China, 1845–1895.* By Frank H. H. King.
20. *China's Wartime Finance and Inflation, 1937–1945.* By Arthur N. Young.
21. *Foreign Investment and Economic Development in China, 1840–1937.* By Chi-ming Hou.
22. *After Imperialism: The Search for a New Order in the Far East, 1921–1931.* By Akira Iriye.
23. *Foundations of Constitutional Government in Modern Japan, 1868–1900.* By George Akita.
24. *Political Thought in Early Meiji Japan, 1868–1889.* By Joseph Pittau, S.J.
25. *China's Struggle for Naval Development, 1839–1895.* By John L. Rawlinson.
26. *The Practice of Buddhism in China, 1900–1950.* By Holmes Welch.
27. *Li Ta-chao and the Origins of Chinese Marxism.* By Maurice Meisner.
28. *Pa Chin and His Writings: Chinese Youth Between the Two Revolutions.* By Olga Lang.
29. *Literary Dissent in Communist China.* By Merle Goldman.
30. *Politics in the Tokugawa Bakufu, 1600–1843.* By Conrad Totman.
31. *Hara Kei in the Politics of Compromise, 1905–1915.* By Tetsuo Najita.
32. *The Chinese World Order: Traditional China's Foreign Relations.* Edited by John K. Fairbank.
33. *The Buddhist Revival in China.* By Holmes Welch.
34. *Traditional Medicine in Modern China: Science, Nationalism, and the Tensions of Cultural Change.* By Ralph C. Croizier.
35. *Party Rivalry and Political Change in Taishō Japan.* By Peter Duus.
36. *The Rhetoric of Empire: American China Policy, 1895–1901.* By Marilyn B. Young.
37. *Radical Nationalist in Japan: Kita Ikki, 1883–1937.* By George M. Wilson.
38. *While China Faced West: American Reformers in Nationalist China, 1928–1937.* By James C. Thomson Jr.
39. *The Failure of Freedom: A Portrait of Modern Japanese Intellectuals.* By Tatsuo Arima.
40. *Asian Ideas of East and West: Tagore and His Critics in Japan, China, and India.* By Stephen N. Hay.
41. *Canton under Communism: Programs and Politics in a Provincial Capital, 1949–1968.* By Ezra F. Vogel.
42. *Ting Wen-chiang: Science and China's New Culture.* By Charlotte Furth.
43. *The Manchurian Frontier in Ch'ing History.* By Robert H. G. Lee.